004.69

D0245086

Things to Check after You Log In

Check Your . . .	What It Is	How to Do It
Requests	Friends asking to connect with you, inviting you to events and groups, or suggesting applications for you	Click the relevant request at the top right of your Home page. If you have no requests, the Requests box won't appear.
Upcoming Birthdays	A list of friends' birthdays occurring within the next few days	Check the Birthdays box in the right column of the Home page. If there are none coming up, it reads, No Upcoming Birthdays.
Inbox	Messages from friends, groups, or events you're a part of or businesses you subscribe to	Click the Inbox link in the blue bar at the top. If there's a number in parentheses, it indicates the number of new or unread messages that you have.
News Feed	A continuous stream of updates about your friends' activities on and off Facebook	Look right at the Home page — it's the largest element on the page!

Find People You Know

What to Do	How to Do It
See which people in your e-mail address book or instant messenger (IM) buddy list are on Facebook	Click Friends in the blue bar at the top and choose Find Friends. Facebook allows you to import from a variety of popular e-mail and IM services.
Search your classmates and co-workers	Click Friends in the blue bar at the top, choose Find Friends, click More Ways to Find Friends at the bottom of the resulting page, and then use the Find Classmates and Find Coworkers links.
Look at your friends' friends	You likely know the people your friends are friends with. To view friends of a friend, go to a profile and click the View All Friends link in the Friends in Other Networks box.
Browse people in your networks	To look through the people in your school, region, or workplace networks, click the Search button above the Quick-Search box on the left-hand navigation bar and then click Browse.
Keep an eye on your friends' feeds	Whenever your friends make new friend connections, stories about those connections appear in their Mini-Feeds, and may also appear in your News Feed. You probably know many of the same people as your friends, so keep your eyes peeled for these stories!

For Dummies™
BESTSELLING
BOOK SERIES

Facebook® For Dummies®

 Cheat Sheet

Celebrate Someone's Birthday on Facebook

What to Do	What It Is	How to Do It
Buy them a gift	A *gift* on Facebook is a special icon designed by famous Macintosh artist Susan Kare. Gifts are often comical or whimsical and cost up to $1.	Go to their profile and click the Send *<Name>* a Gift link under their picture.
Write on their Wall	A *Wall* is an informal public forum on each person's profile. It usually fills with well-wishes on a person's birthday.	Go to their profile, find the Wall box, and enter your message.
Poke them	A *Poke* is a casual gesture that means, "I'm thinking of you." Only the recipient is aware of your poke.	Go to their profile and click the Poke *<Him/Her>* link under their picture.
Write them a note	A *note*, similar to a blog entry, is a free-form post that you can write and share with your friends.	Click Notes in the left-hand navigation bar and then click Write a New Note. Make sure to tag the birthday boy or girl in the note so they see it!

Keep Up with Your Friends

What to Check	What It Is	How to Get There
News Feed	A continuous stream of updates about your friends' activities on and off Facebook	It's integrated into your Home page!
Friends Page	A list of your friends. By default, it shows only your friends who have been active recently as well as what they did (created an event or wrote a new note, for example).	Click Friends in the blue bar at the top of any Facebook page.
Status Updates	A list of your friends' most recent status updates. A *status* is a one- or two-line post from your friends on what they're currently up to.	The Home page shows a few recent status updates. Click the See All link at the top of the Status Updates box to see more.
Photos Dashboard	A list of photo albums recently created by your friends.	Click Photos on the left-hand navigation bar.
Network Portals	The latest news, events, and popular content from your networks.	Click Networks in the blue bar at the top of any Facebook page and then choose the network portal you want to see.

For Dummies: Bestselling Book Series for Beginners

by Carolyn Abram and Leah Pearlman
Facebook Product Managers

WILEY

Wiley Publishing, Inc.

Facebook® For Dummies®

Published by
Wiley Publishing, Inc.
111 River Street
Hoboken, NJ 07030-5774

www.wiley.com

Copyright © 2008 by Wiley Publishing, Inc., Indianapolis, Indiana

Published by Wiley Publishing, Inc., Indianapolis, Indiana

Published simultaneously in Canada

For general information on our other products and services, please contact our Customer Care Department within the U.S. at 800-762-2974, outside the U.S. at 317-572-3993, or fax 317-572-4002.

For technical support, please visit www.wiley.com/techsupport.

Wiley also publishes its books in a variety of electronic formats. Some content that appears in print may not be available in electronic books.

Library of Congress Control Number: 2007943805

ISBN: 978-0-470-26273-3

Manufactured in the United States of America

10 9 8 7 6 5 4 3 2 1

WILEY

About the Authors

Carolyn Abram: One of the first Facebook users on the west coast, Carolyn took her English degree from Stanford University (Class of 2006), and decided the best career move was to get paid to be on Facebook all day long. On the Product Team since 2006, Carolyn has managed voice, language, and tone for Facebook, while contributing as an author and manager of the Facebook Company Blog. Originally from Ardsley, New York, Carolyn currently resides in Palo Alto. She boasts the highest ratio of mess to desk at the office. Her hobbies include hiking, writing, enjoying sunshine, mocking her friends, and Ultimate Frisbee.

Leah Pearlman graduated with a degree in Computer Science from Brown University, where she first signed up for Facebook to find out the name of a boy in a class. Typical. She spent two years at Microsoft learning the product management ropes (seriously, there are ropes) before becoming a Product Manager for Facebook. Since joining, she has worked on a wide range of projects including messaging and the Inbox, News Feed, Pages, and Ads. At the office, Leah's desk is always clean, except sometimes when it's not, and instead of a chair, she sits on an inflatable ball — she has only fallen twice while people were watching. Her hobbies include snowboarding (though she feels pretentious every time she says it), writing (see previous parenthetical comment), and also playing Ultimate Frisbee.

About the Contributor

Blake Ross is currently on leave from Stanford University to oversee development of the new user experience at Facebook. He is three times the dummy as his fellow authors, having written *Firefox For Dummies* in 2005. Or is that twice the dummy? We told you he was dumb.

Deemed *untannable* by scientists, Blake grew up in sunny Miami, Florida, before being shipped out to even sunnier Palo Alto, California. He enjoys writing, playing piano, and programming.

Authors' Acknowledgments

First and foremost, we'd like to thank Blake Ross, double agent and ghost writer extraordinaire. We also could never have started (or finished) this book without the help of everyone at Wiley: Steve Hayes, Nicole Sholly, Brian Walls, and James Kelly, as well as everyone listed on the other side of this page. We don't have space to list everyone on the Facebook team we'd like to thank; everyone who makes Facebook such a great product to work on, write about, and use. Suffice it to say that we'd like to thank Facebook, brought to you by the letters PM, E, D, UO and CO, PR, BD, PMM, HR, OD, OPS, admin, legal, and sales. A special shout-out to the Facebook Status Team — without our status we could never have been held so accountable to this project. Additionally, we'd like to acknowledge the huge role that Neotte and University Café played in caffeinating and feeding us through this process. Finally, we want to thank Pandora for providing amazing music, our laptops for not dying on us, and Facebook Ultimate Frisbee for providing a much needed writing break.

Leah gives her personal thanks to Mom and Dad (in reverse alphabetical order) for the endless supply of you-can-do-its and nose-to-the-grindstone-kiddos. Thanks to Dustin for the support, encouragement, and at least one matzo ball per chapter. Special shout out to brother DJ, nephew Collin, and Uncle Marc for graduating from newbie to Facebook-JV, without the help of this handy how-to. Thanks Maggie and Emily for your sisterly and BFF-erly love, respectively. An obvious, yet totally genuine thanks to Carolyn, if you had an Awesome button, I'd press it. Finally, thank you spell check; without ewe nothing eye right wood make any cents.

Carolyn gives her personal thanks to her entire family — Bill and Barbara Abram (Mom and Dad), Muriel Abram and Anne Berkowitz (Grandmas), Rebecca and Matt Scheck, and Charlotte Abram. Eric Feeny gets special acknowledgement for loving a very busy and stressed-out girlfriend. Thanks also to all of Carolyn's friends who tolerated her writing-induced hibernation from social life (although they were able to stay close via Facebook). Leah beat Carolyn to the Awesome button punch line, so Carolyn can only say, "Thanks" in return. Lastly, Carolyn would like to acknowledge all her teachers over the years, especially Brian Gutherman and Tom Kealey.

In closing, we'd like to thank the millions of Facebook users around the world who are busy connecting, organizing, and generally having fun on Facebook. Keep on signin' on.

Publisher's Acknowledgments

We're proud of this book; please send us your comments through our online registration form located at www.dummies.com/register/.

Some of the people who helped bring this book to market include the following:

Acquisitions and Editorial

Project Editor: Nicole Sholly

Executive Editor: Steven Hayes

Copy Editor: Brian Walls

Technical Editor: James F. Kelly

Editorial Manager: Kevin Kirschner

Editorial Assistant: Amanda Foxworth

Sr. Editorial Assistant: Cherie Case

Cartoons: Rich Tennant (www.the5thwave.com)

Composition Services

Project Coordinator: Lynsey Stanford

Layout and Graphics: Stacie Brooks, Reuben W. Davis, Alissa D. Ellet, Joyce Haughey

Proofreaders: John Greenough, Melba Hopper, Caitie Kelly

Indexer: Potomac Indexing, LLC

Special Help

Teresa Artman

Publishing and Editorial for Technology Dummies

    Richard Swadley, Vice President and Executive Group Publisher

    Andy Cummings, Vice President and Publisher

    Mary Bednarek, Executive Acquisitions Director

    Mary C. Corder, Editorial Director

Publishing for Consumer Dummies

    Diane Graves Steele, Vice President and Publisher

    Joyce Pepple, Acquisitions Director

Composition Services

    Gerry Fahey, Vice President of Production Services

    Debbie Stailey, Director of Composition Services

Contents at a Glance

Table of Contents

Introduction

*F*acebook connects you with the people you know and care about. It enables you to communicate, stay up-to-date, and keep in touch with friends and family anywhere. It facilitates your friendships online to help enhance them in person. Specifically, Facebook connects you with the *people* you know around *content* that is important to you. Whether you're the type to take photos or look at them, or write about your life, or read about your friends' lives, Facebook is designed to enable you to succeed. Maybe you like to share Web sites and news, play games, plan events, organize groups of people, or promote your business. Whatever you prefer, Facebook has you covered.

Facebook offers you control. Communication and information sharing is powerful only when you can do what you want within your comfort zone. Nearly every piece of information and means of connecting on Facebook comes with full privacy controls, allowing you to share and communicate exactly how — and with whom — you desire.

Facebook welcomes everyone: students and professionals; grandchildren (over age 13), parents, and grandparents; busy people; socialites; distant friends; and roommates. No matter who you are, using Facebook can add value to your life. Results are typical.

About Facebook For Dummies

Part I of this book teaches you all the basic tips and tricks to get you up and running on Facebook. This is more than enough for you to discover the value. If you make it through Part III, Facebook may become the most powerful tool in your personal life. Part IV explains how you can leverage Facebook for your business; nearly every person who's brought a business to Facebook has found it to be worth the investment. Finally, Part V explores the creative, diverse, and hilarious ways people have welcomed Facebook into their lives.

Here are some of the things you can do with this book:

✔ **Find out how to represent yourself online in a way that's specific to each member of your online audience.** Friends may see you one way, family another way, co-workers another, and friends of friends yet another (or not at all).

✔ **Connect and communicate with people you know.** Whether you're seeking close friends or long-lost ones, family members, business contacts, teammates, businesses, and celebrities, Facebook keeps you connected. Never say, "Goodbye" again . . . unless you want to.

✔ **Discover how a rich toolset online can help enhance your relationships offline.** Event and group organizational tools, photo-sharing, and direct and passive communication capabilities all enable you to maintain an active social life in the real world.

✔ **Bring your business to the consumers who can bring you success.** Productive audience engagement coupled with deeply targeted advertising can help you ensure your message is heard.

Foolish Assumptions

In this book, we make the following assumptions:

✔ You're at least 13 years of age.

✔ You have some access to the Internet and an e-mail address.

✔ There are people in your life with whom you communicate.

✔ You can read the language in which this sentence is printed.

Conventions Used in This Book

In this book, we stick to a few conventions to help with readability. Whenever you have to enter text, we show it in **bold**, so it's easy to see. Monofont text denotes an e-mail address or Web site URL. When you see an *italicized word*, look for its nearby definition as it relates to Facebook. Facebook pages and features — such as the Friends box or the Privacy Overview page — are called out with capital letters. Numbered lists guide you through tasks that must be completed in order from top to bottom; bulleted lists can be read in any order you like (from top to bottom or bottom to top).

Finally, we, the authors, often state our opinions throughout this book. Though we are employees of Facebook, the opinions expressed here represent only our perspective, and not that of Facebook. We are avid Facebook users and have been since before we joined the company. While writing this book, we took off our "employee hats" and put on our "user hats" to allow us to serve as reliable tour guides, and to share objectively our passion for the site.

What You Don't Have to Read

This book is written with the new Facebook user in mind. Some information pertains to readers looking to use Facebook to launch or expand a business. If you want to get on Facebook primarily to keep in touch with family and friends, feel free to skip these sections. Sprinkled throughout the book, sidebars cover many bits of extra information; these are strictly added points of interest that can be skipped without detriment to your Facebook experience.

How This Book Is Organized

Facebook For Dummies is split into five parts. You don't have to read it sequentially, and you don't even have to read all the sections in any particular chapter. We explain the most generalized functionality — that which applies to just about everyone — up front. The first chapter of each part gives you an overview of the application and functionality covered in that particular part, along with a description of the likely audience for that part. If you're unsure whether a part of this book pertains to you, try reading its first chapter; if you're unsure about a particular chapter, try reading its introduction to decide.

Topics in this book are covered mostly in the order in which most people use each particular feature. We recommend that you feel comfortable with the material in Part I before you move to Part II, and so on. As the book progresses, we dive deeper into specialized functionality that may be relevant only to certain audiences.

Don't forget about the Table of Contents and the Index; you can use these sections to quickly find the information you need. Here's what you find in each part.

Part 1: Getting Familiar with Facebook

Chapter 1 introduces you to Facebook and gives you an overview of the most popular and useful ways different types of people incorporate Facebook into their lives. In the few chapters that follow, we help you get your profile set up and orient you to the site so you can always find your way around. Finally, you discover all the privacy tools and safety tips you need to take full control of your own Facebook experience; when each individual feels safe, the entire Facebook community benefits.

Part II: Representing Your Identity Online

When you're familiar with the basics, Part II helps you create an honest, interactive online presence, linking you with all the people you know in the Facebook community, a community that is getting larger every day. We introduce some of the most popular uses of Facebook, including Photos, and explain how you can tailor the system to meet your specific needs.

Part III: Keeping Connected and Staying in Touch

Part III covers how Facebook can help you stay connected and close with the people you know. We explain the differences between private and public communication, and active and passive interactions, all of which fulfill different needs in different social situations. In this part, you discover how people also keep connected and in touch using Facebook Groups and Events.

Part IV: It's Not Personal: It's Business

Along with providing value for people in their personal lives, Facebook can also help businesses connect with their customers in specialized ways. Whether in the Facebook Platform or in Facebook's spam-free ad system, your business's message can reach consumers in an engaging and uniquely targeted way.

Part V: The Part of Tens

The final section of this book gives fun-to-read and easy-to-digest views on the creative ways people use Facebook. We highlight ten of our favorite Facebook groups from the functional and the absurd. You read about ten very different applications other companies have integrated into the Facebook environment, including one that helps people raise money for nonprofit causes. Finally, ten real-world scenarios provide you a perspective on the value of integrating Facebook with your lifestyle.

Icons Used in This Book

What's a *For Dummies* book without icons pointing you in the direction of great information that's sure to help you along your way? In this section, we briefly describe each icon we use in this book.

The Tip icon points out helpful information that is likely to improve your experience.

The Remember icon marks an interesting and useful fact — something that you might want to use later.

The Warning icon highlights lurking danger. With this icon, we're telling you to pay attention and proceed with caution.

Where to Go from Here

Whether you've been using Facebook for years, or this is your first time, we recommend you start by reading Chapter 1, which sets the stage for most of what we describe in detail in the rest of this book. After reading the first chapter, you may have a better sense of which topics in this book will be more relevant to you, and you can, therefore, flip right to them. However, we recommend that *everyone* spend some quality time in Chapter 4. Facebook is an online representation of a community, so it's important that each person understand how to operate in that community to ensure a safe, fun, and functional environment for everyone.

If you're new to Facebook and looking to use it to enhance your own personal connections, we recommend reading this book from Part I straight through Part III. If you're *so* new to Facebook that you're not even sure that it's for you, you'll find your answer in Chapter 1. (We'll go ahead and ruin the surprise by telling you now that Facebook *is* for you, whoever you are).

You may already be quite familiar with Facebook when you pick up this book. But because the site is constantly growing and changing, there is always more to know. Parts III and IV are the sections of the book that will keep you ahead of the curve. If your primary interest in Facebook is how it can help you advance your business (and you've already made it through Chapters 1 and 4), you can head straight to Part IV, which centers on that topic.

No matter which category you fall into, it's time to get started: Let one hand flip the pages of this book, the other drive your computer mouse, and let your mind open up to a revolutionary way to enhance and experience your real-world relationships.

Part I
Getting Familiar
with Facebook

"I know Facebook is great and you want to be a part of it. But you're my mom - you *can't* be my 'friend.'"

In this part . . .

So, we've persuaded you to read beyond the Introduction. Go team! (You can't see it, but we're high-fiving right now.) Because you started at the beginning, we assume that you have some pretty basic questions, such as

- What is Facebook?
- Am I too old for Facebook?
- How do I use Facebook effectively?
- I know I want to use Facebook, but how do I get started?

These are all great questions for starting a journey into the 'book. In this part, we answer all these and more. We start with the bigger picture of who's using Facebook and how, and then we move into the nitty-gritty of signing up, creating your profile, and finding a few friends. Additionally, we show you how to navigate around the site and protect your information.

Chapter 1

The Many Faces of Facebook

*I*magine trying to get from New York to California some way other than riding an airplane. How about baking a pie (pecan, please) without an oven? Or just try to get to the seventieth floor without using an elevator. Certainly ways are available to achieve those tasks. However, without the right tools, they take longer, come out less-than-perfect, and *really* make you sweat.

Like an airplane, an oven, or an elevator, Facebook is a tool that can make life's *To-Do*s fun and easy. Facebook enables you to manage, maintain, and enhance your social connections. Think about how you accomplish these tasks:

✔ Getting the phone number of an old friend.

✔ Finding out what your friends are up to today.

✔ Making a contact in a city you're moving to or at an office where you're applying for a job.

✔ Planning an event, tracking the guest list, and updating everyone when the time changes.

✔ Garnering support for a cause.

✔ Getting recommendations for movies, books, and restaurants.

✔ Showing off the pictures from your latest vacation.

✔ Telling your friends and family about your recent successes, showing them your photos, or letting them know you're thinking of them.

✔ Remembering everyone's birthday.

The preceding list is merely a sampling of life's tricky tasks that Facebook attempts to help you accomplish. The list could go on, but we need to leave some space in the book to tell you how to solve these problems!

Facebook facilitates and improves all your social relationships — we realize that's a big claim. Almost as big as the claims about the blender that can prepare a seven course meal in six minutes, the pill that can give you the abs of Chuck Norris and the legs of Tina Turner, or the six easy steps that can make you a millionaire. However, Facebook is a little different than these. We won't claim it's so easy your Chihuahua can do it. Getting set up and familiar with Facebook does take a little work (which you know or you wouldn't be starting out on this 360-page journey). Facebook costs only three low payments of $0, but if you aren't totally satisfied, you can be fully refunded. Finally, unlike the blender or the pill, Facebook *will* actually change your life, make it better, more fun, easier, and, did we mention fun?

What Is Facebook?

Think about the people you interacted with in the past day. In the morning, you might have gone to get the paper and chatted with the neighbor. You might have asked your kids what time they'd be home and negotiated with your partner about whose night it is for cooking dinner. Perhaps you spent the day interacting with co-workers, taking time out for lunch with a friend who's in town for business. In the evening, you might have shot off an e-mail to an old college roommate, called your mom (it's her birthday!), and made plans with the gang to get together this weekend. Every day you interact with so many different people in unique ways. You exchange information: "Did you catch the news this morning?" You enjoy another's company: "Who's up for a good joke?" You enrich lives: "I made you something at school today." Throughout your day, most of the decisions you make and actions you take are thanks to or on behalf of someone that you know.

That's a one-foot view of the world in which you're the center. Pan the camera back a ways (farther . . . farther . . . even farther), and you see that each person you interact with — family, friends, the newspaper delivery guy, the lunch lady, and even the people who are writing this book — are at the center of their own realities. So is each person *they* know. The connections between every single person in the world intertwine, interplay, and interlock to form *the social graph*. This living, throbbing, shifting, growing web of human relationships is one of life's most awesome and powerful concepts.

The power of the social graph refers to how information travels quickly and (somewhat) reliably among folks. Facebook's function is to make the social graph accessible, that is, help people keep track of and reach the people they know and help individuals leverage the power of the graph by enabling them to communicate and exchange information with anyone or everyone they trust.

Another powerful aspect of the social graph on Facebook is that it builds and maintains itself. Each member helps define his place in the graph. When you sign up for Facebook, you start by creating your *profile* — a page containing whatever information best defines you. Facebook makes it easy for you to find the profiles of the people you know and establish your virtual connection to them. As a Facebook user, your best interest is to keep your portion of the graph mapped as accurately as possible — form a complete set of connections to the people you know. Facebook can become the single access point for the people you know, so it becomes more useful the more you can confidently find exactly who you're looking for. Because of how Facebook is built, you don't actually have to find everyone you know (imagine the longest game of Hide and Seek ever). After you make a few connections, mutual friends become aware of your presence on the graph, and they seek you out to establish a connection. *Remember:* It's also in their best interest to keep their contact list up to date.

What You Can Do on Facebook

Now that you know Facebook is a means by which you can connect with people, your next question might be, "How?" It's a good question. Such a good question that we spend almost the entire rest of this book answering it. But first, an overview.

Establish a profile

When you sign up for Facebook, one of the first things you do is establish your *Profile*. A profile on Facebook is a social résumé — a page about you that you keep up to date with all the information you want people to know.

If you were handing out résumés in the real world, Facebook understands that you'd probably give a different document to different people. Your social résumé would probably have your phone number, your favorite quotes, and pictures from that crazy night in you-know-where. Your résumé for a potential employer would probably share your education and employment history. Your résumé for your family might include your personal address as well as show off your recent vacation photos and news about your life's changes.

You show different slices of your life and personality to different people, and your Facebook Profile allows you (no, *encourages* you) to do the same. To this end, your profile is set up with all kinds of privacy controls to specify who you want to see which information. Many people find great value in adding to their profile just about every piece of information they can and then unveiling each particular piece cautiously. The safest rule here is to share on your profile any piece of information you'd share with someone in real life. The corollary applies, too: Don't share on your profile any information that you wouldn't share with someone in real life. We provide more detail about the Profile in Chapter 2. For now, think of it like a personal Web page with privacy controls for particular pieces of information. This page accurately reflects you so that you hand the right social résumé to the right person.

The motivations for establishing a profile on Facebook are twofold. First, a profile helps people find and identify you. Each individual is actively (or actively trying) to keep track of the people they know. If your name is something relatively common, such as James Brown or Sarah Smith, it's difficult for people to find you without appropriate identifiers. Facts, such as your home town or your education history, or flipping through your photos, help people find the right James Brown or Sarah Smith.

The second (and way cooler) reason to establish an accurate profile is the work it saves you. Keeping your profile detailed and relevant means that your friends and family can always get the latest information about where you live, who you know, and what you're up to. You no longer have to read your phone number to someone while they fumble to find a pen. Just tell them, "It's on Facebook." If someone wants to send you a birthday present, she doesn't have to ruin the surprise by asking you for your address. When your profile is up to date, conversations that used to start with the open ended, "How have you been?" can skip straight to the good stuff: "I saw your pictures from Hawaii last week. *Please* tell me how you ended up wearing those coconuts."

Connect with friends and build your network

After you join Facebook, start seeing its value by tracking down some people you know. Facebook offers the following tools to help you:

- ✔ **Facebook Friend Finder:** Allows you to scan the e-mail addresses in your e-mail address book to find whether those people are already on Facebook. Selectively choose among those whom you'd like to request a Facebook friendship.

- ✔ **Search:** Helps you to find people whom you expect are already using Facebook.

- ✔ **Browse:** Allows you to look through the profiles of people in your networks (more on networks in a minute) in the hope that you might find some folks you know.

After you establish a few connections, use those connections to find other people you know by searching through their Friends lists for familiar names. Facebook also informs you when your friends are establishing connections with new people in case these are people you also know. We explain how to find friends on Facebook in Chapter 6.

Communicate with other Facebook users

While Facebook grows, it becomes more likely that anyone you're trying to communicate with can be reached, such as a person you met at a dinner party, a professor from college, or a childhood friend you've been meaning to catch up with. Digging up a person's contact information could require calls to mutual friends, a trip to the white pages (provided you know enough about them to identify the right contact information), or e-mail sent to an outdated e-mail address (which may or may not reach its intended recipient). You might have different methods of reaching people depending on how you met the person, or what limited information you have about them.

Facebook streamlines finding and contacting people in a reliable forum. If the person you're reaching out to is active on Facebook, then no matter where they live or how many times they've changed their e-mail address, you reach that person.

Post photos

Since the invention of the modern day's camera in the fifteen hundreds, people have been all too eager to yell, "Cheese!" Photographs can make great tour guides on trips down memory lane but only if we actually remember to develop, upload, or scrapbook them. So many memories fade away when the smiling faces are on an undeveloped roll of film, stuffed into an old shoe box, or forgotten in some folder on a hard drive.

Facebook offers two great incentives for uploading, organizing, and editing your photos:

- ✔ **Facebook provides one easy-to-access location for all your photos.** Directing any interested person to your Facebook Profile is easier than e-mailing pictures individually, sending a complicated link to a photo site, or waiting until the family reunion to show off the my-how-the-kids-have-grown pics.

- ✔ **Every photo you upload can be linked to the profiles of the people in the photo.** For example, you upload pictures of you and your sister and link them to her profile. Whenever someone visits her profile, they see those pictures; they don't even have to know you. This is awesome because it introduces a longevity to photos they've never had before. As long as people are visiting your sister's profile, they can see those pictures. Photo albums no longer have to be something people look at right after the event, and maybe then again years later.

Plan events, join groups

Just about anything you do with other people is easier on Facebook . . . except cuddling. Facebook isn't meant to be a replacement for face time; it's meant to facilitate interactions when face time isn't possible or to facilitate the planning of face time. Two of the greatest tools for this are Facebook Events and Facebook Groups.

Groups are basically Web pages people can subscribe to, or *join*. One group might be intimate, such as five best friends who plan several activities together. Another group could be practical, for example, PTA Members of Denver Schools. Some groups garner support, such as AIDS Awareness. Others exist for solidarity, for example, When I Was Your Age, Pluto Was a Planet (see Chapter 21 for more examples of Groups on Facebook). Groups allow people to come together in the name of some common interest or goal. Depending on the particular group's settings, members may upload photos or videos, invite other people to the group, receive messages, and check on news and updates.

Events are similar to groups, with the addition of being time-based. Rather than joining, users RSVP events, which allows the event organizers to plan accordingly and allows attendees to receive event reminders. Facebook Events is often used for something as small as a lunch date or something as big as a march on Washington, D.C. Sometimes events are notional rather than physical. For example, someone could create an event for Ride Your Bike to Work Day and hope the invitation spreads far and wide (through friends) to promote awareness. At Facebook headquarters, Events are used to plan company meetings, happy hours, ski trips, and more. Read more about Facebook Groups and Facebook Events in Chapters 12 and 13, respectively.

Try out applications

Facebook Photos, Groups, and Events are only a small sampling of how you use Facebook to connect with the people you know. In Chapter 18, we explain in detail *Facebook Platform*. In short, Facebook is a service that helps you maintain connections with your friends, but any company can build the tools, or *applications*, that allow that connectivity. Photos, Groups, and Events are tools that are built on top of the Facebook Platform; they aren't core to the notion of connecting with your friends but are useful features to use in conjunction with your contacts.

Examples of applications that have been built by other companies include tools to help you edit your photos, create slideshows, play Scrabble with friends across the globe, divvy bills among people who live or hang out together, and exchange information about good movies and books. After getting a little more comfortable with the Facebook basics, you can try out literally hundreds of applications. We simply mention it here to pique your curiosity about the potential; Chapter 9 gives all the juicy details about third-party applications.

Promote your business

Say, you have something to sell, that fancy blender maybe. How do you get people's attention? You don't go to a deserted parking lot and yell, "Hey! Buy my blender!" do you? Of course not. You go to where the people are, and the people are on Facebook. Although anybody can (and should) use Facebook to connect with their friends and family, some use it to connect with their patrons, fans, or supporters. In addition to their personal profiles, people create additional profiles to promote their band, business, brand, product, service, or self, in the case of celebrities or politicians. These profiles are similar to user profiles in that they're a page on Facebook meant to:

- Represent a specific real-world entity.
- Consist of truthful, necessary information required to engage with that entity.

These profiles differ from user profiles in that the relationships are essentially one way. We may have a relationship to Starbucks, but Starbucks doesn't really have a specific relationship with us, which leads to a number of differences in the functionality of business profiles. We discuss the details of those differences and explain the benefits of promoting your business on Facebook in Chapter 16.

Chapter 17 discusses how you advertise your business without, or in addition to, establishing a business profile on Facebook. Because Facebook users enter detailed information about themselves (and their actions on Facebook reveal even more about the kinds of people they are), Facebook can offer a compelling advertising platform by allowing advertisers to reach a targeted audience based on who people are and what they like.

Facebook also offers another kind of targeting, which is *social targeting*. When your friend buys something, you're often more likely to buy it than someone whose friend didn't buy it or someone who didn't *know* their friend bought it. When Facebook shows you an ad, wherever possible, it tries to inform you whether any of your friends had an experience with that product, service, or business. In fact, if you have a friend who bought an item in an ad, you're more likely to see that particular ad than someone with friends who haven't purchased the item. This type of targeted advertising is a win-win for business owners and users because business owners don't have to waste money or dilute their message on people who don't care, and users are more likely to see ads for products that actually interest them — or, at the very least, tell them something about their friends' purchasing habits.

What You Can't Do on Facebook

Facebook is meant to represent real people and real associations; it's also meant to be safe. Many of the rules of participation on Facebook exist to uphold those two goals.

Note: There are things you can't do on Facebook other than what we list here. For example, you can't message multiple people unless you're friends with all of them; you can't join the school network of a school you didn't attend (or a workplace network of a company you don't work for); and you can't spin hay into gold. These rules may change how you use Facebook, but probably won't change *whether* you use it. We separate out the five rules in this section because, if any are a problem for you, you probably won't get to the rest of the book.

You can't see just any profile

When Facebook launched, it didn't let just anyone sign up. Only people with an e-mail address from a particular school could join. When someone signed up, she would be automatically placed in a network corresponding to her particular school. The primary purpose of a *network* was, and still is, to enforce one simple rule: Only people in the same network can see each other's profiles without explicitly asking for permission. If you want access to the profile of a person outside your network, you must search for that person, and then, when you find the listing, request to add that person as a friend. If the person being added doesn't know you, he can reject the friend request and thereby keep his profile private. If the person you contact confirms he knows you, you both have access to each other's profiles. We talk more about networks in Chapter 11.

You can be in up to five networks, including one high school network, one region network, and three college and/or workplace networks. By joining a network, you gain access to profiles of others in that network. This rule has roots in both of the primary motivations for all rules on Facebook. First, because Facebook is meant to mimic real life, you only "run into" the people on Facebook that you'd run into in real life. For example, if you live in Providence, then you might potentially see someone else who lives in Providence. If you attend Brown University, you're very likely to run into other students at Brown, so Facebook grants you access to these profiles. Second, although users have all the controls they need to keep their information protected, some people aren't as concerned with safety as they probably should be. Therefore, Facebook raises the barrier to gaining information about other people as best it can while limiting the site's usability as little as possible. Read more about this in Chapter 4.

You can't lie

Okay, you can, but don't, especially not about your basic information. Lying about your identity is a violation of the Facebook Terms of Use and grounds for profile deactivation. In other words, thank you, bye-bye. Although many people try, Facebook doesn't let anyone sign up with an obviously fake name like Marilyn Manson or Fakey McFakerville. Those who do make it past the name checks, will likely find their account tracked down and deactivated.

A few fake accounts survive on Facebook undetected for a very long time because the Facebook user operations team goes after people who are breaking serious and safety-compromising offenses first. So, if you're considering setting up a fake profile to test our claim, you're probably better off just going outside to play. Take a Frisbee.

You can't be twelve

Or younger. Seriously. Facebook takes very seriously the law that prohibits minors under the age of 13 from creating an online profile for themselves. This rule is in place for the safety of minors, a particular safety Facebook takes extremely seriously. If you or someone you know is under 13 on Facebook, deactivate (or make them deactivate) the account now. If you're reported to the Facebook user operations team, your account is deleted instantly, and Facebook (Carolyn and Leah as well) will be very unhappy. Because Facebook is so vigilant about keeping minors off the site, if you're under 13, know that the people you hang out with won't be on Facebook either. If you happen to be over 13 and looking for people under 13, check out the next section for what else you can't do.

You can't troll

We can't stress this enough, and putting it in bold definitely isn't enough stress. We could add underline, italics, or all caps. Let's try.

YOU CAN'T TROLL.

Facebook is about real people and real connections. It's one thing to message a mutual friend or the occasional stranger whose profile implies being open to meeting new people and the two of you have matching interests. However, the moment the people you contact have a problem with you sending unsolicited messages, your account is flagged; if the behavior continues, your account is deactivated.

Imagine going to a coffee shop and introducing yourself to each and every person while they try to mind their cup of Joe. That is how we view the sending of unsolicited messages on Facebook, and the user operations team will make like an angry barista and kick you to the coffee shop curb.

You can't upload illegal content

Supporting United States law is something Facebook would have to do regardless of its position on pornography (where minors can see it), copy righted material, hate speak, depictions of crimes, and other offensive content. However, doing so is in line with Facebook's goal of being a safe, happy place for its users. Don't confuse this with censorship; Facebook is all about freedom of speech and self-expression, but the moment that compromises anyone's safety or breaks any law, disciplinary action is taken.

How Is Facebook Different from Other Social Sites?

Several social sites besides Facebook try to help people connect. Some of the most popular sites are MySpace, Friendster, Orkut, LinkedIn, Windows Live Spaces, Bebo, Meebo, Match, and QQ.

In some cases, these sites have slightly different goals than Facebook. LinkedIn, for example, is a tool for connecting with people specifically for career networking. MySpace initially started out as a way for small, local bands to gain popularity outside of the politically-complicated music industry by creating a space for people to connect with others who had similar tastes in music. Match.com is a social networking site specifically geared toward people looking to date. Alternatively, other sites have the same goals as Facebook; they just have different strategies. Orkut, for example, doesn't allow anyone to sign up until they've received an explicit invitation. MySpace (and Spaces) has options that allow anyone to view anyone else's profile and allow anyone to create a user profile for any (legal) purpose, such as band promotion. Some of these sites also give users complete customization over the look and feel of their profile, whereas Facebook maintains a pretty consistent design and expects users to differentiate their profiles by uploading unique content.

These subtle differences create vastly different user behaviors. It's difficult for us to spend much time talking neutrally about what these differences are because Facebook prides itself on taking examples of how other social utilities run their sites and improving upon their models wherever possible.

Rather than an explicit comparison between Facebook and other sites, the following lists some of the things that differentiate Facebook from its primary competitors:

- ✔ **On Facebook, you see only the profiles of people in your networks or people you've explicitly contacted.** There's no getting around it. Read more about what this means in Chapter 10.

- ✔ **Facebook allows very little customization of your profile's design.** This frustrates some people who want to use their profile for total self-expression. However, Facebook has found that the value gained from having uniform profiles, which eases site navigability, outweighs the benefits of self-expression through page design. If you want to be a unique flower on Facebook, upload interesting photos, write riveting notes, or set your religious views to something snarky, such as Church of Jack Bauer.

- ✔ **Facebook has different kinds of profiles for users and for businesses.** Other sites allow, and even encourage, people to create a profile for any purpose, be that managing your friends or promoting your band or business. However, Facebook believes that these different entities — individuals versus anything that requires promotion — have very different goals (and therefore needs) in a social networking space. Similarly, people expect to interact with people differently than how they'd interact with businesses or celebrities they don't personally know. To satisfy these differences, Facebook offers each camp a profile with very different features that optimize the different goals.

Who's Using Facebook

Originally, Facebook was created as a way for students at a particular college or university to find and connect with each another. In fact, when Facebook launched, only those people with a verified college e-mail address were permitted to sign up.

After the success of the university-only model, Facebook opened its doors to high school students in the United States as well. High school students don't have e-mail addresses to verify which high school they attend; therefore, Facebook has a fairly complicated system that relies on students verifying one another before gaining access to a particular high school network.

Facebook took off in high schools with such momentum that Facebook next opened its doors to workplace networks. Workplace networks followed the same model as the college networks — in order to join, you had to sign up with a verified e-mail address, this time, from a particular corporation. Therefore, workplace networks existed only for the companies big enough to offer its employees e-mail addresses, such as Microsoft, Apple, Amazon, and others.

Finally, in the fall of 2004, rather than opening any more doors, Facebook just knocked down its walls. Today, anyone with any e-mail address is welcome to join the Facebook party. The privacy rules from day one still exist: People only have access to the profiles of those who are in the same networks or who have explicitly established each other as friends. People who now sign up outside of a school or workplace network can join a regional network. For example, the people in the Seattle network automatically gain access to the other profiles in the Seattle network.

The ability for everyone in a mutual region to see one another's profile may sound a little scary because the implicit trust that comes from sharing a school or company with somebody doesn't exist by virtue of sharing a city. Just because someone has access to your profile, though, doesn't mean they have access to all your information. Put under lock and key the parts of your profile you *don't* want to show to people in your region network. Chapters 4 and 5 go into much greater detail on how to protect yourself and your information.

Here are two reasons Facebook made the leap from *verified networks* (those in which you must offer some kind of proof of identity, such as an e-mail address, in order to join) to the region networks:

- ✔ **Facebook was offering a tremendous amount of utility to the people who had access to it.** Before opening to the general public, about 85 percent of registered users were logging in at least once per month, and 75 percent of those people were logging in daily. Numbers like that proved Facebook creators were onto something special and that other people — in addition to students and employees of large corporations — could gain value from access to Facebook.

- ✔ **For any given user, Facebook provides more utility when more people that the user would like to connect with are active on Facebook.** This reason for allowing any and everyone on Facebook is a little less obvious, so we offer this example as an explanation:

  A University of Colorado alumnus wants to throw himself a birthday party. At college, he used Facebook to plan his events and manage his guest lists, but now some of his friends are older and were out of college before Facebook became popular. Creating the event on Facebook could lead to an incomplete guest list. If he chooses not to use Facebook, he might end up using a less efficient means of communicating, such as e-mail, which requires that he dig up the e-mail address of everyone he wants to invite and then manage all the RSVPs as they flood his Inbox. He might also decide that it's not worth the hassle and invite only people who are on Facebook. Facebook actually allows him to create an event and generate special invites to those not on the site, but he still has to locate those friend's e-mail addresses and enter them on Facebook.

Significant to the utility of the social graph is its reliability. Having a single source to find and interact with friends, mutual acquaintances, family, or others with shared interests and beliefs would be one of the greatest solutions to many of life's most complicated tasks. Managing our relationships with everyone we know or want to know is the service Facebook is trying to provide. To anyone for whom Facebook has become the primary source for information and interaction, the moment someone in particular isn't represented on Facebook, the whole service becomes less powerful because its reliability for finding whomever you're looking for is reduced. To that end, welcoming everyone onto Facebook was a way to make the service more valuable to those already using it.

A majority of Facebook users are not, nor have ever been, part of a school network, and most of Facebook's growth is in demographics other than high school or college. In the following sections, we talk about how people in different demographics use Facebook. Note that these cases aren't exclusive to the particular category they're listed under; people in workplace networks might use many of the same features and functionality as students, and international users clearly span all three of the demographics. These sections simply emphasize the general trends in particular demographics and highlight some of the differences between them.

Students of the 'Book

Students live in somewhat of a unique environment in that the shared affiliation to the same school implies a level of trust. This allows students to create profiles for themselves, comfortable with the knowledge that only other students at their school (and people they manually verify) can see that information. Because of the close quarters and accountability of their peers, students are perhaps the most open about the information they exchange on Facebook. As long as students are safe about the information they choose to share (see Chapter 4), this abundance of information flow is actually a very good thing that can make their lives and relationships extremely rich.

Students use Facebook for all kinds of fun and practical things:

- **Getting information:** Students can easily connect with others who live in their dorm or take the same classes. This can be great for (approved) collaboration on class work, finding out when homework's due, or borrowing a book for research.

- **Planning events:** A big source of student engagement is event planning. Say, Tau Phi Beta wants to plan an event. The fraternity's officers can create the event page on Facebook, and with a few clicks of a few buttons, invite everyone they want to. They can specify whether the invite should go only to those initially invited — say, a Tau Phi Beta brothers-only dinner — or whether anyone can be invited (a must for a giant frat party — er, *fundraiser*). This is just one example, but Events is rampant across universities. Every club, dorm room, sports team, and group of friends organize their events on Facebook.

✔ **Tagging photos:** Photos is one of the most popular features on Facebook. Students regularly engage in a lot of memorable activities, such as dances, games, and rallies. Generally a large number of students and a nearly-as-large number of cameras attend these events. We hear many students confess that in the time it takes them to hop a shuttle or stumble to their dorm room, someone has already uploaded photos from the event to Facebook. No sooner does a student experience a magical moment than she gets to remember it.

One of the fancy aspects of Facebook Photos is that each photo can be tagged with links to the profiles of the people in the photo. All the photos a particular person is tagged in are aggregated into one album, so when you look at a person's profile, you see all the photos he's ever been tagged in. After a big night on campus, students can see all the pictures their friends took or go straight to all the photos of them. Narcissistic maybe, but also human.

✔ **Keeping up with friends from home:** Sometimes college can feel like its own little universe, especially for those who travel far from home to attend. By establishing friend connections with those friends they _don't_ see every day, they can more easily stay in touch. When they upload photos from the University Gala, friends from home can send a message to say, "Nice dress!" or "Who's the boy?" An RSVP to an event, such as the National Championship Dinner, informs friends from back home of their friend's recent success. And, even though students often get caught up in the action of campus life, sometimes they'll hear a song or read a passage that reminds them of a friend back home. Rather than digging for the e-mail address or finding time to call, they can just use Facebook to drop their friend a _thinking of you_ Wall post, Poke, or message. (Find out more about these options in Chapter 10.)

✔ **Flirting and gossip:** We should've stuck this bullet point first because it's probably the biggest piece of the time-spent-on-Facebook pie. Mmmm, Facebook pie. Throughout this book, you read about messaging, poking, chatting, and gifting, which are all ways that students virtually bat their eyelashes at one another — and avoid doing their homework.

Everyone has the ability on their profile to inform people who they're looking to meet (women, men, or both) and for what purpose (relationship, dating, friendship, and so on). Those already in a relationship can link to their significant other for the world to see. Provocative _Wall posts_ (one friend can write a public message on a friend's _Wall_), intriguing photo uploads, and changing relationship statuses are all sources of juicy gossip without which high school or college just wouldn't be the same.

The School of Life

Chronologically speaking, there's only a small difference between someone nearing the end of their school career (whether that be high school, college, or graduate school) and someone starting life after school. But these two phases share a few other similarities. During school, most people have a set crowd of folks they interact with. They're very familiar with the city or town they live in and the daily routine (class, sports, studying) they've been doing for years. After school, things can change. Many folks move to new cities, start new jobs, and meet new people. Their groups of friends start to disperse (geographically and emotionally), and creating environments for social interaction requires more effort when people cut out lunch time, study hall, or Friday nights at the student center. Because Facebook is all about nurturing relationships, when the nature of people's relationships change, their usage of Facebook changes as well. After school, people find different kinds of utility from their social graph.

✔ **Moving to a new city:** Landing in a new city with all your worldly belongings and an upside down map can be hugely intimidating. Having some open arms or at least numbers to call when you arrive can greatly ease the transition. Although you might already know some people who live in your new city, Facebook can help connect with all the old friends and acquaintances you either forgot live there or have moved there since you last heard from them.

When Leah first moved to the Bay area, she filtered her friends list to everyone in the San Francisco and Silicon Valley networks. The final list probably contained four times as many people as she remembered living in the area. She sent messages announcing her imminent arrival and then connected with her various contacts to get settled into an apartment, meet other people, and find doctors, bike routes, Frisbee leagues, and restaurants. Even if you don't have friends or acquaintances in your new city, someone you know probably does. Your friends can give you names of people to look up when you arrive — use Facebook to do that.

✔ **Getting a job:** Recently, more and more people began using Facebook as a tool for managing their careers as well as their social lives. If you're looking at a particular company, find people who already work there to get the inside scoop or to land an interview. If you're thinking about moving into a particular industry, browse your friends by past job and interests to find someone to connect with.

✔ **Finding activity partners:** Many folks would agree that it's harder to meet people after they leave school. Facebook is a great tool for meeting new friends with similar interests, activity partners, or even potential love interests. You can browse profiles of people in your network based on various kinds of information, such as age, political views, and specific interests. Plenty of online sites offer these kinds of services, but the reason Facebook works particularly well is that the connection you make is often based on mutual acquaintances, making them less awkward, better informed, and safer.

Putting Facebook to work at work

Facebook is still finding it's footing within the workplace networks. Therefore, it's tricky to generalize how people in workplace networks use Facebook because it really depends on the particular workplace. However, here are some uses we've heard about anecdotally:

- Getting to know co-workers and putting names to faces.

- Hosting events specific to the company. Facebook uses Events to plan company parties and host happy hours.

- Using Groups for people in the company with similar interests or needs. This may range from those with similar athletic endeavors, carpool requirements, or artistic interests.

- Buying and selling on Facebook Marketplace with people they trust within their company.

- Post and share stories about the company relevant to the business.

Facebook maturing

Facebook isn't just for students. Anything you've heard to the contrary is dated information. Like we mention before, the fastest growing group of Facebook users is those for whom school is a distant memory. Many of these folks find the same value in Facebook as people in other demographics; however, they also use it for some different kinds of interactions.

Keeping in touch with family

These days, families are often spread far and wide across state or country lines. Children go to college, parents travel for work, grandparents move to Florida. These distances make it hard for families to interact in any more significant way than gathering together once per year to share some turkey and pie (pecan, preferably). Facebook offers a place where families can virtually meet and interact. Parents can upload photos of the kids for everyone to see, grandparents can write notes about what everyone is up to, and college students can gather support for a cause, plan a graduation party, or show off their class schedule — great information for family members who might have a hard time extracting the information in other ways.

We often hear parents and older family members say they feel being on Facebook might infringe on their kid's social life. If you fit this description, we have a few comments for you:

- **You might be right that your kids want you nowhere near their social life.** If that's the case, and you respect that, then don't "friend" them. Exist within your social graph on Facebook, and let them exist within theirs — you never have to interact with one another whatsoever. Not joining Facebook because your kids are using it is like not eating ice cream because your kids eat ice cream. Sure, you *can* go for ice cream together (or be friends on Facebook), but you certainly don't have to. Don't deprive yourself of the sweet creamy deliciousness just because your kid might be offended that you have similar taste in desserts.

✔ **You might be wrong that your kids don't want you on Facebook.** Depending on your kids' age and personality, they might actually prefer that you join Facebook. Some kids, especially the college-aged or twenty-somethings, are very busy and active. It can be hard for them to remember to call home, let alone call the grandparents, aunts, and uncles. Even when they do, they might leave out interesting information about their lives simply because they forget (this hypothetical is coming from personal experience). Still, kids should reach out to their relatives, and the relationships can be much stronger when everyone is on Facebook. Relatives can always see the latest news even when they've been out of touch for some time; they can also connect in a lightweight way in between longer phone conversations. (See Chapter 10 on communicating through Facebook.)

✔ **Kids are *really* good at using Facebook.** If you are Facebook friends with your children and they want to upload something they don't want you to see, they know exactly which privacy controls to put in place so that you don't see it. Whether this is a relevant concern to you, we recommend sitting down with your kids (sometime after the birds-and-bees conversation but before the how-to-pay taxes conversation) and figuring out how to happily cohabitate on Facebook.

Facebook reunion

Thanks to life's curve balls, whoever your friends are at any given time might not be the people in your life at another. People you consider to be most important in your life fade over the years so that even trying to recall a last name causes you pause. The primary reason for this is a legitimate one: There are only so many hours in a day. While we make new, close friends, others drift away because it's impossible to maintain many intense relationships. Facebook is an extremely powerful tool; however, it hasn't yet found a way to extend the number of hours in a day, so it can't exactly fix the problem of growing apart. Facebook can, however, lessen the finality and inevitability of the distance.

Assuming Facebook achieves the longevity and reach it's striving for, those who have started using Facebook at a young age (13 is the minimum) will, at an old age, actually have a lead on every single person they've ever been friends with. This extremely powerful concept actually alters how people have and un-have human relationships. Thirty years after you last speak to someone, you might have a funny memory, something important to share, or just genuine curiosity about that person's whereabouts. If you keep them on your Facebook Friends list, it doesn't matter how many times you both move, change your phone numbers, or get married and change your name, you can still get in touch with each another. If that concept scares you, Facebook also has the tools to explicitly sever connections with people you'd rather didn't find you.

Because Facebook is fairly new (and the fact that you're reading this book), you probably don't have your entire social history mapped out. Some may find it a daunting task to create connections with everyone they've ever known, which we don't recommend. Instead, build your graph as you need to or as opportunity presents. Perhaps you want to upload a photo taken from your high school graduation to tag various classmates. Search for them on Facebook, form the friend connection, and then tag them. Maybe you're thinking about opening a restaurant, and you'd like to contact a friend from college who was headed into the restaurant business after graduation. Perhaps you never told your true feelings to the one that got away — your unicorn. For all these reasons, you might find your cursor in the Facebook Search box.

Frequently, we receive reports from adopted children who connect with their real parents or estranged siblings who find each other on Facebook. Carolyn recently told a story about how her sixth grade bully found her on Facebook to apologize for how he terrorized her.

Organizing groups

Unlike students, adults don't often have the luxury of participating in a lot of events organized by other people. Instead, they organize their book clubs and cooking groups or gather to watch sporting events and have dinner parties. Facebook Groups can add value to all these events. Creating a group on Facebook for your book club makes it easy for someone to update everyone each week about times, dates, locations, who should bring what, and what everyone should read before attending. People can join and leave groups as they see fit, so you never have to worry about notifying those who've moved or are no longer interested in your group.

For one-time gatherings, such as a Super Bowl party, Facebook Events offers a great solution. All you have to do is fill out the guest list and event description — the rest takes care of itself. For the three days prior to the event, everyone receives a reminder on their Facebook Home page, so they have no excuse for not showing (unless someone invited them to a better party). If you want to ensure your guest list is accurate or that people don't forget, message everyone who RSVP'd (attending or tentative, that is) or who hasn't replied. After the event is over, upload photos or leave funny comments and quotes on the event's Wall. Your Super Bowl party is forever immortalized online — and everyone who RSVP'd has total access.

The Birth of the 'Book

In the old days, say, three or four years ago, most college freshmen would receive a thinly bound book containing the names and faces of everyone in their matriculating class. These *face books* were useful for matching names to the students seen around campus, or for pointing out particular people to friends. There were several problems with these face books. If someone didn't send their picture in, they were incomplete. They were outdated by junior year because many people looked drastically different, and the book didn't reflect the students who had transferred in or who were from any other class. Finally, they had little information about each person.

In February of 2004, Mark Zuckerberg, a sophomore at Harvard, launched an online "book" that people could upload their photo and personal information to, which solved many of these problems. Within a month, more than half the Harvard undergraduates had created their own profiles. Zuckerburg was then joined by others including Dustin Moskovitz and Chris Hughes to help expand the site into other schools. Your very own author, Carolyn Abram, was the first non-Harvard student to receive an account. During the summer of the same year, Zuckerberg, Moskovitz, and another partner, Andrew McCollum, moved the company to Palo Alto, California, where the site and the company kept growing. By December 2004, the site had grown to one million college students. Every time Facebook opened to a new demographic — high school, then work users, then everyone — the rate at which people joined the site continued to increase. In November of 2007, the site reached 50 million active users (defined as unique accounts that accessed the site in the last 30 days), and the company reached 400 employees. At this point, Facebook's growth shows no sign of slowing.

Le Facebook International

Facebook launched in universities in the United States and then spread to U.S. high schools. As a result, it wasn't until the fall of 2006 (when Facebook opened to everyone) that Facebook started making a showing in any other countries. When Facebook finally ventured into Canada and the United Kingdom, it took off fast, like Nick Cage fast. Many people speculate that the reason for Facebook's insta-popularity in these countries, more so than in the United States, came from the fact that citizens in Canada and the U.K. (and, randomly, Norway) didn't have the same stigma that U.S. citizens had: that Facebook was only meant for students. People in the U.S. had heard the buzz about Facebook for two years when it was only for students. This stigma has been a significant hurdle for Facebook's growth in older U.S. demographics. Because Facebook left this stigma behind when it crossed international borders, it's achieving massive penetration among Anglophones worldwide.

In the beginning of this chapter, we offer two motivations for Facebook's transition from allowing only students to encouraging everyone to join the site. The first is the ability to offer more people a valuable service, and the second is that Facebook becomes more useful to its existing members if each individual can reliably find anyone they're looking for on the site. This logic applies to Facebook's next big move — non-English speaking markets.

Chapter 2

Adding Your Own Face to Facebook

*I*n Chapter 1, we cover why you want to join Facebook. Here we actually get you signed up and ready to go on Facebook. Keep in mind a couple of things when you sign up. First, Facebook gets exponentially more useful and more fun when you start adding friends. Without friends, it can feel kind of dull. Second, your friends might take a few days to respond to your friend requests, so be patient. Even if your first time on Facebook isn't as exciting as you hope, be sure to come back and try again over the following weeks. Third, you can have only one account on Facebook. Facebook links accounts to e-mail addresses, and your e-mail address can be linked to only one account. This system enforces a world where people are who they say they are on Facebook.

What Do You Need to Do to Sign Up?

Officially, all you need to join Facebook is a valid e-mail address. When we say *valid*, we just mean that you can easily access the messages in that account because you're e-mailed a registration confirmation. Figure 2-1 shows the sign-up page. As you can see, you need to fill out a few things:

✔ **Full Name:** Facebook is a place based on real identity. It's not a place for fake names or aliases. Numerous privacy settings are in place to protect your information (see Chapter 4), so use your full real name to sign up.

✔ **Email:** You need to enter your valid e-mail address here. If you want to join a school or work network automatically, use your school or work e-mail.

✔ **Password:** Like with all passwords, using a combination of letters and numbers is a good idea for your Facebook password.

✔ **Date of Birth:** Enter your date of birth. You can hide this information on your profile.

✔ **Security Check** (not shown): The security check on Facebook is in the form of a CAPTCHA. A CAPTCHA is that funky-looking word-in-a-box. Computers can't read CAPTCHAs, but humans can. Asking you to solve a CAPTCHA is Facebook's way of keeping out robots who want to spam you, while still letting you sign up. You see the CAPTCHA after filling out your information and clicking Sign Up.

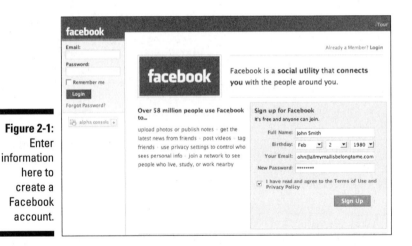

Figure 2-1:
Enter information here to create a Facebook account.

After you've filled out this information and agreed to the Terms of Service and Privacy Policy, click Sign Up Now. You're sent a confirmation e-mail; click the link in that e-mail to finish the sign-up process. When you log in to Facebook for the first time, Facebook will take you through a series of steps that it believes will help you get started and find your friends. These steps focus on entering information that will help you find friends either immediately or later on. For example, these steps ask you to use the Friend Finder,

---

Is Facebook just for college students?

No. Most emphatically, no. This is a common misconception mainly because Facebook started as being exclusive to college students. Facebook's origins, even its name, are rooted in college campuses, but its utility and nature aren't limited to being useful to only college students.

Everyone has networks of friends and people with whom they interact on a day-to-day basis. Young or old, in college or working, this is true. Facebook tries to map these real-world connections to make it easier for people to share information with their friends.

If you're reading this section thinking maybe you're just too old for Facebook, you're wrong. More and more people in older age demographics are signing up for Facebook every day to keep in touch with old friends, share photos, create events, and connect with local organizations. Almost everything we discuss in the book is non–age-specific.

Obviously, how people use the site can be very different at different ages, but you will discover these nuances when you use Facebook more and more. Generally, you should feel confident that you and your friends can connect and use Facebook in a meaningful way.

---

which we cover in Chapter 6. The Friend Finder checks your e-mail address book and matches e-mails to Facebook accounts. This means you can immediately send friend requests to people you know.

The set-up wizard has a tendency to change depending on what kind of e-mail address you join with and whether or not a friend invited you to use Facebook, so instead of going through every possibility for what Facebook will look like when you first log in, we suggest you read the "Joining a Network" section, as well as the "Education and Work history" segment of the "Setting Up Your Profile" section. These concepts definitely come into play as you are prompted for information in the set-up process.

Joining a Network

The word *network* can be a bit overused around Facebook from time to time. After all, isn't Facebook a giant network? Aren't your friends, with whom you have direct connections, a network? What about if you're using Facebook for business networking? When getting started on Facebook, you're prompted to join a network. In this context, *network* refers to a group of people with a real-world connection but who might not actually know each other.

Each of the four types of networks has a real-world counterpart. High school networks and college networks mirror high school and college campuses, workplace networks mirror companies and businesses, and regional networks mirror real-world neighborhoods. Joining a network (a process that we cover in detail in Chapter 11) expands your Facebook experience beyond only confirmed friends.

Networks are the building blocks of and privacy on Facebook. The default privacy setting on Facebook is that only confirmed friends and people in your networks can see your full profile. Say Carolyn belongs to the Stanford University network, and Leah belongs to the Brown University network; they can't see each other's profile unless they become friends. If Leah transfers to Stanford, she can (by default) then see Carolyn's profile without needing to be her friend.

Why join a network?

Joining a network allows you to see more people's profiles. The tradeoff here is that most people in that network can also see your profile, but with awareness and smart privacy settings (see Chapter 4), you should be able to expose some information comfortably to this larger group.

Joining a network gives you access to Network pages, where information from that network is compiled and displayed. For example, you're able to see upcoming events for your school or region. Network pages also bring to light interesting posted items, notes, and groups that are gaining popularity on a day-to-day basis.

Finally, joining a network makes connecting to the people around you easier. When you're in a network, you can easily search for the people you meet from day to day, and you can probably see their profiles and discover more about them.

Some people get a little anxious about joining networks because they think it makes them too visible. *Remember:* Even a larger network has only a fraction of the total number of people on Facebook. (The London network, for example, has more than one million people, but that's still less than one-fiftieth of Facebook.) Your profile is always off-limits to the vast majority of people on Facebook.

Which networks should you join?

The most important thing to consider when you join a network is which networks map your life. Think of yourself at a dinner party, introducing yourself to someone you've never met. If you were to say, "Hello, I work at the Daily

Planet," you'd probably want to join the Daily Planet workplace network. If you say, "Hello, I live in Metropolis," then you probably should join the Metropolis region network. Maybe you say some combination, "Hello, I work at the Daily Planet and live in Metropolis." In that case, you can join both networks. Maybe you'd even say, "Hello, I work at the Daily Planet, and I graduated from Metropolis University." Then you would probably want to join the Metropolis University network with your alumni e-mail address. From these details, you can decide which networks it makes sense to join; however, keep in mind these limitations:

- ✔ **You cannot join a high school network unless you're actually in high school.** High School networks cannot, for security reasons, accommodate high school alums or even teachers.

- ✔ **You can join college and workplace networks only with authenticated e-mail addresses.** If you've already graduated from college but want the capability to see classmates, request an alumni e-mail address from your alma mater. Without it, you won't be able to join that school's network.

- ✔ **You can join only one region network at a time.** If you introduce yourself at a party as, "I live in Metropolis, but I'm from Gotham," you have to pick one of those region networks to join.

To join your most relevant networks, look for the links on the big blue bar at the top. Click the arrow next to Networks for a drop-down menu, and then click Join a Network. Figure 2-2 shows the options you see if you haven't yet joined any networks.

To join your workplace or school network(s), you need an e-mail address from your company or school.

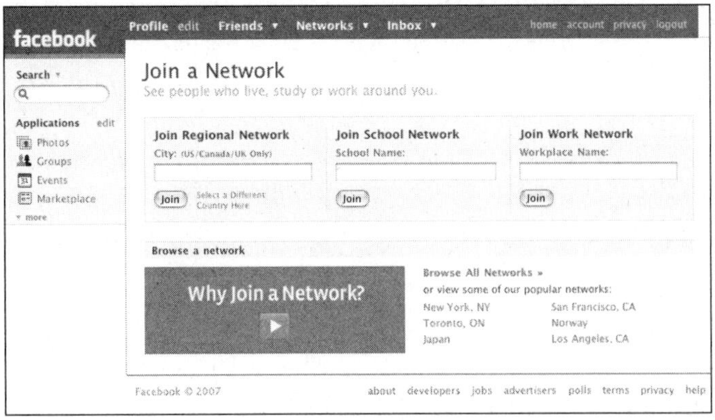

Figure 2-2:
Look no farther than this page to find a network to join.

facebook

Profile edit   Friends ▾   Networks ▾   Inbox ▾   home account privacy logout

Search ▾

Join a Network
See people who live, study or work around you.

Applications   edit
📷 Photos
👥 Groups
📅 Events
🛒 Marketplace
▾ more

Join Regional Network
City: (US /Canada/Uk Only)

(Join)   Select a Different
            Country Here

Join School Network
School Name:

(Join)

Join Work Network
Workplace Name:

(Join)

Browse a network

Why Join a Network?
▶

Browse All Networks »
or view some of our popular networks:
New York, NY   San Francisco, CA
Toronto, ON   Norway
Japan   Los Angeles, CA

Facebook © 2007   about developers jobs advertisers polls terms privacy help

Setting Up Your Profile

You're probably thinking, "Didn't I set up my profile when I joined?" The answer to that is, not quite. Your account is what you already created; however, your *profile* — what people can see about you — is probably still blank. We talk more about the bigger picture of profiles and what they mean for you in Chapter 5. For now, just say that setting up your profile is important so that when you start to find friends and friends start to find you, they can identify who you are, and that you really are you. The main pieces we cover here will help people figure out who you are.

To edit this information (and any other information on your profile), look for the Edit link next to the word *Profile* on the big blue bar at the top. Figure 2-3 shows the page for editing basic information; you can select any of the other tabs to edit that information as well. As you edit this information, you may wonder who can see it. By default, your confirmed friends and people in your networks can see this basic information. Sensitive stuff like your contact information will be available only to your confirmed friends by default. You can restrict this further using your privacy settings, if you choose (see Chapter 4).

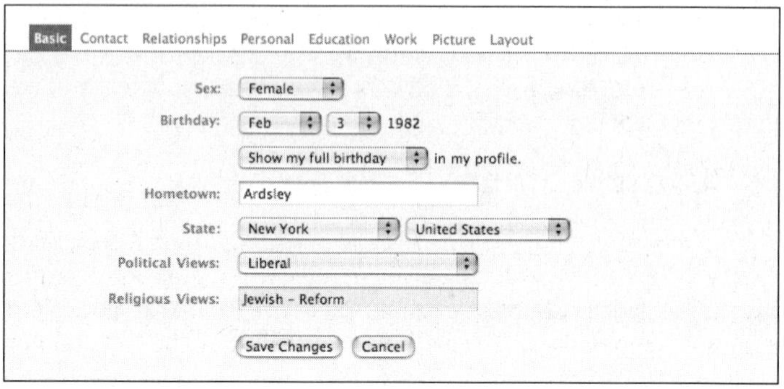

Figure 2-3:
Updating
your basic
information.

Throughout the rest of this chapter, we detail four of the tabs shown in Figure 2-3. Here, we briefly describe the others, which get more attention in Chapter 5:

- ✓ **Contact information:** Facebook has an amazing ability to be a one-stop address book. Because of the ability to restrict visibility, you can share your phone number, address, e-mail addresses, and screen names easily. The Contact tab has built-in privacy drop-down menus that enable you to control who sees what.

- ✓ **Relationships:** Information entered on the Relationships tab pertains to you being or not being in a relationship, what sort of relationship that is (married, engaged, or . . . it's complicated), or what sort of relationship you're looking for. Although Facebook is not a dating site, it can be useful in ascertaining if a potential date is even looking for a relationship or is already in one. Additionally, if you are in a relationship, you can link yourself to that person on Facebook by entering their name in this tab.

- ✓ **Personal:** Personal information includes a lot of free-form fields. For example, you can enter your favorite books, movies, activities, TV shows, and music. You can also enter representative quotes, as well as tell people "about me."

- ✓ **Layout:** The Layout tab offers some instruction for how to change the layout of your profile.

Basic information

Basic information — the information that appears at the top of your profile next to your profile picture and below your name — is a sort of "at-a-glance" window into you. It includes your hometown and your political and religious views. All these fields are optional, but it helps people know the most, well, basic information about you very quickly.

Education and Work history

Entering your education and work history usually helps people identify how they know you when you request a friend or send someone a message. Additionally, if someone performs a search for a certain class year from your school, you'll appear in the search results, and old friends can get in touch with you.

Profile picture

Your profile picture is another way that people can identify you, especially if you have a common name. A few considerations about profile pictures that fit into the larger idea of a profile are covered in Chapter 5. For now, keep these points in mind when choosing a profile picture:

✔ **Make a good first impression.** Your profile picture is one of the first ways people interact with your profile and how you choose to represent yourself. Most people pick pictures that are more or less flattering, or that represent what's important to them. Sometimes, profile pictures include other people — friends or significant others. Other times, the location matters. If the first photo you see of someone is at the beach versus at a party or sitting at his desk, you might draw different conclusions about that person. What picture represents you?

✔ **Consider who will see your profile picture.** By default, a small version of your profile picture appears in search results that are visible to all of Facebook. So, generally, people who search for your name can see that picture. You can control this with privacy settings. For more about privacy settings, see Chapter 4.

✔ **Remember that you're not stuck with it.** After we put all this pressure on you to represent yourself and let people identify you, keep in mind that you can easily change your profile picture at any time. Is it the dead of winter, and that photo of you on the beach last summer just too mocking? No problem; simply edit your profile picture.

Do You Trust Me? Getting Verified

As we say over and over, Facebook is a Web site for real identity and real people. To protect this fact, Facebook has systems in place to detect any fake profiles. Fake profiles might be jokes (for example, someone creating a profile for their dog), or they might be *spammers* (robots creating accounts to send thousands of fake friend requests). Regardless, they're not allowed on the site.

You, however, aren't fake or a spammer; how does Facebook know that? Facebook figures that out by verifying you. Now, you may start out verified, or it may take a little while. To figure out whether you still need to get verified, look at these questions:

✔ **Did you join with an *authenticated* e-mail address?** *Authenticated* e-mail addresses are ones that not just anyone can get. For example, Google provides e-mail addresses to its employees that end with a specific domain. You can't have that address unless you work for Google. Most colleges and workplaces have authenticated e-mail addresses. If you joined with one of these, you were automatically verified.

✔ **Do you have an authenticated e-mail address that you didn't join with?** Joining a network with your authenticated e-mail address also serves to verify you. (Refer to Figure 2-2 to see how you join an authenticated workplace or school network.)

✔ **Do you not have an authenticated e-mail address?** You will need to get verified as you use the site. To do that, keep reading this section.

Without an authenticated e-mail address, Facebook unfortunately has to assume the worst about you. It's afraid you might send spam or inappropriate content to people on Facebook. It's suspicious and paranoid. But it wants to trust you, so it's going to start testing you.

Remember the CAPTCHA you filled out when you joined? Until Facebook trusts you, you will continue to see these when you interact with other people on Facebook. Through normal use of the site, eventually Facebook will believe you are not, in fact, malicious, and it will stop showing you CAPTCHAs wherever you turn. You can forgo having to solve many of these by instead being verified through your mobile phone.

To get verified via mobile, follow these steps:

1. **Search for someone and click Add to Friends.**

2. **On the Add to Friends pop-up that appears (shown in Figure 2-4), click the Verify Your Account link (located beneath the CAPTCHA).**

   A new Confirm Your Phone pop-up appears, as shown in Figure 2-5.

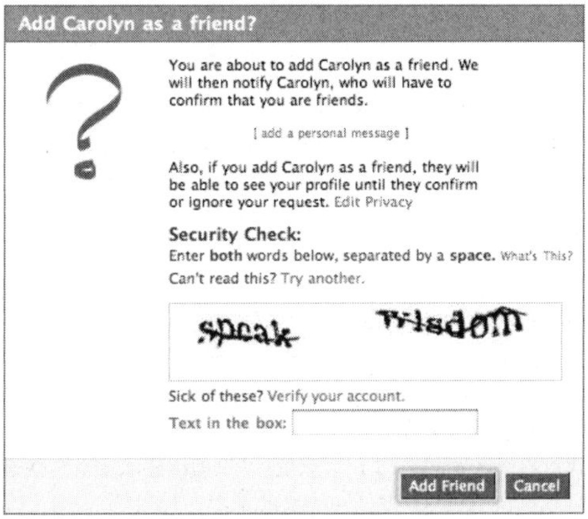

Figure 2-4: Still seeing a CAPTCHA like this? End the madness with mobile verification.

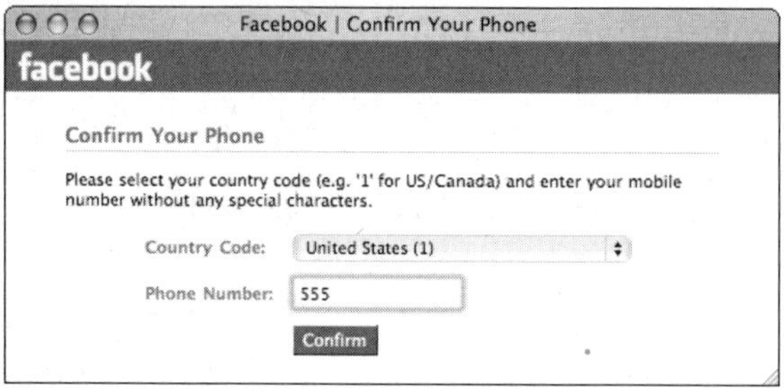

Figure 2-5:
Confirm
your phone
to prove
you're real.

Facebook | Confirm Your Phone

facebook

Confirm Your Phone

Please select your country code (e.g. '1' for US/Canada) and enter your mobile
number without any special characters.

Country Code: United States (1)   ⬍

Phone Number: 555

Confirm

3. **Select your country and enter your mobile phone number.**

4. **Check your mobile phone for a text message that should contain a
   code.**

5. **Enter the code into the Code field in the Confirm your Phone pop-up.**

6. **Press Confirm.**

Facebook won't send you any other mobile messages unless you choose to
opt into Facebook Mobile. (For more information about Facebook Mobile, see
Chapter 14.)

If you're already verified, you won't see a CAPTCHA. You might not be able to
use mobile verification if your phone can't receive text messages, but don't
worry, you'll still get verified eventually just by being a normal user of
the site.

Chapter 3

Finding Your Way

- -

In This Chapter

▶ Finding your way around Facebook

▶ Configuring the left column

▶ Looking around after logging in

▶ Reading about friends on News Feed

▶ Learn about what's new, now, and next in the right column

- -

*F*acebook is composed of two main components: the Frame and the Canvas. *The Frame* includes the blue bar at the top, the navigation column of links and icons underneath the Facebook logo, and the links along the bottom. Understanding the elements of the Frame is important because no matter what link you follow, what page you load — wherever you are on Facebook — the Frame stays visible and virtually unchanged. (The two exceptions to this are the new message indicator next to Inbox, which we explain in Chapter 10, and the customization of the Applications in the left column, which we explain later in this chapter.) Think of the Frame more like a faithful puppy than a creepy stalker, and be comforted that no matter where you find yourself in the depths of the Facebook Web site, you can always find your way home via the Frame.

The Canvas — the big rectangle that encloses everything else — is very different from the Frame. The name refers to the potential of this space. Just about anything can appear on the Canvas: search results, friends' customized profiles, photo albums, invitations to events, your privacy settings, and so on. Anything a developer can dream up might appear because Facebook and non-Facebook developers can build applications for Facebook. Just about the only thing that will never appear on the Canvas is a song or audio clip that plays the second you load the page. When you click any link on the Frame or within the Canvas, you don't feel like you're jumping Web pages because the Frame remains unchanged. It feels like you're repainting the Canvas with a new picture.

In this chapter, we show you the three components of the Frame and explain the Home page, which is what you see on the Canvas when you log in. Consider the rest of this book to be a long explanation of what else you might see on the Canvas because that is where the Facebook action happens.

The Blue Bar on Top

We both happen to spend a lot of time in coffee shops working alongside writers, students, business people, and hobbyists — all drinking steamy beverages and manning laptops. We can always tell at a glance when someone is browsing Facebook by the big blue bar across the top of the page. The blue bar is home to the most important links on Facebook. When you can sufficiently navigate the blue bar, kick off your shoes and put up your feet (unless you're in a coffee shop) because you'll undoubtedly feel comfortable on Facebook. Figure 3-1 lists the blue bar links from left to right, and what you need to know about each:

✔ **Facebook:** The Facebook logo in the top left of the page serves two purposes. The first purpose is to remind you what Web site you're using, lest you should forget. When you hover your mouse over the Facebook logo, you see a little house appear — the second purpose. No matter where you are on Facebook, all you have to do is click this icon (say, "There's no place like home!") and you're back at the Facebook Home page.

Search for a person, group, event, application, or business here.

Click here to go home. The blue bar links The Notch

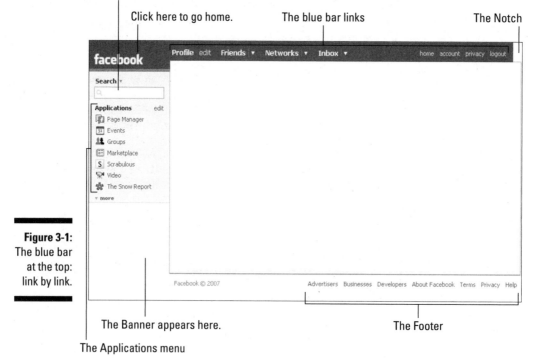

Figure 3-1:
The blue bar at the top: link by link.

The Banner appears here. The Footer

The Applications menu

✔ **Profile:** Next to the Facebook logo, you find a Profile link (see Chapter 2). Clicking Edit, which appears right next to Profile, takes you to your Profile settings. This isn't normally something you need to access in a hurry. But you never know when your relationship status might change or when you'll discover a new favorite TV show you want to list, so be comforted knowing that the ability to make these changes is always a click away.

✔ **Friends:** The Friends link takes you to a list of all your Facebook friends. This might be everyone you've ever known depending on how active you are on the site. If you're anything like us, clicking Friends gives you the sensation a magician must feel with the wave of the wand: *Poof!* Everyone you know appears. Click the arrow next to Friends to see the following options:

- *Status Updates* shows you a list of friends and their current statuses.

- *Online Now* filters your Friends list to those who've been active on Facebook in the last five minutes.

- *Recently Updated* indicates whether your friends have updated their profiles.

- *Recently Added* sorts your Friends list by the recency of your Facebook friendship

- *All Friends* shows you a listing of your friends in alphabetical order.

- *Invite Friends* enables you to invite friends who aren't yet on Facebook to join the site.

- *Find Friends* provides a quick way to find friends who are on Facebook but not yet your Facebook friends.

✔ **Networks:** Clicking Networks takes you to your primary network's page (see Chapter 11), while clicking the arrow next to Networks allows you to jump to any of your networks, browse other networks, or join a new network. *Note:* You can actually edit any of your network settings by clicking Join a Network (confusing terminology, we confess). These settings include updating your status at a school from student to alumni, selecting your primary network, or leaving a network.

✔ **Inbox:** Anyone on Facebook can send you a message unless you change the messaging privacy settings. The Inbox is where you retrieve those messages. The number of new or unread messages you have in your Inbox is shown in parentheses next to the Inbox link. Clicking the arrow next to Inbox takes you to messages you've sent, the compose window for sending a new message, or the Notifications page, which is described in Chapter 10.

✔ **Home:** The Home link works the same as the Facebook logo; it's just more explicit about where it takes you — the Home page. Leah personally never uses it because no adorable house appears on mouse over.

✔ **Account:** You see here four tabs, each containing anywhere from a handful to several settings. It can be almost overwhelming how many options you have to configure your Facebook account. These settings are described independently throughout this book in each setting's relevant context.

✔ **Privacy:** Privacy is one of the cornerstones of the Facebook experience, and is defined in great detail in the very next chapter. Many people set all their privacy settings when they're first getting familiar with Facebook, and rarely change them afterward. However, the fact that this link follows you around the site serves as a constant reminder of the importance of privacy to the Facebook experience, and should you ever want to change a privacy setting, having the link live on the frame ensures that you have no trouble doing so.

✔ **Logout:** Use this link to explicitly log out of Facebook. This is particularly important on computers that others might have access to, as some can do a lot of damage to your social life with free reign over your Facebook account. *Note:* One other way to log out of Facebook is to end your browser session. However, if you have the Remember Me option selected, you won't ever be logged out until you explicitly hit Logout. That option keeps you logged in despite closing the browser; therefore, only use it on a personal computer.

On the Left: Search, the Applications Menu, and the Banner

For simplicity's sake, we're grouping Search, the Applications menu, and the Banner into this section, even though their only relationship is their physical location on the site: the left side of the Frame.

Search

The left side Search box is the quickest way to start a search. The Search box is most effective if you know some or the entire name of the person or thing (group, event, application, band, business, and so on) that you're looking for. You can also access more detailed people-search options on the Search page, which you access by clicking Search. For more on finding friends, see Chapter 6.

People often try a few popular types of queries that the Search box isn't designed to handle. Searching for elements of Facebook itself, such as Photos or Privacy doesn't give you what you're looking for. A better way to discover, or navigate to, a particular feature of the site is to scroll to the bottom of the page and click Help. The Help page features a different search box specifically designed for these types of queries. Another common misuse of the Search box is entering attributes of people or things, such as *Events happening this Saturday in Denver* or *Liberal men in Seattle*. To find events or groups in a particular location, go to a particular region's Network page via the Network link, and look at popular groups or upcoming events. To browse people who match a particular set of criteria, click the arrow next to Search and choose Browse. There, you can use the options on the right to filter your search results. The other search options that appear under the arrow next to Search are actually the same as the options on the Search page; see Chapter 6.

The Applications menu

In Chapter 1, we introduce the term *application* as it's defined on Facebook. *Applications* are the services that leverage the core Facebook elements, including Profile information, Friend associations, the Facebook Calendar, and Inbox. These enable you to engage in more specific and sometimes niche activities.

When you join Facebook, you see six default applications already added to your account:

Photos

✔ The Photos application enables you to browse your friends' recent photos, view photos in which you're tagged, and upload your own photos. For more details on Photos, see Chapter 7.

Groups

✔ Groups on Facebook can be created by any user for any reason, and are usually meant to bring people together (virtually) around common causes or interests. The Groups link on the Applications menu takes you to a page for viewing groups recently joined by your friends, groups to which you belong that have recently been updated, or generally popular groups that you can browse. See Chapter 12 for more details on Groups.

Events

✔ The Events application is most often used to enable people to organize real life events with guest lists, reminders, and a space to add relevant comments and photos. The Events link on the Applications menu takes you to a page for viewing your upcoming and past events, friends' events, and other popular events that you can browse. For more on Events, see Chapter 13.

Marketplace

✔ The Marketplace is where Facebook users can buy and sell items, find or offer services, and hunt for jobs or applicants. Clicking Marketplace takes you to the marketplace in your primary network, but you can quickly access listings from other networks, listings made specifically by your friends, or items you've listed. You can read more about the Facebook Marketplace in Chapter 8.

Posted Items

✔ The Posted Items application allows people to highlight interesting content from the Web or Facebook and provides them a forum for discussion. Clicking Posted Items, which is located beneath More on the Applications menu, takes you to a list of items recently posted by your friends as well as links to your posted items and other popular posted items. To read more about Posted Items, see Chapter 8.

Notes

✔ Known to techy-types as a blogging tool, Notes offers users a blank page for sharing thoughts, anecdotes, tirades, diatribes, and more. The Notes link, located beneath More on the Applications menu, gives you quick access to notes recently written by and about your friends. You also get quick access to notes you've written and other popular notes. For more about Notes, see Chapter 8.

The applications described here are simply the defaults you have upon signing up, but ultimately you have complete control over which applications you add to your Facebook experience. You're free to remove or add as many applications as you like from the hundreds developed by Facebook (which we cover in Chapter 8) or other companies (which we cover in Chapter 9).

Each time you add an application on Facebook, you have the option of adding a quick link to that application on your Application menu (refer to Figure 3-1). The quick link shows at the top of your hidden quick links, which you can see by clicking More. The Applications menu can hold as many applications as you like, but can only show seven on the Frame. To access a hidden quick link, click More and then click the specific application name. To customize which applications are shown, click More and then drag and drop the applications above or below the divider.

If you add an application but choose *not* to add a quick link, you can still access it by clicking Applications. If you decide later you would like to add or remove a quick link to a particular application, click Applications, scroll to the specific application, click Edit Settings, and then check or uncheck Left Menu.

The Banner

Right underneath the Applications menu, in the shape of a rectangle, is *the Banner* — the primary reason Facebook is free. The ad spot underneath the Applications menu is the *Banner Ad*. Facebook pays its engineers, its hardware costs, and gets its lunch money by placing a few advertisements throughout the site. This spot is currently contracted to Microsoft's adCenter, a service that delivers a particular ad via some loose targeting parameters. (Male users of Facebook shouldn't hold their breath hoping for a Victoria's Secret advertisement, and women shouldn't wait for a Gillette Mach 3 ad.) Both Facebook and adCenter earn revenue when people click the Banner ad.

The Footer

At the bottom of every Facebook page, you see a set of links collectively called *the Footer*. The Footer is the catch-all for important information about Facebook the social network, Facebook for business, Facebook the company, and the Facebook policies. Descriptions of each link follow.

- ✔ **Advertisers:** Explores two of Facebook's primary promotional offerings, Facebook Pages and Social Ads. In Chapters 16 and 17, we cover these advertising solutions in great depth.

- ✔ **Businesses:** If you're looking to use Facebook to enhance your businesses, this is the page to read. The Businesses page offers an overview of the Facebook business offerings including Social Ads, Facebook Pages, Beacon, Insights, Platform, and Polls. Most of these features are discussed in Part IV of this book.

- ✔ **Developers:** Most of the applications you can add to your Facebook profile are written by developers who don't work at Facebook. Some of these outside developers write Facebook applications to help their business, some are students creating applications for programming classes, and some are simply developer hobbyists. If you're interested in creating a new Facebook application, this is your link.

- ✔ **About Facebook:** Takes you to the About Facebook page. Here, you can read about some key features of Facebook, see the latest headlines from the Facebook Blog, discover the newest Facebook features, and see links to recent articles written about Facebook. Also, follow this link to discover all the job opportunities at Facebook.

- ✔ **Terms:** Though this link might see the least traffic of all the links on the site, it's one of the most important. Facebook is eerily adept at catching users who break the Terms of Use in any damaging way. For the sake of those who use the site in a respectful way, Facebook takes violations of the Terms of Use seriously. The use of fake birthdays, fake names, pornographic or copyrighted content, and spam-like behavior are all grounds for disabling an account.

- ✔ **Privacy:** Details the Facebook Privacy Policy, which states

    Facebook's Privacy Policy is designed to help you understand how we collect and use the personal information you decide to share, and help you make informed decisions when using Facebook.

✔ **Help:** The Help page gives you all sorts of tools for finding out how to use the site, how to stay safe on Facebook, and where to send in your suggestions about how the site might be improved. ***Remember:*** Many of the Facebook applications are written by external developers (not Facebook); if you're having trouble using one of these applications, the Facebook Help page offers methods for contacting those developers directly.

The Home Page

The Home page refers to what you see on the Canvas when you first log in to Facebook. It's comprised of two major sections: News Feed and, um, the right column, which doesn't have a name but rather a theme, which we cover in just a minute.

News Feed

Ever pick up the morning paper and read about a foreign election or a famous actor's arrest, and wonder what any of this has to do with you? Stop wondering. Staying in touch with current events enables you to do anything from making casual conversation at a barbecue to changing the world.

Now, imagine if your morning paper, news show, or radio program included an additional section that featured articles solely about the *specific* people you know. This is News Feed. As long as your friends are active on Facebook, you can stay up-to-date with their lives via News Feed. A friend might post photos from his recent birthday party, another might write a Note about her new job, and several others might RSVP to a wine-tasting party that you might be interested in attending as well. All these might show as stories in your Facebook News Feed. Recently, in her News Feed, Leah read that 12 of her friends attended a Lymphoma research fundraiser, a friend moved to Seattle, and another friend arrived in Bali for her honeymoon — plus 22 other stories of this kind.

A bonus of News Feed: You can often use it to stay up-to-date on current events just by seeing what your friends are talking about. In one morning's News Feed, Leah found out that a friend was excited about Barack Obama's choice for campaign chair, another friend was intrigued by Donald Rumsfeld's position at Stanford, and a third friend found that day's Dilbert cartoon relevant to anyone working in technology. We're not recommending you rely on News Feed for all your current event news, but sometimes it can be a decent proxy.

For the most part, News Feed shows the actions that your friends are taking on Facebook, such as photo uploads, comments, Wall posts, profile changes, and others. Sometimes, however, you may read about what your friends are up to in life through their interactions on the rest of the Web. A feature called *Facebook Beacon* allows other sites (such as Blockbuster.com, Yelp, eBay, and others) to publish stories to Facebook — with the user's permission. For example, Carolyn might write a review on Yelp or Leah might rent The West Wing, Season 2 on Blockbuster, and they can have those stories printed in their friends' News Feeds.

Every story is preceded by an icon, which serves two purposes. The first is to denote which type of story it is. (Relationship statuses, for example, are noted with a heart icon.) The second purpose is the procrastinator's dream. Clicking any of these icons filters your News Feed to only stories of that kind but includes many of the stories that have already fallen off the bottom of your News Feed. For example, clicking the green speech bubble with quotation marks filters your News Feed to all recent stories about comments people have made on photos, notes, or on a Wall, and so on. Filtering your News Feed to a particular story type also reveals a menu of all story types, shown in Figure 3-2. Here, you can quickly filter News Feed to any particular story type that interests you.

Figure 3-2: Sampling of News Feed story types.

Network Stories

Relationship Stories

Group Stories

Event Stories

Photo Stories

Edit Profile Stories

Note Stories

Posted Item Stories

Wall Stories

Video Stories

Friend Stories

Status Stories

Discussion Stories

Gift Stories

Sponsored Stories

Marketplace Stories

Poll Stories

How News Feed works

News Feed generates a list of interesting stories about what your friends have been up to. On the backend of News Feed is a whole lot of math. You might be connected to 10, 100, or 500 friends on Facebook, many of whom take actions on the site that reflect news in their real lives. The average Facebook user has 105 friends, though clearly some users have about 3 and others have 600. Collectively, your friends take, on average, about 20,000 actions on Facebook per day. If you are one of the users increasing the average, it's nearly impossible for you to keep up with all these actions. Additionally, because your Facebook friends range from your very best friend to some girl you went to elementary school with, many of these actions aren't particularly interesting.

In order to keep the number of News Feed stories you receive manageable and to maximize the relevance of the stories, News Feed tries to calculate which people and story types most interest you. How? News Feed gives a weighting to each Facebook friend based on various factors, such as whose profiles you view often, whom you've messaged recently, whom (according to friend details) you're close to, and more. Next, Facebook figures out what types of stories you might like, such as photo uploads versus status updates versus who wrote on whose Wall. This calculation is based on general story-type popularity (people most often click through to see Photo upload stories, for example), what types of stories you've seen too many or too few of recently, and other factors. Finally, News Feed takes into account how recent these actions occurred, giving higher weight to stories that happened most recently. All these calculations come together to deliver you approximately three to six different News Feed stories every hour.

Obviously, the fewer friends you have active on Facebook, the higher the percentage of total actions you see in your News Feed; however, the more Facebook friends you have, the more often the stories are of greater diversity and interest.

News Feed preferences

Sometimes, the quantitative calculations of News Feed just don't equal reality. When you read a story in News Feed, you have an immediate emotional reaction. If it's a great story, you can press the Thumbs Up icon that appears in the upper right of every News Feed story to help News Feed understand your particular tastes better. If it's a terrible story, a misleading story, or a boring one, clicking the x in the upper right similarly tunes News Feed to your preferences. These controls help Facebook adjust your News Feed over time and inform the company about story types that people like or dislike. Therefore, changes to the product reflect user preferences. Other times, you know specifically why you like or don't like a story. Perhaps you have an ex whose profile you view from time to time, but you'd rather not read about that person in your News Feed. Maybe you have a friend who always posts interesting stuff, and you'd like to see most of the stories about her. Maybe you simply love receiving stories about friends writing on each other's Wall, but you don't care that much about when friends, no matter how much you like them, change their profile information. For these general cases, alter your News Feed more dramatically by clicking Preferences in the top of the News Feed header.

The Preferences link at the top of News Feed, across from the News Feed header, adds a qualitative aspect to the News Feed calculations. Clicking this link gives you a place to express your explicit interest or disinterest in specific story types and people. On the top half of the page, you see several sliders corresponding to story types. For story types you find interesting, increase the corresponding slider; for those you like less, move the slider down. *Note:* These settings are relative to one another. Positioning a slider all the way up or down doesn't mean that you receive all or none of that particular story type; it simply indicates relative preference of story types, which News Feed uses to adjust its calculations.

On the bottom half of the screen, you see two buckets that can hold the names of 40 friends. Putting names into the bucket on the left means you're more likely to see stories about these friends than if you hadn't put them in the bucket; adding names to the right bucket means you see fewer stories about these friends. Again, note that these are relative settings. You might still miss a few stories about friends in the More bucket, and you might still see occasional stories about friends in the Less bucket. This is particularly true if you have very few friends. News Feed would rather show you stories you might be less interested in than show you no stories at all.

Sponsored stories

Occasionally, no more than twice a day, you might see a story in News Feed that has nothing to do with your friends. These are *sponsored stories,* the content of which is provided by an advertiser who pays for the placement. Like the Banner, sponsored stories pay the Facebook electricity bill, help stock the company snack room, and ensure that employees have health insurance — all while keeping Facebook free to users. Sponsored stories can always be identified with the icon to the left of this paragraph.

New, Now, and Next

On the right side of the Home page, next to News Feed, you find a somewhat random smorgasbord of what's new, what's now, and what's coming up next on Facebook.

✔ **Notifications:** The Notifications page tells you about all the actions your friends have taken directly relating to you. Perhaps someone has tagged you in a photo, written on your Wall, or given you a virtual gift — all of that is listed on the Notifications page. When you have a new notification, a flag appears in the top right of the Home page to alert you. Read more about notifications in Chapter 10.

- ✔ **Requests:** Requests are similar to notifications, but they require a specific reply. An example of a request is someone on Facebook wanting you to confirm that you two are friends. The request contains links to accept or ignore the friend's request. Another example is an invitation to an event to which you should RSVP. The request contains links to RSVP Attending, Not Attending, and Tentatively Attending. When any request is pending, a link to it appears in your right column above Status Updates. If nothing shows there, you have no unanswered requests.

- ✔ **Updates:** After you've pledged allegiance to a particular band or business on Facebook, that business can send news and updates to your Inbox. A flag in the right column informs you that you have a new update waiting. Read about Updates in Chapter 16.

- ✔ **Pokes:** Read about Poke in Chapter 10. Just know for now that if you receive a Poke, you find out about it on the Home page.

- ✔ **Status Updates:** Use this section to let your friends know what you're currently up to by clicking the blue text next to your picture. Note that Facebook enforces the use of the present tense by allowing you to fill in the blank after *is*. While some Facebook users find this construction limiting, others value how it encourages people to fill in what they're up to right then, instead of an abstract free-form tagline. To see the three most recent friend's statuses, click Show Friend Updates. To see even more, click Show All.

    Clicking your profile picture in Status Updates takes you to your profile. Some people prefer this to the Profile link at the top of the frame.

- ✔ **Upcoming Events:** Reminders about all events to which you're invited show in this column for three days prior to the start of the event unless you RSVP Not Attending.

- ✔ **Birthdays:** The Birthdays field shows you which friends have birthdays in the next three days. Clicking See All gives you a snapshot of all your friends' birthdays as well as access to shelling out a little cash to send them a virtual gift or post a Happy Birthday flier. You won't see birthday reminders for those friends who have chosen to hide their birthday information from their profile.

- ✔ **Invite Your Friends:** This section doesn't particularly fall into the new, now, or next theme, but if getting someone you care about to join Facebook would improve your Facebook experience, you have easy access to invite them. Click the icon in the Invite Your Friends box to invite friends to Facebook.

- ✔ **New Stuff:** This box serves as a promotional area for new things being offered around the site. Here, you might see the newest gift in the virtual gift shop (see Chapter 8), recent Marketplace listings in your networks, and more. Refreshing your Home page refreshes the contents of this box.

- ✔ **The Next Step:** Here, you find out about new or popular features of Facebook or paid promotions for various groups, events, and contests.

What is *The Notch?*

In the top right of the Facebook page, the blue bar of the Frame doesn't extend as far as the edge of the Canvas. This gap was nicknamed *The Notch* by Facebook employees during the vetting of this particular design. As far as we know, no such (mis)alignment exists on any other page on the Internet. What's the frequency, Facebook?

We describe at the start of this chapter that the ever-constant Frame holds the tools Facebook provides to enable your experiences, whereas the Canvas, and the content in it, belong to you. It's the Canvas that shows your profile, your photos, your friends, and so on. From a developer's perspective, the Canvas is the blank slate on which they "wow" you with their applications.

Facebook can be thought of as a platform that runs in the background supporting your online identity and your interactions with the people you know. The Notch, combined with the subtle shadow around the Canvas, gives the appearance that the Facebook Frame is laying beneath the Canvas, which is lifted, front and center. The design of the site is meant to artistically represent the relationship between the Facebook Web site and the community it supports.

Chapter 4

Privacy and Safety on Facebook

. . . .

. . . .

*U*nfortunately, a lot of horror stories are out there about the Internet, especially about social networking sites. A lot of them involve teenagers and predators, some of them involve identity theft, and others involve far less salacious (but no less real) problems, such as spamming and computer viruses. The bad news is that these things are out there. The good news is that Facebook has some of the most granular privacy controls on the Internet, enabling you to share real information comfortably on Facebook.

Facebook has created a trusted environment that provides three major assets to you:

  ✔ **In general, people create real accounts for themselves, and people are who they say they are on Facebook.** This means that the community enforces a standard of reality. When people ask you to view their Web cast or click some mysterious link, those actions are reported by the community and are removed from Facebook. This also means that it's easy to tell a real person from a fake one and that you can make informed choices about with whom you interact online.

✔ **Facebook provides granular privacy controls that are built into every feature on the site.** We discuss how these work in depth in this chapter. Before we get to that, however, we talk a bit about privacy in general and how Facebook approaches it.

✔ **The Facebook default is to allow only a small number of people — your networks and confirmed friends — to see your profile.** This means that even if you never touch your privacy settings, only a tiny, tiny fraction of the people on Facebook can see your profile. This doesn't even include things like your contact information, for which the default is that only confirmed friends can see it.

The Win-Win of Privacy

Would you display your phone number on a public billboard? Probably not. Would you write it down for your friends to hold onto? Probably yes. What Facebook has learned is that the more people control their information, the more likely they are to share it. If they feel confident that only those people whom they want will see their phone number, they post it on Facebook. The win-win of privacy is that the more you share, the better it is for information flow among you and your friends. So, when you share more information, your friends share more information. You win in that your information is shown to the people you want to see it, and not to the people you don't. Your friends win because they can have access to more information about you. Therefore, you win again because you have access to more information about them. And then, well, the cycle keeps building.

Keeping this in mind, using your privacy options wisely is the best way to share the right information with the right people. Using your privacy options wisely is also the best way to keep your information from the wrong people. With this control, Facebook becomes a place where you can share very personal things — not just in a "my phone number is private" way, but also in an "I'm writing notes for my friends only" way (and a blog that anyone could find). Because of the privacy controls, Facebook is a place for you to truly share your life the same way you do in the real world.

Privacy Options

To start, take a gander at the Privacy Overview page, as shown in Figure 4-1. You access this page by clicking Privacy in the big blue bar on top.

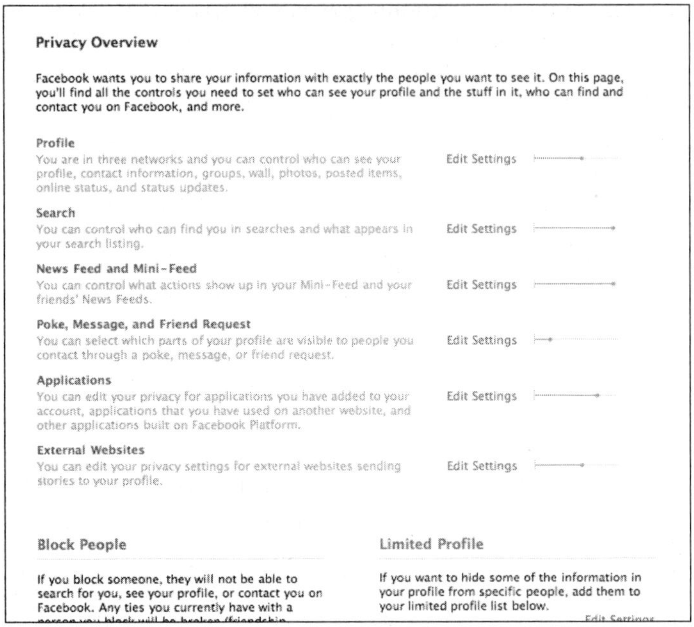

Privacy Overview

Facebook wants you to share your information with exactly the people you want to see it. On this page, you'll find all the controls you need to set who can see your profile and the stuff in it, who can find and contact you on Facebook, and more.

Profile
You are in three networks and you can control who can see your profile, contact information, groups, wall, photos, posted items, online status, and status updates.   Edit Settings

Search
You can control who can find you in searches and what appears in your search listing.   Edit Settings

News Feed and Mini-Feed
You can control what actions show up in your Mini-Feed and your friends' News Feeds.   Edit Settings

Poke, Message, and Friend Request
You can select which parts of your profile are visible to people you contact through a poke, message, or friend request.   Edit Settings

Applications
You can edit your privacy for applications you have added to your account, applications that you have used on another website, and other applications built on Facebook Platform.   Edit Settings

External Websites
You can edit your privacy settings for external websites sending stories to your profile.   Edit Settings

Block People

If you block someone, they will not be able to search for you, see your profile, or contact you on Facebook. Any ties you currently have with a person you block will be broken (friendship,

Limited Profile

If you want to hide some of the information in your profile from specific people, add them to your limited profile list below.
                                    Edit Settings

Figure 4-1:
The Privacy
page.

That's a lot of sections, but we break it down by going through what each section controls:

- ✔ **Profile:** The Profile section controls who can see what on your profile. If you click through to this page, you find controls for your profile as a whole, as well as individual settings that control who sees your Status updates, videos of you, photos of you, your online status, your friends, your Wall, every part of your contact information, and every application you add. We talk about what the setting options are in "Limited Profile and custom settings," a little later in this chapter.

- ✔ **Search:** The Search section controls who can find you in a search for your name on Facebook. This section also controls whether your public search listing gets indexed in outside search engines. In addition, you can decide what sorts of ways people can interact with you after they do find you in search. For example, you can decide that strangers can't Poke you, but they can add you as a friend.

- ✔ **News Feed and Mini-Feed:** *News Feed* is a constantly updating list of stories about your friends' actions on Facebook. News Feed appears on your home page. *Mini-Feed* is a list of your recent activity on Facebook that appears on your profile. This section lets you decide what sorts of actions generate Mini-Feed stories in your profile and News Feed stories in your friends' News Feeds.

✔ **Poke, Message, and Friend Request:** This section applies only to people who aren't in your network and who aren't your friends. Basically, when you Poke, message, or add folks that you're not already connected with as a friend, they can see certain parts of your profile. You can decide which parts you want to let them see.

✔ **Applications:** Applications built on top of Facebook Platform are sometimes built by Facebook and are sometimes built by other people. (For more information on adding applications, see Chapters 8 and 9.) The Applications section of the Privacy page controls what applications interact with your information as well as what information they're allowed to interact with.

✔ **External Websites:** Through a program called Beacon, Facebook enables you to generate News Feed and Mini-Feed stories from other Web sites. The External Websites section is where you control which Web sites are allowed to send stories to your Mini-Feed and your friends' News Feeds. This also controls whether you are notified about such stories.

✔ **Block People:** *Blocking* someone on Facebook is more or less the digital equivalent to some combination of a restraining order and a witness protection program. For the most part, if you add someone to your Block List — either on this page or on his profile page — he will never see any traces of you on Facebook.

✔ **Limited Profile:** We get into this in more detail in "Limited Profile and custom settings," later in this chapter. For now, know that Limited Profile is a way to keep certain individuals from seeing a lot of information that you want most of your friends to see.

When you change any of your settings on these pages, you must click Save in order for Facebook to apply them.

For most of these sections, a very common-looking drop-down menu appears. The drop-down menu is basically the starting point for deciding who sees what. You see similar drop-downs when you create photo albums and upload videos. Instead of going through each and every drop-down option, we cover some general options for restricting (or granting) privacy.

Network privacy

In Chapter 3, we talk about joining a network and how that is a way of affiliating yourself with other people who have something in common with you — a school, a location, or a company. When you join a network, you're usually saying, "I choose to trust people who have this thing in common with me to see my profile." Now, that might be completely accurate if you're joining a college network. However, if you're joining a regional network of over 1,000,000 people (see London, UK), you might not want to trust all those people. Network level privacy is pretty stringent in the grand scheme of Facebook, however. Rules are imposed upon people to prevent them from changing networks too often — therefore, "trolling" for people to harass or spam.

Network level privacy (plus friends) is the default for Facebook. This is the case because, in general, you do trust the people you work with, go to school with, or even live near you with more information than you'd entrust to the world at large. Still, at a network level, you can't know absolutely everyone who can see that piece of information about you.

Friendship

Adding a friend is basically extending a level of trust. By default, you're comfortable with them being able to see all your information. If you aren't comfortable with them, don't add them as a friend. One of the tightest presets for privacy is Only My Friends. Unlike Friends of Friends and network level privacy, you have complete control over this list: You can remove people if you don't want them to see your information anymore, and you can add people who you do want to see your information. This aspect of friendship — its implication on your privacy — is the number-one reason to *never* accept friend requests from people you don't know or know and don't trust.

Limited Profile

Officially, friendship is the smallest possible circle that you can restrict some piece of content to. However, at some point, at least one person creeps onto your Friend List that you do know and do trust but just don't want seeing the *Wild and Crazy Night* photo album. Maybe it's a co-worker you don't want seeing that you joined the *I Hate My Co-worker* group. Maybe it's a family member who writes a message in response to every status update, inundating your inbox. For many college athletes, information found on Facebook can incriminate them for violating certain honor codes.

For this reason, Facebook offers a *Limited Profile* to help you control which of your friends see what.

A *Limited Profile* is a version of your profile that you can create to prevent friends from seeing your profile. Here's how to adjust your Limited Profile:

1. **Go to the Privacy Overview page by clicking the link in the big blue bar on top.**

2. **Click Edit Settings underneath Limited Profile in the bottom right.**

3. **Edit what appears in your Limited Profile by using the check boxes on the left side of that page (as shown in Figure 4-2).**

   When you select (check) or clear (uncheck) something, the preview on the right side automatically updates.

4. **(Optional) Edit which photo albums appear in your Limited Profile.**

After you select what goes in your Limited Profile, select who sees your Limited Profile.

1. **From the Limited Profile Settings page, look for the Person text box underneath Limited Profile list.**

2. **Start adding people's names.**

   When you start typing, your friends' names appear.

3. **When you find the friend you want, click Add.**

4. **Repeat Steps 2 and 3 for as many friends as you want to add to your Limited Profile list.**

5. **Click Save to save your settings.**

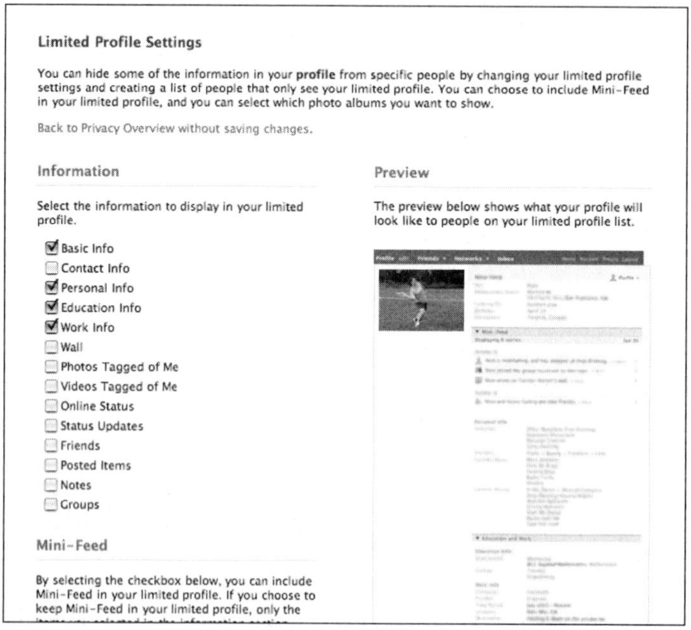

Figure 4-2:
The Limited
Profile page.

Anyone you add to your Limited Profile list sees only the things that are included in your set Limited Profile. Keep in mind that if something is checked in your Limited Profile but then you turn off the feature in general, the people on your Limited Profile list can see more than the rest of your friends.

Personal Responsibility to Safety

No one wants anything bad to happen to you as a result of something you do on Facebook. Facebook doesn't want that. You don't want that. We don't want that either. Facebook tries to keep it from happening by giving you all these privacy options. We are trying, right now, to keep it from happening by telling you about these options and explaining how they work. You're the third piece of the picture. You also have to make an effort to be smart and safe online. If you and Facebook both do your parts, the chances of something bad happening become incredibly small.

So what is *your part* as opposed to *Facebook's part?* Your part is to be aware of what you're putting online and on Facebook by asking yourself a few questions:

> Is what I'm putting on Facebook legal or illegal?

> Would I be embarrassed by it being on my refrigerator at home?

Regardless of the answer to these questions (we actually don't judge people based on their refrigerators), you need to be the one to choose whether displaying it on Facebook is risky. If it's risky, you need to be the one to figure out the correct privacy settings for showing it to the people you want — and not to the people you don't.

Your part, like most things on Facebook, is equivalent to the part you play in your everyday life to keep yourself safe: you know, the alleys you don't walk down at night, buckling your seatbelt when you get in a car, locking the door before you go to sleep at night, flossing. Add these to your list:

> I use my Facebook privacy settings wisely.

> I am careful about what information I expose to lots of people.

It Takes a Village to Raise a Facebook

Another way in which you (and every member of Facebook) contribute to keeping Facebook a safe, clean place is in the reports that you submit about spam, harassment, inappropriate content, and fake profiles. Facebook assumes that your friends aren't putting up bad stuff, but when you're looking at content of people you're not directly connected to, you should see a little Report link beneath it. This is true for Photos, Profiles, Groups, Posted Items, Applications, Pages — seriously, everything. When you click one of these links, you see the Report page.

The various Report options that you see might vary, depending on what you're reporting (a message as opposed to a photo, for example). These reports are submitted to the Facebook user operations team. The team then investigates, taking down inappropriate photos, disabling fake accounts, and generally keeping Facebook clean, safe, and un-obnoxious.

When you see content that you don't like — for example, an offensive group name or a vulgar profile — don't hesitate to report it. With the entire Facebook population working to keep Facebook free of badness, you wind up with a pretty awesome community.

After you report something, Facebook's User Operations team evaluates it in terms of violating Facebook's Terms of Use. This means pornography, fake profiles, and people who send spam get taken down, disabled, or warned, respectively. However, sometimes something that you report might be offensive to you but doesn't violate the Terms of Use and, therefore, will remain on Facebook. Due to privacy restrictions, User Operations may not always notify you about actions taken as a result of your support, but rest assured that the team handles every report.

Behind the Scenes

Facebook's part in keeping everyone safe includes a lot of manpower and technology power. The manpower involves responding to the reports that you and the rest of Facebook submit, as well as proactively going into Facebook and getting rid of content that violates the Terms of Service.

The technology power that we talk about is kept vague on purpose. We hope that you never think twice about the things that are happening behind the scenes to protect you from harassment, spam, and pornography. Moreover, we hope that you're never harassed, spammed, or *porned* — the official verb form meaning "being assaulted by accidentally seeing unwanted porn" — but just so you know that Facebook is actively thinking about user safety and privacy, we talk about a few of the general areas where Facebook does a lot of preventive work.

Protecting minors

Again, we keep this section purposefully vague to avoid becoming *Gaming Facebook's Systems For Dummies*. In general, we want you to note that people under the age of 18 have special visibility and privacy rules applied to them. For example, users under the age of 18 don't have Public Search Listings created for them. Public Search Listings enable people to be found in outside search engines, such as Google. Facebook decided, in this case, never to expose minors in this way. Would anything bad have happened if Facebook had decided otherwise? Probably not, but better to be safe than sorry.

Other proprietary systems are in place that are alerted if a person is interacting with the profiles of minors in ways they shouldn't, as well as systems that get alerted when someone targets an ad to minors. Again, with reference to the Personal Responsibility part, as a teenager (or as the parent of a teenager), you are responsible for understanding privacy and safe behavior on Facebook. Facebook tries to prevent whatever it can, but at the end of the day, you have to be a partner in that prevention.

You must be at least 13 years old to join Facebook. No one younger than that should have an account.

Preventing spam

Ah, spam, that delicious little can of . . . something once meat-like? Male-enhancement medications? Prescription drugs delivered to your door? Everyone can agree that spam is perhaps the bane of the Internet, all too often sliming its way through the cracks into e-mail and Web sites — and always trying to slime its way into Facebook as well.

The spam reports that you provide are incredibly helpful. Facebook also has a bunch of systems that keep track of the sort of behavior that spammers tend to do. If you haven't read this yet, hop to Chapter 2 for the scoopage on CATPCHAs. Those are part of the first line of defense against spammers creating multiple dummy accounts (the bad kind of dummy, unlike you), that can be used to harass people with FREE MALE UPLIFTING ads. The spam systems also keep track of messaging people too quickly, friending too many people, and other such behaviors that tend to reek of spam. Sometimes, you might get hit with a warning to slow down your poking or your messaging. This is the spam system at work, and it's why Facebook has remained relatively spam free over the last four years.

Part II

Representing Your Identity Online

The 5th Wave — By Rich Tennant

"Mr. President, North Korean President Kim Jong-il just sent you a Super Poke."

In this part . . .

One thing you hear repeatedly in this book is this idea of Facebook reflecting real life. On Facebook, like in real life, you define yourself and your experience. This part focuses on giving you knowledge of the tools you use to define yourself on Facebook.

Between your personal profile and the applications that you choose to use, there are hundreds of ways to connect to family and friends — both old and new.

Chapter 5

Building Out Your Profile

Your Facebook Profile is more than just a bunch of information — it's how you represent yourself to your friends, family, and others. Think of your profile as the equivalent of getting dressed in the morning. What does it say to the world when you roll out in jeans and a T-shirt, jeans and a button-down shirt, or a suit? You probably get dressed and leave the house at least seven times per week; one day might be a jeans-and-tee kind of day, and another might be a power suit kind of day. If you think about what you expressed to the world in the last week based on what you wore, you can start to get a feel for what your profile is.

Your Facebook profile is not about altering who you are but rather representing yourself. Think of it as an advertisement or a billboard for you. What do you want people to know about you? What do you want people to think about you? People think of looking at a Facebook profile as the equivalent of an introduction. How do you want to be introduced?

In Chapter 2, we cover the basics of your profile, profile picture, education, and work history. In this chapter, we talk about tailoring the other fields to represent who you are.

Advanced Profile Features

In Chapter 2, you fill out your basic information, workplace, education history, and then add a profile picture. You probably notice that several more tabs are available for you to edit. You can find them by clicking Edit in the big blue bar on top. These information tabs include

✔ **Contact:** Privacy settings are a very useful part of Facebook because people can share their telephone numbers, e-mail addresses, and other contact information without the whole world seeing. This enables incredibly useful features (such as Facebook Mobile; see Chapter 14), and the ability to track down someone's e-mail address and phone number — even if you were accidentally left off his "I'm moving/changing jobs/changing names" e-mail. For your own contact information, share what you're comfortable sharing and try to keep it up to date. We talk more about the privacy settings that protect this information in the "Choosing Who Can See What" section, later in this chapter.

✔ **Relationships:** Although Facebook is not a dating site, it includes your relationship information (that is, if you fill it out) as part of your most basic information. As you meet people and become their friends on Facebook, if you do happen to be in the market, knowing whether they are single and interested in your gender is incredibly helpful information. Also, the Relationships section is where people in a relationship link themselves to each other's profiles.

✔ **Personal:** Your personal information comprises your favorites: activities, movies, books, TV shows, music, and quotes. Additionally, you complete the kind-of-intimidating About Me section. Fill out the fields how you see fit, but remember: This "clothing" presents you to the Facebook world.

Edit the Personal tab of your profile directly from your Profile page by scrolling to the box labeled Information and then clicking the field you want to edit. Change the text in the box and then click outside the box to save your changes.

✔ **Layout:** The Layout tab isn't where you go to edit the layout of your profile; it's just a place for information about the layout. We talk about this aspect of profiles later in this chapter.

And I will call it . . . Mini-Feed

Mini-Feed is a personalized list of news stories about you. Any public action that you take on the site automatically creates a Mini-Feed story that is added to the top of your Mini-Feed. *Public actions* are changes that other people can see. For example, when you upload a photo album, your friends can see it, so this shows in your Mini-Feed. Comparatively, your friends can't see when you message someone, so this doesn't show in your Mini-Feed.

Mini-Feed displays only information that people can see based on your privacy settings. For example, if you create a Secret event, the people invited to that event can see in your Mini-Feed that you created it. No one who was not invited can see it when they look at your profile.

Facebook uses Mini-Feed to help keep your friends updated on what you're doing by always putting the most recent actions on the top. If you haven't talked to a friend in a while, you might visit her profile page and see that she recently attended an event or posted photos from a vacation. You might see a history of status updates, something like these: "Leah is now experiencing writer's block," followed by, "Leah is starting to make progress on her chapter," and then, "Leah is Yay! One down!"

Choose what stays in your Mini-Feed by deleting stories you don't like. Next to any story, look for a small *x* in the right corner (see Figure 5-1). When you click this and then click Hide Story, the story is deleted from your Mini-Feed. Therefore, keep the information that you like on Mini-Feed longer and erase the actions that you don't think are interesting or relevant. For example, when Leah finds a typo in her status message and updates it to correct the typo, she erases the first status update because it seems redundant.

Even though Mini-Feed and News Feed have similar names, they aren't linked in the Facebook system. If you erase a story from your Mini-Feed, it might still appear in your friends' News Feed.

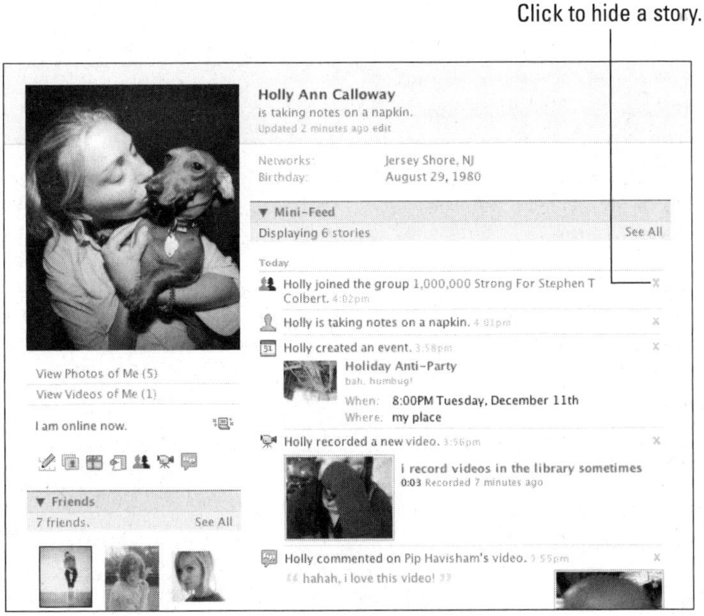

Click to hide a story.

Figure 5-1: Check out the variety of stories that appears in Mini-Feed.

Profile action links

Profile action links are the small text links that live below your profile picture. Most of these allow quick access to common actions that others may want to take on your profile. Keep in mind that the links you see on your profile might be different from the links you see on other profiles. For example, someone visiting your profile sees an Add *<Your Name>* as a Friend link but doesn't see the Edit My Profile link that you see.

The default links that others see on your profile are

- ✔ View More Photos of *<Your Name>*
- ✔ Send *<Your Name>* a Message
- ✔ Poke *<Your Name>*!

These are the most common ways that people interact with you on Facebook. They make sure that you're you by looking at the photos of you, and then they get in touch through either a message or a Poke. When they arrive at your profile, they know (and so do you) exactly where to look to do these things.

When we talk about adding applications to your profile in Chapter 8, we discuss that applications can add action links to your profile. That way, when people view your profile, they can see View Videos of *<Your Name>*, Play Scrabulous with Me, and Pet *<Your Name>*'s (fluff)Friend, in addition to the usual View Photos of *<Your Name>*.

The Friends box

The *Friends* box lives below your profile action links and displays thumbnail photos of six of your friends. These photos are displayed randomly, so if you really love dynamic content, refresh the page repeatedly to see new friends appear. Friends is one of a few boxes that is anchored to your profile. This is a reminder that although your profile is a big piece of your Facebook experience, your friends are a big piece, too. Additionally, looking at this box on your friends' profiles is a nice way to discover people you know. You might suddenly see the thumbnail of Michael Bluth and think, Oh my gosh, I want Michael Bluth to be my friend, too!

When you look at other people's profiles, you see an extra box of friends that never appears when you look at your own profile: the Mutual Friends box. The *Mutual Friends* box shows a random sampling of friends you have in common with the profile you're viewing; it doesn't appear if you have no friends in common. Say that Leah and Carolyn are friends with Blake. When Leah looks at Carolyn's profile, she sees Blake in the Mutual Friends box. When Carolyn looks at Leah's profile, she sees the same. When Blake looks at his profile, however, he doesn't see a Mutual Friends box, although he may see Leah and Carolyn in his regular Friends box.

Wall you need is love

The Wall is the most interactive part of your profile where your friends leave *Wall posts* (messages) as public displays of affection. You might find Wall posts a slightly more lightweight form of sending a message; it's usually a quick "Hey, I'm thinking of you" rather than a long missive about the most recent happenings in your life. We discuss the Wall in terms of communication in Chapter 12, but here are some things to keep in mind about the Wall on your profile:

- ✓ **Your friends can leave love in many forms.** You might find messages that include attachments from other applications or see Wall posts in the form of video, photos, or posted items.

- ✓ **Only your friends can leave love.** If you don't like one of the posts on your Wall, delete it. If someone in particular keeps leaving bad messages, remove him as a friend. Only friends can write on your Wall. Real friends wouldn't treat you badly.

- ✓ **You can share the love.** Go write on some of your friends' Walls. It puts a little sunshine in their day.

- ✓ **Rules of etiquette apply.** Generally, people don't write on their own Wall. If you're feeling itchy to write on a Wall, say hello to one of your friends.

Applications (that is, everything else)

In the preceding sections, we refer to the various boxes on your profile. To name a few, you have your profile picture, Mini-Feed, Friends, Information, and your Wall, which, basically, is one long box. However, when you visit other profiles, you might notice many more boxes. These are added to your profile when you add content to your account. Groups, for example, is an application that has a box on your profile. If you join a group, the name of that group appears in your Groups box. When you open a Facebook account, you also get Photos, Notes, Posted Items, Events, and Marketplace boxes. Additionally, applications can be added via Facebook Platform, which we cover in Chapter 8. Numerous third-party applications, such as Virtual Bookshelf and (fluff)Friends, are also available (see Chapter 9).

Understand that many applications have a box that goes in your profile, and these boxes can be placed in any order that you like.

1. **Hover your mouse over a box's blue title bar.**

2. **Click and drag the box to wherever you want it to be on your profile.**

   Pay attention to error messages; some boxes can be in only certain columns of the profile.

3. **Release the mouse when the box is where you want it.**

Figure 5-2 shows a box getting moved from one column to another. Your changes are saved automatically, but can always be moved back from whence they came.

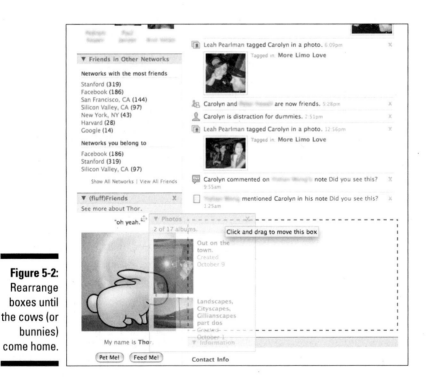

Figure 5-2:
Rearrange boxes until the cows (or bunnies) come home.

Profile-Building Strategies

Similar to spending a large chunk of time with someone you met only once or twice, a profile is a set of small nuances, subtle hints, and larger traits that help you decide whether you and another person are destined to be friends.

To say you have a strategy when you talk to someone for a length of time may be a bit of an overstatement. Your strategy is probably to just be yourself. That's what your strategy should be on Facebook, too. Here are a few reasons why people create a profile and a few things to keep in mind as a result.

Building a profile for yourself

With so many people using their real names to connect with their real friends on Facebook, clearly, a huge reason people build profiles is for their own social life. Yes, you can connect with friends, but you build a profile to help organize your life and represent your personality to the world. When you build a profile, build something that makes you think, "This is a cool guy/gal. Man, I'm cool." *Warning:* Saying that aloud, however, is not cool.

- ✔ **Be yourself.** Fake information is boring. If you haven't read *Crime and Punishment,* don't add it to your Favorite Books lists to make yourself look smarter. People want to get to know you; represent as many parts of yourself that you feel are relevant to the people you meet. If you've read *Crime and Punishment* but also have a thing for supermarket romance novels, don't be afraid to admit it. This is you — the profile.

- ✔ **Make deliberate choices about what you share.** We talk more about privacy options later in this chapter and in Chapter 4, but it's worth noting that one of the biggest ways you represent yourself is in what you choose to share via Facebook. If you want to import your secret blog onto Facebook for all your friends to read, go for it. Bring that once-secret information into the "conversation" where people can read all about you. If you don't want your friends to know your most candid thoughts about life, don't put them on Facebook.

- ✔ **Keep your profile updated.** You're a dynamic and multi-faceted individual. If you can't represent all your facets on a two-dimensional screen, let time be a part of the representation of self. As Carolyn has gotten older, for example, she's moved from profile pictures of herself at themed-parties to profile pictures that include her and her sisters. The later photos aren't a judgment on the earlier ones, just a natural reflection of the way she feels about herself. Her representation has changed.

 ✔ **Be a trendsetter.** Don't be afraid to add things to your profile that aren't necessarily part of everyone else's profiles. If none of your friends write notes, but you think you have something to say, add a Notes box to your profile and start talking. Keep an eye out for new features and functionality. (Facebook is constantly upgrading and improving different products.) When something sounds interesting, try it and see whether you like it.

Building a profile for promotion

Profiles that are primarily for promotion are relatively new in Facebook-land. Introduced in November 2007, *Pages* — an online presence for brands, businesses, stores, restaurants, and artists — enable *non-people entities* — companies, movies, and more — to engage with Facebook users in a truly meaningful way. Find out more about setting up a Page in Chapter 16.

For the moment, though, pretend that you already created a Page for your café, band, or dental office. Then think about the goals behind your creating a Page. If you're an aspiring musician, maybe you want more exposure and airtime via your existing fans, spreading your music. If you're with a major corporate brand, maybe you want to allow consumers to engage and affiliate, spreading your brand to their friends. If you represent a local shop, maybe you want to gather feedback from your customers on how to improve their shopping experience.

Regardless of your goal, here are a few tips to help you:

 ✔ **Be real.** People on Facebook want to connect to something alive and engaging. Ditch your canned slogans and phrases; give real information about yourself and your product.

 ✔ **Engage with your fans/consumers/customers/patrons.** Facebook users can give you feedback and opinions about your product or service, which amounts to free focus group results from your consumers. Ask what they think of your new record, clothing line, or menu item. Don't be afraid of negative feedback; use it to make your product better.

 ✔ **Keep your profile updated.** Users return to profiles that have new and relevant information. If your page remains static, it grows stale and has little or no activity. Don't waste this opportunity.

 ✔ **Don't be misleading.** Keep your members informed about how often they can expect message updates, offers, deals, and more. Don't use deceptive language to trick people into taking actions; you only hurt your brand as well as the success of your Page in the long term.

Representing yourself to family, friends, and the world

We use the words *reflection* and *representation* a lot in this chapter. Facebook is truly a mapping of reality — drawing lines between your friends and your profile. Of course, the reality that you see might be different from what your friends see. Maybe you see a friend (Jessica) as witty and sarcastic, but others see her as downright mean. And how does Jessica see herself? No one knows except Jessica, but you can probably tell how she views herself based on her Facebook profile.

When you create a profile on Facebook, you aren't just representing yourself. You also reflect how you see yourself. We're getting a little bit meta, but keep in mind these two pieces that people see. You are giving folks a window into you. What do you want them to see?

All this comes back to making choices about the information you put in your profile. If someone has a window into your living room, how do you arrange the sofa pillows — and what do you move into another room?

The other issue is that whom you represent to your parents, siblings, or kids is different from the person you represent to your friends. And that person is completely different from whom you represent to your co-workers, which is maybe even different from how you represent yourself to your boss. Continuing our living room analogy: You clean your living room from top to bottom when your boss comes over, straighten up for your parents' visit, and maybe just let your friends deal with a few dust mites under the couches.

After you build your profile (or clean your living room), you have two ways to choose what you're representing and to whom. In the next chapter, we cover how to represent yourself by selecting whom you add as a friend and to whom you expose yourself. In the next section, we cover the other side: controlling the information you think represents your but maybe doesn't represent you to *everyone*.

Choosing Who Can See What

We cover privacy and security in Chapter 4, but as you build your profile, remember that all the information it contains can be controlled, almost line by line. You choose who can see each bit of information. At any time, the maximum number of people who can see your full profile is all the people in your networks — only a fraction of the total number of people on Facebook. Therefore, the default settings are already rather restrictive, more so in the case of sensitive data like your contact information.

Know your options

Generally, you see the following options in any drop-down menu about profile privacy:

- ✔ **All My Networks and All My Friends:** Anyone in your networks and all your friends can see that piece of information.

- ✔ **Some of My Networks and All My Friends:** This option will only appear if you have more than one network. You will then be able to select which Networks are allowed to see your profile. Your friends and people in those networks will be able to see your information.

- ✔ **Only My Friends:** Only your friends can see that piece of information.

- ✔ **Only Me:** When you look at your profile, you'll be able to see that piece of information, but no one else will.

- ✔ **No One:** This removes that type of information from your profile entirely.

We say *that information* or *that piece* of information instead of *your profile* because each piece of your profile is controlled separately.

Figure 5-3 shows the Privacy Settings for Your Profile page, which you reach by clicking Privacy on the big blue bar across the top and then clicking the Profile link. Each aspect of your profile gets its own drop-down box. Here, no one can see your online status, certain networks can see the photos of you, only your friends can see your status updates, and all your networks and friends can see your Friends box.

We also throw another log (of confusion) on the fire by introducing you to the Limited Profile Settings page, shown in Figure 5-4. Access this page by clicking Privacy on the big blue bar and then clicking the Limited Profile link in the lower right.

Your *limited profile* is intended for blocking individual people (not groups of people) from having access to certain parts of your profile. For example, in your workplace network, you might be completely comfortable with your co-workers seeing your photos but not your boss. If you put your boss on your Limited Profile List and deselect the Photos check box, she won't be able to see your photos even though she's in the same network as you.

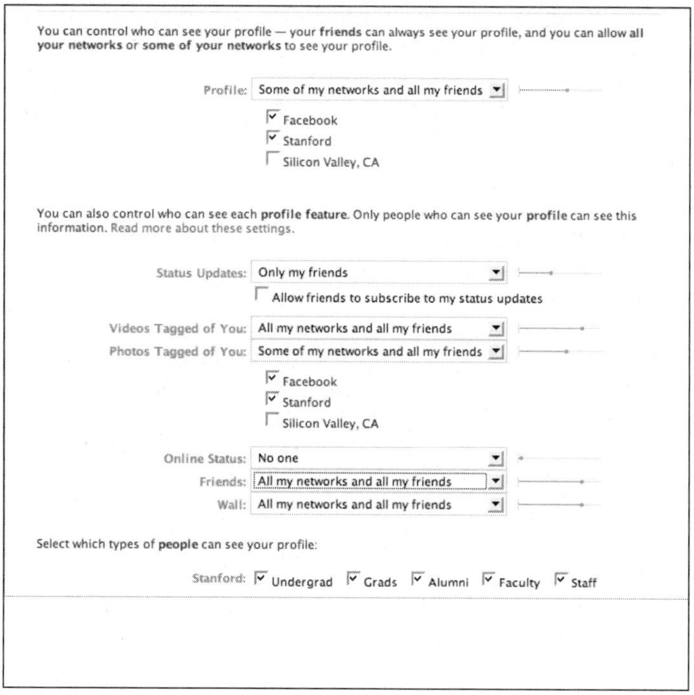

You can control who can see your profile — your **friends** can always see your profile, and you can allow **all your networks** or **some of your networks** to see your profile.

Profile: [Some of my networks and all my friends ▼]

☑ Facebook
☑ Stanford
☐ Silicon Valley, CA

You can also control who can see each **profile feature**. Only people who can see your **profile** can see this information. Read more about these settings.

Status Updates: [Only my friends ▼]
☐ Allow friends to subscribe to my status updates

Videos Tagged of You: [All my networks and all my friends ▼]
Photos Tagged of You: [Some of my networks and all my friends ▼]

☑ Facebook
☑ Stanford
☐ Silicon Valley, CA

Online Status: [No one ▼]
Friends: [All my networks and all my friends ▼]
Wall: [All my networks and all my friends ▼]

Select which types of **people** can see your profile:

Stanford: ☑ Undergrad ☑ Grads ☑ Alumni ☑ Faculty ☑ Staff

Figure 5-3: Adjusting your profile's Privacy settings.

Limited Profile Settings

You can hide some of the information in your **profile** from specific people by changing your limited profile settings and creating a list of people that only see your limited profile. You can choose to include Mini-Feed in your limited profile, and you can select which photo albums you want to show.

Back to Privacy Overview without saving changes.

Information

Select the information to display in your limited profile.

☑ Basic Info
☐ Contact Info
☑ Personal Info
☑ Education Info
☑ Work Info
☐ Wall
☐ Photos Tagged of Me
☐ Videos Tagged of Me
☐ Online Status
☐ Status Updates
☐ Friends
☐ Posted Items
☐ Notes
☐ Groups

Mini-Feed

By selecting the checkbox below, you can include Mini-Feed in your limited profile. If you choose to keep Mini-Feed in your limited profile, only the

Preview

The preview below shows what your profile will look like to people on your limited profile list.

Figure 5-4: Decide what can (or can't) be seen on the Limited Profile Settings page.

Your profile is in the eye of the beholder

Because of the general options we discuss in the preceding section, infinite views of your profile exist. Each person has a different combination of networks and friendships, so generalizing what any particular person is seeing is difficult.

Almost everything is visible on your profile, but don't worry. Just because you see your phone number and address when you click Profile, doesn't mean that everyone sees it, too.

In general, these are the two distinct groups of people to consider when thinking about your profile privacy: a group of people that you can't control, and a group of people that you can control. The group you don't control are settings that include some (or all) of your networks. The group you do control is your Friend List, your Limited Profile list, and any other friends lists you make. When you're deciding on privacy, simply ask whether you're comfortable with these groups seeing your sensitive information.

Contact information

Obviously, your contact information is the most sensitive information that you put on Facebook. It's also incredibly useful because it means you have an auto-updating phone book of all your contacts that never gets lost and never goes away. However, you don't want anyone, even if they're in your network, seeing your home address and phone number.

For this reason, your Contact setting defaults to Only My Friends. Increase its visibility if you choose, but by limiting it to only the people you confirm are your friends, you make it incredibly likely that the people you want to contact you can do so.

Another great privacy feature of Contact is that you control each piece of information. To check out these options, click Edit next to Profile in the big blue bar at the top and then select the Contact tab. See what's available in Figure 5-5.

For example, you might have a work e-mail address that you want people in your workplace network to see but not people in your school network. You might also have an e-mail address that you send all your e-mail notifications to although you don't want anyone e-mailing you there. If that's the case, set the work e-mail address to Some of My Networks and All My Friends and the other e-mail address to No One.

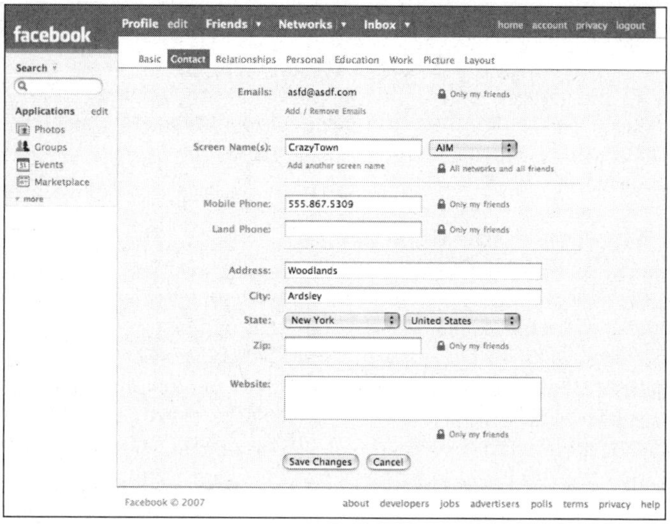

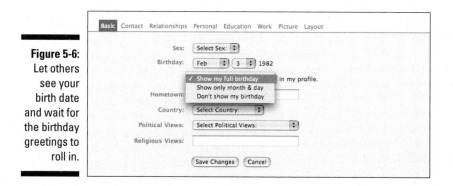

Figure 5-5:
Not everyone needs to see your personal e-mail address.

Your birthday

Your birthday is another sensitive piece of information that has specific privacy controls in Facebook. To get to these privacy controls, click Edit on the big blue bar. You land on the Basic tab, which is where your birthday is. As shown in Figure 5-6, a drop-down menu lets you hide your birthday entirely, or simply hide your birth year. Keep in mind that if you hide your birthday entirely, no one is notified about your birthday, so you won't get nearly as many "Happy Birthday" Wall posts.

Figure 5-6:
Let others see your birth date and wait for the birthday greetings to roll in.

Honesty's the best policy

We talk a lot in this chapter about representation and showing yourself to the Facebook world. Metaphors about clothing aside, all people care about on Facebook is getting to know you. Facebook is a great way to build closer relationships with people, and lying on your profile does not help accomplish this. In fact, lying just makes other people think that they should lie, too. The utility of Facebook is destroyed by having fake names, fake birthdays, fake work histories, and so on. Facebook is a great place to get real information. If you are uncomfortable with certain pieces of information being shared, we have two solutions for you:

- ✔ **Don't share anything that makes you uncomfortable.** If having your phone number up is just too creepy for you, so be it.

- ✔ **Become well acquainted with Facebook's privacy options.** Using the privacy options enables you to limit certain people or certain groups of people from accessing your information. This is certainly the better choice for enhancing your Facebook experience.

Chapter 6

Finding Facebook Friends

*H*undreds of sayings abound about friendship and friends. We looked up a bunch of them online, and we boiled them down into one catch-all adage: Friends, good; no friends, bad. This is true in life, and it's also true on Facebook. Without your friends on Facebook, you find yourself at some point looking at a blank screen and asking, "Okay, now what?" With friends, you find yourself at some point looking at photos of a friend's high school reunion and asking, "Oh, dear. How did that last hour go by so quickly?"

Most of Facebook's functionality is built around the premise that you have a certain amount of information that you want your friends to see (and maybe some information that you don't want *all* your friends to see, but we get to that later). So, if you don't have friends that are seeing your profile, what's the point in creating one? Messages aren't that useful unless you send them to someone. Photos are made to be viewed, but if the access is limited to friends, well, you need to find some friends.

On Facebook, all friendships are *reciprocal,* which means if you add someone as a friend, they have to confirm the friendship before it appears on both profiles. If someone adds you as a friend, you can choose between Confirm and Ignore. If you confirm the friend, congrats, you have a new friend! And if you ignore the friend, the other person won't ever find out.

Now that we made you feel as though you're the last kid picked for the team in middle-school dodge ball, we're also here to tell you to have no fear because there are many ways to find your friends on Facebook. If your friends haven't joined Facebook, invite them to join and get them to be your friends on Facebook as well as in real life.

What Is a Facebook Friend?

Good question. In many ways, a *Facebook friend* is the same as a real-life friend (although, to quote many people we know, "You're not real friends unless you're Facebook friends"). However, subtle differences exist among your real life friends, your Facebook friends, and a few Facebook-specific things about friendship that you should know.

A reflection of reality

The first and foremost definition of Facebook friends is that they're just friends. These are the people you hang out with, keep in touch with, care about, and want to publicly acknowledge as a friend. These aren't people you met on Facebook but rather the same people you would call on the phone, stop and catch up with if you crossed paths at the grocery, or invite over for parties, dinners, and general social gatherings.

In real life, there are lots of shades of friendships. Think of the differences between acquaintances, a friend from work, an activity buddy, an "ex-significant other but we're still friendly," and a BFF (best friend forever). In real life, these designations are always shifting — say, when you start calling up an activity buddy for advice, or it turns out that you and your significant other really can't be just friends. On Facebook, though, all these nuanced relationships are still your friends.

There are ways to account for these different relationships using Friend Lists, which we discuss later in this chapter. For the most part, though, all friendships are created equal on Facebook. When people see your Friend List, they see a big list that can be sorted only by networks, not your personal designations of *best friends* and *too awkward to say no*.

A contact

A Facebook friend is also a contact, meaning that you are giving all your Facebook friends a way to get in touch with you. In many cases (depending on privacy settings and what information you choose to share), you are also giving your friends access to other info, such as your phone number, address, and e-mail address.

In return, your friends become your contacts: You can always contact them through Facebook, in addition to having access to their phone numbers, addresses, and e-mail addresses.

A privacy implication

One important thing to remember when you send and confirm friend requests is that friends get access to your profile. This is similar to the preceding section, but it bears repeating. Accepting a friend request is the same as saying, "I want this person to be able to see everything about me." The tightest *pre-set* value for privacy on anything — photo albums, profile information, your Wall, and so on — is Only My Friends.

What this means, practically speaking, is that you trust every one of your Facebook friends with your Facebook information. Remember that the number of people who can see your profile by default is very low; everyone else who wants to see your profile must first become your friend. So when you accept a friend request (or send one), just remember that you're letting your friend access your information.

That might sound a bit scary, but this is similar to the access we give friends in real life. The only difference is that in real life, this process happens gradually, as opposed to at the click of a button. At some point, a person you know becomes someone you enjoy spending time with, care about, and are willing to listen to. This sort of friendship intimacy is akin to the intimacy of letting someone see your profile. In addition to that, it's a way to acknowledge to the world, "Hey! This is someone I care about."

A News Feed implication

News Feed is a constantly updating list of stories about all the actions your friends take on Facebook, as well as a few stories about actions your friends take on other sites. Think of News Feed as a personalized cable news show. Instead of reporting on everything happening around the world, it reports on everything happening around *your* world. News Feed stories might be something like "Blake wrote on Will's Wall" or "Eric was tagged in a video." All these stories link to relevant content about your friends. Also, News Feed selects the most interesting stories to show you, so depending on your friends' actions, you get a pretty good variety of stories about different people.

After you add people as friends, they start appearing in your News Feed. This is awesome if you're actually friends with a person because then you see his status, what sorts of photos he uploaded, and so on. However, if you're less interested in that person, this is potentially irritating. Do you really care when *<person you met once but will never see again>* joins a new group or writes a new note? If the answer is yes, that's great. If the answer is no, you probably don't want to send a friend request.

The Facebook Friend Philosophy

You might hear different reports on the rules for Facebook. You might hear that it's rude to ignore a friend request. Pay no attention to these ugly rumors. The truth about Facebook Friend etiquette is here.

Choose your friends wisely

Generally, you send friend requests to and confirm friend requests only from people you actually know. If you don't know them — *random friend requests* — click Ignore. For all the reasons enumerated in the preceding section — your privacy, News Feed, and reflection of reality — don't declare friendship unless some kind of relationship actually exists. Remember the lecture you got about choosing good friends when you were in high school? It's every bit as true now. Accept a friend request that you shouldn't, and the next thing you know, you're fleeing for the border on the back of a motorcycle belonging to some guy who insists his name is Harley. Trust us: It will happen exactly like that.

It's quality, not quantity

Another common misperception about Facebook is that it's all about the race to get the most friends. This is very, very wrong. Between the News Feed and privacy implications of friendship, aim to keep your Friend List to the people you actually care about. Now, the number of people you care about — including the people you care about the most and those you care about least — might be large or small. The average number of friends that a person has on Facebook is around 105. Does a person with 105 friends care about them all equally? Probably not. Does this mean that person is shallow? No. It means that this person is keeping up with and keeping track of all the friends that have come and gone through a lifetime. Changing jobs, schools, and locations also comes with new friends, but that doesn't displace the fact that you care about the old.

Should you aim to have 125 friends? No. Carolyn's mom has a great Facebook experience with fewer than 20 friends. With that number, she still can share her photos with her friends, play Scrabulous with people she knows, and have a pretty active News Feed. Aim to have all the people you care about on your Friend List. Maybe that's a big number, or maybe it's a small number; the part that counts is that you want to see them in that list, smiling back at you.

Finding Your Friends on Facebook

Now that we impressed upon you how important friends are, you might be feeling a bit lonely. How do you get to the people you want to be your friends? Facebook is big, and if you're looking for your friend John, you might need to provide some more detail. Facebook has a couple of tools to show you people you might know and want to be your friend, as well as a normal search-by-name functionality for finding specific people.

If only real life had a Friend Finder

Friend Finder is a tool that matches e-mail addresses from your e-mail address book to people's profiles on Facebook. Because each e-mail address can be associated with only one Facebook account, you can count on your matches finding the right people that you already know through e-mail.

With your permission, Friend Finder also invites those people who don't have a Facebook account that matches the e-mail in your address book to join Facebook. If they join from an invite that you send, they have a friend request waiting from you when they join.

To use Friend Finder, you need to give Facebook your e-mail address and e-mail password. Facebook doesn't store this information: It just uses it to retrieve your contacts list that one time.

Chances are that you came across Friend Finder when you first set up your account. The following steps make several foolish assumptions: namely, that you use Web-based e-mail (Hotmail, Gmail, Yahoo! Mail, and so on), that you haven't used Friend Finder before, and that the address book for that e-mail has a bunch of your friends in it. We cover other options, such as a client-based address book or using an AIM Buddy List, later.

1. **From the Friends drop-down menu in the big blue bar on top, choose Find Friends (the last option on this list).**

   Figure 6-1 shows the default Friend Finder page.

2. **Enter your e-mail address into the Your Email field and then choose your e-mail domain from the drop-down menu.**

   For example, if your e-mail address is dummy@hotmail.com, *hotmail* is the e-mail domain. If you don't see your domain on this list, skip the rest of these steps; unfortunately, you won't be able to use Friend Finder for your Web e-mail.

3. Enter your e-mail password (not your Facebook password) into the Password box and then click Find Your Friends.

If Facebook finds any matches with the e-mails in your address book, you see a page that looks similar to Figure 6-2. If it doesn't find any friends, go to Step 4. These are the people that Facebook thinks you might know. By default, they're all selected; if you click Add to Friends, all these people are sent a friend request from you.

Figure 6-1:
An unfilled
Friend
Finder.

Figure 6-2:
The Friend
selector
portion of
Friend
Finder.

4. **Decide whether to:**

   - *Add everyone as a friend.* Click Add to Friends.

   - *Not friend anyone.* Click Skip.

   - *Add many people as a friend.* Deselect the check box to the left of the person's name that you don't want to be friends with. After you deselect the people you don't want, click Add to Friends.

   - *Add a few people as friend.* Deselect the Select All Friends option at the top of the screen, and then add back anyone that you want to add as a friend by selecting the check box next to their name. When you're ready, click Add to Friends.

   After you click either Add to Friends or Skip, you land on the Invite portion of Friend Finder. It should look something like Figure 6-3. These are e-mails that have no matches on Facebook.

5. **(Optional) Invite people to join Facebook and become your friend.**

   Similar to adding friends, you can

   - *Invite all these contacts.* Click Invite to Join.

   - *Invite none of these contacts.* Click Skip.

   - *Invite many of these contacts by deselecting the ones you don't want to invite.* Use the check boxes to the left of their e-mails and then click Invite to Join.

   - *Invite some of these contacts to join.* Deselect the Select All/None check box on top. Then reselect the ones you want to add by using the check boxes to the left of their e-mails and clicking Invite to Join.

Figure 6-3: The Invite portion of Friend Finder.

After doing all this, we hope you manage to send a few friend requests. Your friends need to confirm your requests before you officially become friends on Facebook, so you might not be able to see your friends' profiles until that confirmation happens.

If that whole experience yielded nothing — no friends you wanted to add, no contacts you wanted to invite — you have a few options. You can go through these steps again with a different e-mail address. You should probably use the one that you use for personal e-mail (from where you e-mail your friends and family). If that's not the problem, you have two more ways to use Friend Finder.

Import an Address Book

If you're someone who uses a *desktop e-mail client* — a program on your local computer that manages your e-mail (like Microsoft Exchange, or Entourage) — create a CSV file of your contacts and import it so that Facebook can check it for friend matches. The way to create your CSV file depends on what e-mail client you use. Here's how to get the right instructions:

1. **Go to the Find Friends page (by choosing Find Friends in the Friends drop-down menu in the big blue bar on top).**

2. **Select the Email Application option.**

   This expands a window that looks similar to Figure 6-4.

3. **If you already have a CSV file created, import it here.**

   After you do that, you're taken through Steps 4–5 from the preceding section.

Email Password:

Find Your Friends

We won't store your login or password or email anyone without your permission.

AIM Instant Messenger Find your AIM buddies on Facebook

Email Application Outlook, Apple Mail, etc.
Upload a contact file and we will tell you which of your contacts are on Facebook.
Read how to create a contact file here.

Outlook
Outlook Express
Windows Address Book
Thunderbird
Palm Desktop
Palm Desktop (vCard)
Entourage
Mac OS X Address Book
Other

Still having problems? Contact us.

Contact File: Choose File no file selected

More Ways to Find Friends »

Figure 6-4:
Importing a
CSV file.

Also, if you're on a PC, you may have an option to simply import your Microsoft Outlook Address Book.

4. **If you don't have a CSV file already created, click the How to Create a Contact File link and follow the instructions; then import the file, and follow Steps 4–5 in the preceding section.**

AIM Friend Finder

This option works for you only if you use AIM as an instant messenger (IM) client for chatting with your friends. The biggest difference is that any invitations you send via the AIM Friend Finder are delivered via IM. Thus, instead of sending your friends an e-mail asking them to join, they get an instant message from Facebook Bot. Again:

1. **Go to the Find Friends page (by choosing Find Friends in the Friends drop-down menu in the big blue bar on top).**

2. **Click AIM Instant Messenger.**

   The page expands to what's shown in Figure 6-5.

3. **Enter your AIM screen name and AIM password and then click Find Friends.**

4. **Follow Steps 4–5 for the regular Friend Finder.**

If none of these methods yield any results for you, don't worry; you'll find friends in other ways, and you can still use the site.

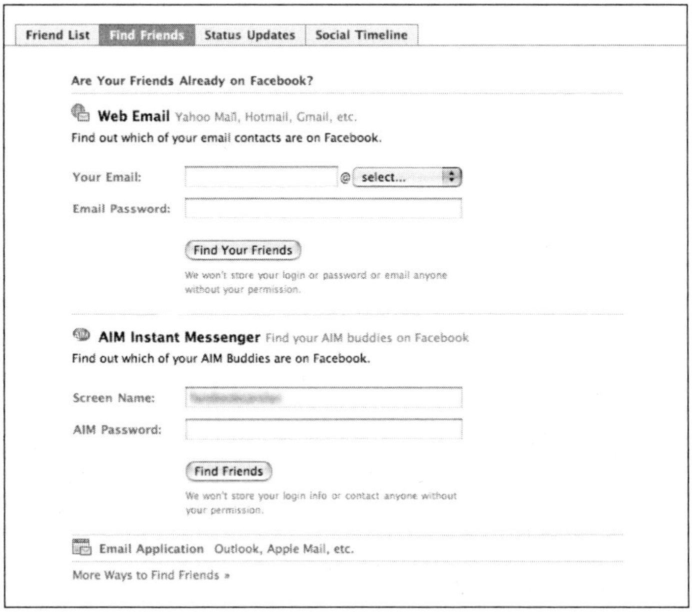

Figure 6-5:
The AIM Friend Finder.

Find what you're looking for: Search

Friend Finder is a great way to build your Friend List quickly without a lot of work. After you build it out a bit, though, what if you think other people might want to be your friends? Facebook Search has a few different methods that let you search for groups of people you might know; Facebook Search also offers you the capability to seek out certain friends by name.

Coworker Search

Coworker Search is based on information that people enter into their profiles about their work history. Generally, people enter the company they worked for and the dates they worked there. Coworker Search lets you search for people who work at the same places you do (or did). Depending on the size of the place where you worked, this sort of search might yield entirely too many people or not enough (if not all of your co-workers have joined Facebook). To account for the "too many" problem, search for specific names at specific companies, if you wish. Name search can be as general or as specific as you need. (Hmm. Remember John, who sat a few cubicles over?) Like with many types of searches, though, the more specific you are, the more likely you are to find what you're looking for.

To get to Coworker Search:

1. **Click the drop-down arrow next to the word Search above the Applications menu on left and then click Find Coworkers.**

   You land on the Search by Company page, as shown in Figure 6-6.

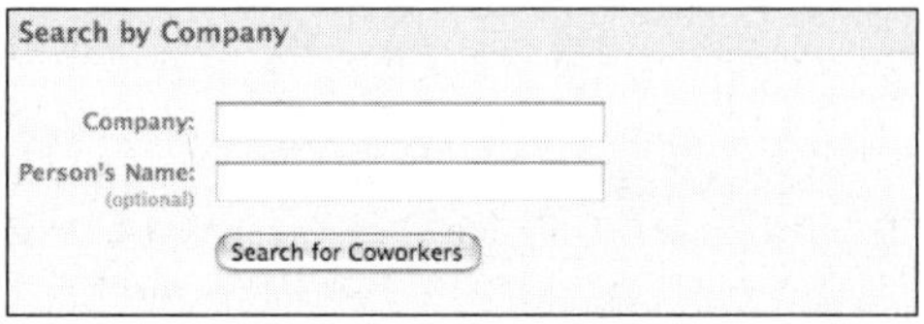

Figure 6-6: Coworker Search.

> Search by Company
>
> Company: [   ]
> Person's Name: [   ]
> (optional)
>
> (Search for Coworkers)

2. **Start typing the name of the company you want to search.**

   The Company field tries to autocomplete what you're typing.

3. **(Optional) If you want, enter a specific person you're looking for.**

4. **Click Search Coworkers.**

   Voilà! A list appears of people who listed that company in their profiles.

Classmate Search

Classmate Search is similar to Coworker Search in that it takes the information from people's profiles to create a big, searchable index. Classmate Search is even better, perhaps, because you can easily find your friends from high school, college, graduate school, and so on. Ever wonder what that awkward kid from the dining hall wound up doing? Look no further.

To get to Classmate Search:

1. **Click the drop-down arrow next to the word Search above the Applications menu on the left; then click Find Classmates.**

   You land on the Search by High School/Search by College page, as shown in Figure 6-7.

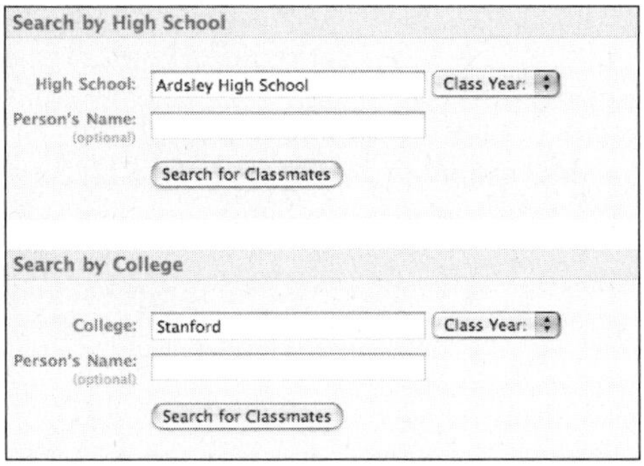

Figure 6-7: Classmate Search.

Search by High School	
High School:	Ardsley High School Class Year: ⬦
Person's Name: (optional)	
	Search for Classmates

Search by College	
College:	Stanford Class Year: ⬦
Person's Name: (optional)	
	Search for Classmates

2. **Choose to search for high school or college classmates.**

   Despite the two boxes here, you can search for only one at a time.

3. **Enter your high school or college, as well as your graduating year.**

   The graduation year can be huge in filtering the results to the people you actually know. If you just search for *Harvard,* you get over 500 results, which is too many to sift through looking for that one person you knew once upon a time. Limiting it to a certain graduation year makes it easier to find more people that you actually know.

   If you list your educational info in your profile, the fields for Classmate Search are pre-filled with your college and high school.

4. **Click Search for Classmates.**

   See whether you know anyone in the search results.

Quick-Search

In directing you to Classmate Search and Coworker Search, we keep bypassing the convenient-sounding Quick-Search box. The Quick-Search box is (more or less) what it sounds like. You enter a name of someone you want to find on Facebook, press Enter, and very quickly get a list of search results.

If Friend Finder hasn't yielded any results and you still don't have very many friends, try thinking of some people that you know are on Facebook. Enter their full name into the Quick-Search box and see whether that finds them. Read results, lather, repeat.

Keeping Track: Friend List Management

After you do all this work finding and adding your friends, at some point, you might get a little overwhelmed and yell, "Stop the madness!" at your computer. This might freak out your computer, so here are some ways to spare your computer's feelings and keep your friend list under control.

Creating and applying Friend Lists

Friend Lists (plural) are subsets of your giant Friend List (singular). You create Friend Lists as you see fit. You can use them for messaging and for general organization of where your friends fall in your inner-friend hierarchy.

The options for Friend Lists are virtually limitless. You can have 1500 friends on each list, people can be on more than one list, and you can make up to 100 Friend Lists. Your lists can be for silly things (Girls Night Out Girls), real-world needs (Family), or general bucketing (co-workers).

Whether it's Tuesday Ultimate Players or Random Acquaintances, use Friend Lists for all sorts of conveniences. To create a Friend List:

1. **From the Friends drop-down menu in the big blue bar on top, choose Friend List.**

2. **Click the Make a New List button (on the right side of the screen).**

3. **In the new space that opens for the list, name your list.**

   Maybe something like *Dummies* for the Dummies Team (see Figure 6-8).

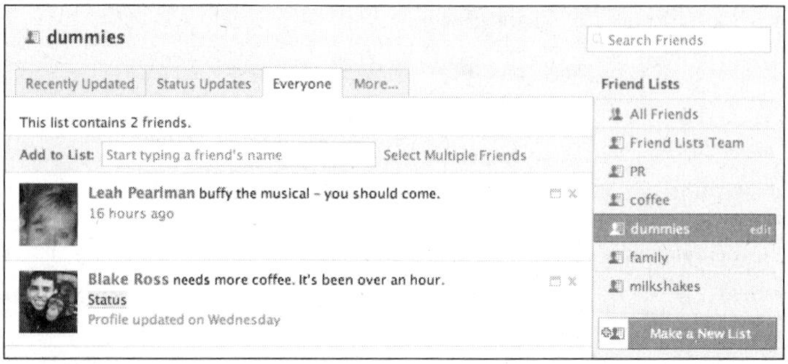

Figure 6-8:
Friend List
creation.

4. **Input the names of the people who belong on this list and then press Enter.**

   While you type, your friends' names autocomplete.

5. **Select the name you want and then press Enter.**

   If you're planning on adding a lot of friends at once, click the link to Select Multiple Friends. This opens the multi-friend selector, where you can select a lot of friends with a few clicks. You see what this looks like in Figure 6-9.

6. **When you finish adding friends the quick way, click Save.**

   After you select the friends you want, your list saves automatically. You can add and remove friends from a list at any point in time.

Applying Friend Lists, like creating them, can happen in many places, which means that it's hard to enumerate them all in the next few paragraphs. Generally, after you create a friend list, you can enter the name of a Friend List almost anywhere you enter a friend's name. The most prominent place you use this is for messaging groups of people.

Messaging on Facebook is fairly straightforward. If you message the same seven people every day, save yourself some time by using Friend Lists. You can create a "Daily News" Friend List, and messaging that list is a vast improvement over typing out everyone's name and then realizing — a bit too late — that you forgot someone.

Figure 6-9:
Adding many friends to a Friend List at once.

When you want to message a Friend List, open a composer window as you normally would, and start typing the name of the list you want to message in the *To:* field. The Friend List name is among the names of your actual friends, so you can actually message a list in addition to a single person.

Friend Lists are private, so even if the group you're messaging is known in your mind as Annoying Co-workers, all that your annoying co-workers see is a list of their names.

Spring friend-cleaning

Every now and then, no amount of Friend Lists can hide the fact that you just have too many friends you don't care about anymore. This isn't your fault: After all, you can't help being popular. If it's cluttering your News Feed, though, it's time to do a little *friend pruning*.

No, this doesn't mean waiting for your friends to shrivel in the sun. Instead, go to your huge master Friend List and start working your way through all your friends. The rules that apply for friend pruning are similar to the rules for spring-cleaning: If you haven't used it in six months, you can probably throw it out. If you haven't even thought about a friend in a few months, or if you can't remember why you accepted a friend request in the first place, it's okay to remove that person as a friend. When you're looking at your Friend List, you see a small x at the right of that person's listing. Just click the x to remove your friend, and that friend is gone.

Don't worry — your friends are never told that they've lost a coveted place on your Friend List. Chances are that if you had no contact over several months, they won't notice, either. You merely disappear from his Friend List (and he from yours), and both move on happily with your lives.

Chapter 7

Using Facebook Photos

In This Chapter

▶ Uploading, editing, and tagging your photos

▶ Tracking photos of you

▶ Understanding and using privacy rules for your photos

*F*acebook Photos is the leading photo-sharing application on the Web. This may sound surprising because entire sites are dedicated to storing, displaying, and sharing photos, whereas photos are just one piece of the Facebook puzzle. Because of your Friends connections, Facebook can become the one-stop shop for tracking all the photos of you, all the photos you've taken, and all the photos of your friends.

The Photos Page

The Photos page is where you land when you choose Photos in the Applications menu on the left. A lot of fun and interesting information lives here. Photo albums your friends have recently added take the bulk of this page. Looking at your friends' photos is a great way to keep in touch and feel involved when you can't always be there. Lots of photo albums get delivered to you via News Feed (see Chapter 3), but if that's not enough, you can check out what's available from the Photos page.

Figure 7-1 shows that you can get to pages that display all the photos your friends have recently been tagged in, all your photos, and all the photos of you. Throughout this chapter, we show you how you can do all this with your photos.

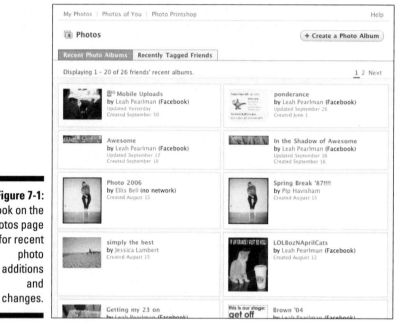

Figure 7-1:
Look on the
Photos page
for recent
photo
additions
and
changes.

Uploading Photos

Facebook is a great place to keep your photos because you can easily organize them into albums and share them with all the people who might want to see them. You can upload albums for anything — a party, a trip, or just a collection of photos you want people to see.

When you upload photos to Facebook, you're asked to categorize them into albums. Even if you upload a single photo, it's considered its own album. Each album can have no more than 60 photos. To get started, follow these steps:

1. **Go to the Photos page by choosing Photos in the Applications menu.**

2. **Click the Create a Photo Album button in the top-right corner.**

   The Add New Photos page appears, as shown in Figure 7-2. You see the following fields:

   • *Name:* This is what displays as the Album title. This field is required.

   • *Location:* Usually, this is where the photos were taken. This field is optional.

   • *Description:* Whatever you feel best describes the album. This field is optional.

- *Visible To:* This is the privacy setting for this particular album. You get to decide who can see what. We talk more about photo privacy later in this chapter.

- *Show this in my limited profile:* This is another privacy option that's covered later in this chapter.

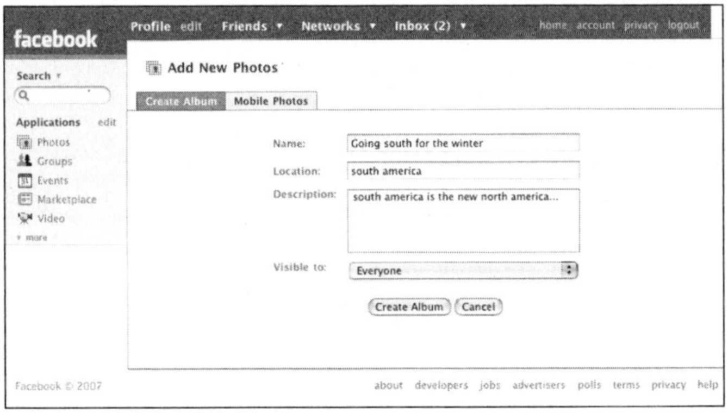

Figure 7-2:
Enter details about your photo album here.

3. **Enter at least a name for your album and then click the Create Album button.**

   You can edit this information later if you choose.

   After you click Create Album, a JavaScript applet opens within the window for viewing photos. Facebook uses a JavaScript applet to bring your photos from your computer's hard drive to Facebook. The first time you do this, you will see a pop-up asking whether you want to trust this applet, as shown in Figure 7-3.

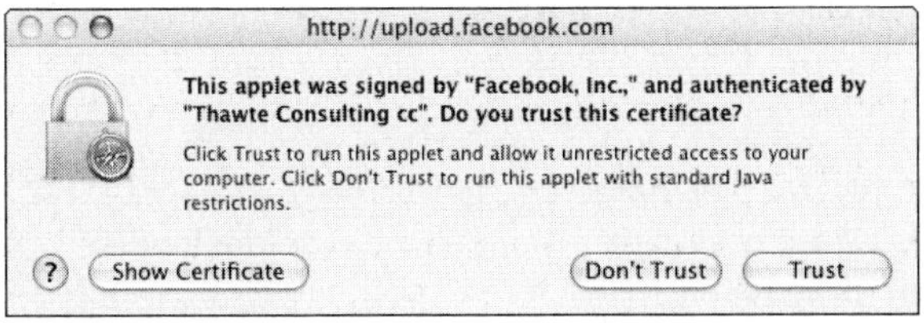

Figure 7-3:
When you see this screen, click Trust to use Facebook.

4. Click Trust.

Figure 7-4 shows a screen taking you through the photo upload flow. Your screen displays a directory of your hard drive folders, and from there you can navigate to the folders where your pictures are.

5. Select which photos you want to upload or just choose Select All.

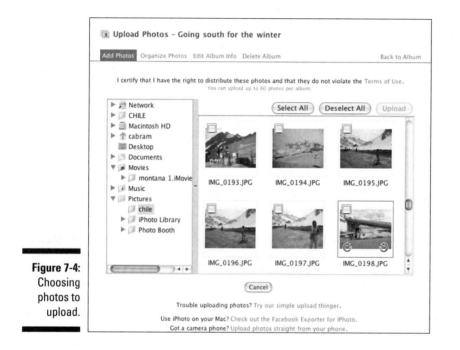

Figure 7-4:
Choosing
photos to
upload.

6. After you select the photos for your album, click Upload.

A pop-up displays the progress of your upload. This might take a few minutes. You're then taken to the Edit portion of the album creation process, which we discuss next.

If, for some reason, the java applet doesn't work, you can use the Simple Uploader to add photos. As shown in Figure 7-5, the Simple Uploader lets you browse your computer manually, photo by photo, for the files you want to add to your album. The Simple Uploader takes more time than the java applet, so we don't recommend it.

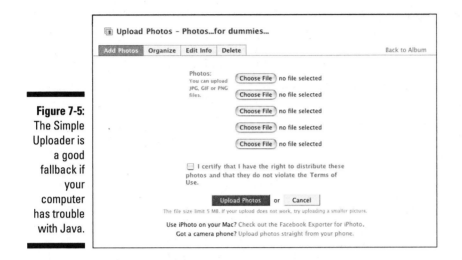

Figure 7-5:
The Simple
Uploader is
a good
fallback if
your
computer
has trouble
with Java.

Editing and Tagging Photos

After uploading the photos for your album, you have several editing options. To edit an album at any time, click Photos (in the Applications menu), click My Photos, and then click Edit Album beneath the album title you want to modify. Across the top of Figure 7-6 are the following links:

- **Edit Photos:** Here, you can add captions to your photos, tag your friends in individual photos, choose which photo will be the album's cover, and move a photo into one of your other albums.

- **Add More:** Your albums can have up to 60 photos. If you have fewer photos than that, you can return to the uploader and add more photos.

- **Organize:** You can rearrange the order of the photos in your album here.

- **Edit Info:** We mention earlier in the chapter that you can change the album name and other info you added when creating the album; you click this button to do that.

- **Delete:** This it how you delete an entire album.

If you want advanced editing options, such as red-eye reduction or cropping, you either need to do these on your computer before uploading photos or use another photo-editing application on Facebook. (For details about adding applications to your profile, see Chapter 8.)

After you finish all your captions, tags, and other edits, click Save Changes at the bottom of the page. If you don't do this, and you click anywhere else to change pages, your captions, tags, and photo order are lost.

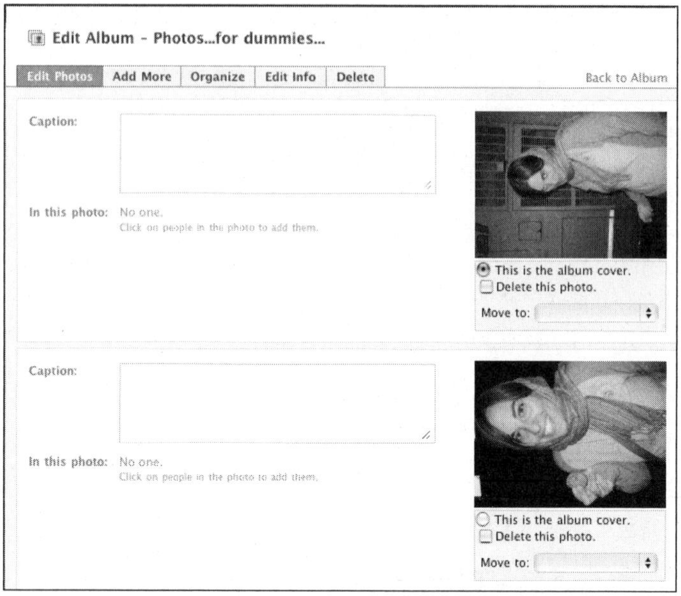

Figure 7-6:
All about
your album.

Adding captions to your photos

The Edit Album screen (refer to Figure 7-6) is a long list of your photos, displayed as thumbnails. The boxes next to the thumbnails are where you can enter captions. Facebook has no rules regarding a caption — you can leave it blank, you can talk about where the photo was taken, or you can make a good joke about its content.

At this point, you can select which photo you want to be the *album cover* — the photo people see with the album title and description. Remember to save your changes.

Tagging your photos

Tagging — the part of Facebook Photos that makes the application so useful for everyone — is how you mark who is pictured in your photos. Imagine if you took all your photos, printed them out, put them in albums, and then created a giant spreadsheet cross-listing the photos and the people in the photos. Then you merged your spreadsheet with all your friends' spreadsheets. This is what tagging does. When you tag a friend, it creates a link from her profile to that photo, and notifies the friend that you've tagged her. Your friends always have the option to remove a photo tag that they don't want linked to their account.

Figure 7-7 shows what the photo tag box looks like. To tag a photo from the Edit Album screen

1. **Hover the mouse over the photo you want to tag.**

   The mouse switches from an arrow to a target symbol.

2. **Click the face of the person you want to tag.**

3. **In the pop-up that appears, begin typing the name of any friend. The list below will auto-complete; as soon as you see your friend's name, select it with your mouse.**

   Additionally, as you tag an album, the people you have already tagged will be saved to the top of the entire list just in case they are in more than one photo (see Figure 7-7).

   After you select the friend, his name appears under the caption in the In This Photo field. You can tag yourself by typing your name or just *me*.

4. **Remember to click Save Changes when you're done.**

If you have a friend in one of your photos who isn't on Facebook, you can still tag her. While you type her name, your Friend List eventually becomes blank, and a field for entering an e-mail address appears. Enter your friend's name into the top field and her e-mail address into the bottom field. Your friend's name appears in the tagged list, and a notification is sent to her e-mail so that she can see the photo without being on Facebook.

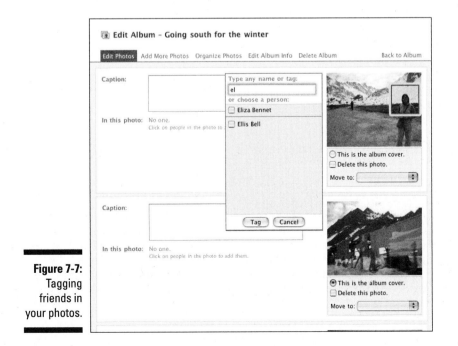

Figure 7-7:
Tagging
friends in
your photos.

Rearranging photos

After saving your captions and tags, you can organize the photos in your album. Figure 7-8 shows the Organize Photos screen, which provides the order in which your photos appear. You can drag and drop these photo thumbnails into any order, and they will appear in that order. Remember to click Save Changes when you're done organizing.

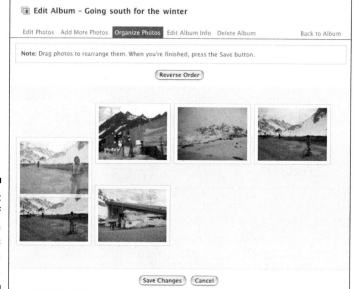

Figure 7-8: The order of photos in an album is never set in stone.

Congratulations, you've just created your first Facebook photo album that you can share with friends and family!

You can edit your album at any time by going to the Photos page, clicking My Photos, and then clicking Edit Album beneath your album title.

Viewing Photos of You

When we say *photos of you* we're referring to photos that have you tagged in them. You could have tagged these yourself, or your friends may have tagged you in their photos. The most common way to see all the photos of you is to click the View Photos of Me link under your profile picture. (If you don't see this link, you know that no one has tagged you in any photos yet.) Most of your friends can also see this link right below your profile picture, but the photos they can see might differ. For more on this, see the upcoming "Photos Privacy" section.

You can browse all the photos of you that you've tagged as well as the photos that others have tagged. Remember, if any photo of you has a tag that you don't like, you can always remove the tag from the photo. ***Note:*** If there's a photo you don't want on Facebook at all, even after you've removed the tag, you have to get in touch with your friend and ask him to remove the photo.

Generally, your friends can comment on any of your photos, and you can comment on any of theirs. (See Chapter 10 for more information on communicating through comments.) You can delete comments you leave as well as any comments on your photos that you don't like or think are inappropriate. You can see all the comments on one of your albums by going to the Photos page, clicking My Photos, and then selecting the albums with the comments you want to see. This takes you to the album view; you see thumbnails of the first 20 photos in the album. If you look on the bottom right, the little number next to the View Comments link tells you how many comments are in that album.

If you're curious about all the things that have been said about your photos over time, you can go to the Photos page, click My Photos, and then click View My Photo Comments. This displays all the comments from all your albums.

The Profile Picture Album

Facebook creates one album for you automatically: the Profile Picture Album. Every time you upload a new profile picture (see Chapter 2), it's added to the Profile Picture Album.

You can access this album by clicking your current profile picture. This takes you to an album view, where you can see all your past profile pictures. If you click Edit Photos, you can caption, tag, and delete photos, similar to uploading albums.

You can automatically turn any photo from this album back into your profile picture by clicking the Make Profile Picture link underneath the right corner of the photo. You will also see this link underneath any photo in which you are tagged.

Photos Privacy

The two pieces of privacy in terms of your photos are privacy settings on a per-album basis and privacy settings related to photos in which you're tagged. The interaction between your friends' Tagged Photos privacy settings and your Album Settings can sometimes be a bit confusing, so we separate them for now.

Sharing albums with non-Facebook users

If all your friends and all the people you want to see your photos are already on Facebook, sharing photos is easy. You can see their albums, and they can see yours, all in one place. Tags and News Feed help people know when new photos are posted; comments let people talk about those photos. However, most people have at least a few friends who aren't on Facebook. Here are two ways to share your albums with them:

✔ **Using Share:** Share is covered in more depth in Chapter 10, however, to use Share to send a photo album to a friend, go to the album view and then click the Share button at the bottom right of the page. A pop-up asks you to enter a friend's name or an e-mail address. If you enter your friend's e-mail address, and add any message content (optional), your friend receives an e-mail from Facebook providing a link to all the photos in the album.

✔ **Using copy and paste:** In album view, go to the bottom of the page, where you see the Public link. Copy and paste this link into an e-mail, blog, or anything else on the Internet, and anyone who clicks that link can see your album.

Album privacy

Say you create an album titled *Day at the Beach*. One of the first choices you make about your album is the privacy level. The following are your Visible To options in order from strict to open:

✔ **Only My Friends:** Only confirmed friends can see the photos in *Day at the Beach*.

✔ **Some of My Networks and All My Friends:** People in certain networks are excluded from being able to see this album although typically, they can see your profile. Say, for your *Day at the Beach* album, you decide that not everyone in your region network needs to see photos of you in a bathing suit. You could remove the visibility from your region network, while still letting your friends and people in your workplace network see the album. (For more information on joining a network, see Chapters 2 and 11.)

✔ **All My Networks and All My Friends:** Anyone who can see your profile can see your *Day at the Beach* album.

✔ **Everyone:** This setting means that all of your networks and all of your friends can see your photos, and, in addition, friends of people who are tagged in the album can also see your photos. For example, if Leah is friends with Carolyn but not with Blake, and she tags Carolyn in a photo (assuming they are not all in the same network), and Blake is friends with Carolyn, he will be able to see the photo. If Carolyn is not tagged, even though she can see the album, Blake cannot. The "everyone" in this context are all the people looking at photos you've tagged.

✔ **Show in My Limited Profile:** This option regulates whether the people on your Limited Profile list can see this album. Your *Limited Profile* is a version of your profile that you create to restrict certain parts of your profile from view. You then select friends who should see your Limited Profile. If you have certain friends you do not want to see your photo album, add them to your Limited Profile List and uncheck this box.

If you haven't added anyone to your limited profile list yet, this option will not appear. (For privacy and safety details on Facebook, see Chapter 4.)

Photos of You privacy

The beauty of creating albums on Facebook is that it builds a giant cross-listed spreadsheet of information about your photos — who is in what photos, where those photos were taken, and so on. You're cross-listed in photos that you own and in photos that you don't own. However, you still have control over who sees these photos of you from your profile. To set these preferences, go to the Privacy page (the link is on the big blue bar on the top) and click the Profile link. You notice drop-down menus for many parts of your profile; look for the Photos Tagged of You option.

You have several options for this setting:

✔ **Only Me:** No one but you can click through to see these photos.

✔ **Only My Friends:** Only your confirmed friends can click through to see these photos.

✔ **Some of My Networks and All My Friends:** Your confirmed friends as well as people in certain networks who can see your profile can click through to see photos of you.

✔ **All My Networks and All My Friends:** Anyone who can see your profile can click through to see all the photos of you.

Keep in mind that the photos of you that are owned by other people might have privacy settings that the album's owner set. Although you let all your networks and friends see the photos of you, certain people might not be able to see all the photos because of privacy settings on other people's albums.

Chapter 8

Facebook Applications

- -

- -

*F*acebook offers you a ton of cool things to do: add photos and videos, write notes and messages, share links, give gifts, save the world, save the cheerleader . . . the possibilities are truly endless. In this chapter, we get into the basics of almost all these things, so that when your friends look at your profile, they say, "Wow, this is cool."

In Chapter 3, we discuss how Facebook's menus are divided into core elements and applications. Facebook's core elements (collectively, the *platform*) are things like your profile, your friends, and your messages; you access these elements through the blue bar on top. Without your friendship connections, your Facebook profile is kind of just another Web page floating all alone in the void of the Internet. Without your profile, your connections are merely a tangle of strings, without the ability to understand who is connected to whom. Without the ability to communicate along these strings connecting these profiles, well, you're still going to feel a bit alone.

Without this platform, Facebook just doesn't work. However, these aspects of Facebook are only some of the cool things listed at the top of this chapter. What about the photos? What about the videos? The zombies? The cheerleaders? All these other parts of Facebook are *applications*. Applications are features built on top of Facebook's core. Facebook Photos, which we discuss in Chapter 7, is a decent way to upload photos to the Internet. However, it's the best way to *share* photos on the Internet because it takes advantage of your profile and friendship connections. When applications are built on top of the Facebook Platform, awesomeness ensues.

Applications can be built by Facebook or by third-party developers. You have to *add* third-party applications to your account, whereas most of the applications developed by Facebook (though not all of them) are waiting for you when you sign in. You learn about the distinctions as we move through this chapter. We cover adding third-party applications in Chapter 9.

Facebook engineers built all the applications we talk about in this chapter. Most of them you find in your left-hand Applications menu, squeaky clean and ready for you to get started. The only exceptions to this are Mobile and Politics (and sometimes Video), but we don't want to get ahead of ourselves.

To add Facebook applications that are not pre-added, click on the By Facebook filter on the Application Directory. This is covered in greater depth in the upcoming sections, Politics, Mobile, and Video.

Photos

Chapter 7 covers Facebook Photos. With Photos, you upload albums of 60 photos each and then reorder, caption, and tag the photos. *Tagging* is compiling who is in each of your photos. The profiles of friends that you have tagged link to your photos via the View Photos of *<Name>* link underneath every tagged person's profile picture.

The best part about the photos tagging feature is that you and your friends have a communal and ever-expanding repository of photos. Anywhere you go with a computer, you can access any relevant photos that you want to revisit or show off.

Groups

When Facebook started, all it had was profiles, friends, and messages. Quickly people started making profiles for things that weren't quite people — John Kerry (representing a school's Democrat organization), The Manune (representing eight men who lived together), Ultimate Frisbee (representing the sport that we love so very, very much). People wanted a way to connect with an idea, person, or group of people that wasn't necessarily included in the word *Friend;* having these entities, however, meant that profiles weren't reliably real people. In order to keep profiles as people profiles, Facebook created the Groups application. Groups gives people a way to represent other parts of their lives on Facebook. Groups are currently used to reflect real-life affiliations, such as *The Ultimate Players Association* and *Westchester Is the Bestchester*, as well as humorous or funny statements, such as *Dunkin Donuts is kind of a big deal in my life.*

Creating and joining groups is a way to express yourself to your friends; all the groups you join are listed on your profile in the Groups box. To learn more about creating and joining groups, check out Chapter 12.

Events

Events are, unsurprisingly, a way to plan, invite, and manage an event that you're hosting. Events have features that are similar to a group, but have the added, and important, feature of being time-sensitive. Events also plug into Facebook's Calendar, which means that you can manage your parties, dates, and personal time all in one place. With the Events application, you send people invites through Facebook as well as via e-mail. Events can be a great way to ensure your friends know about the big You-a-pa-looza that's coming up. See Chapter 13 for more about events.

Notes

Notes are blogs. Similar to blogs, Notes are ways of writing entries about your life, your thoughts, or your latest favorite song and sharing them with your Facebook friends.

Like Photos, the beauty of Notes lies in the ability to blog without needing to distribute a Web address to friends so that they can check it out. Instead, your friends are connected to your profile. Therefore, when you start writing, they find out about it through News Feed.

If you already keep a blog, import it into Notes and distribute it to your friends through that application.

Writing a note

No specific rules of etiquette dictate the proper length of notes or even the contents of notes. Some people like to keep them short and informative, other people like to take the extra space to say everything they want to say about a topic. Go crazy, or not. Feeling uninspired? Pick a favorite funny memory, awkward moment, or topic that really gets people thinking. Write something short about it, and see what your friends have to say in their ensuing comments. Getting started on your first note is pretty straightforward.

1. **Open your Notes page using the Notes link in the left-hand Applications menu.**

   Don't forget, it may live below the More link at the bottom of the Applications menu.

2. **On the Notes page, click the Write a New Note button in the top right.**

   A blank note appears, as shown in Figure 8-1.

3. **In the Title field, add your title.**

4. **In the Body field, start writing about anything.**

5. **After you finish writing, click Preview.**

   Preview opens a preview of the note, so you can have one last glance-over before you publish. If you're unhappy with your preview, go to Step 6; otherwise, go to Step 7.

6. **Click Edit on the right side of the note to return to the Write Note screen.**

   Make edits to your heart's desire.

7. **When you're happy with your note, click Publish.**

   Voilà! You shared your note, and your thoughts, with anyone who can see this on your profile.

The next sections take you through the steps of formatting — and otherwise getting fancy with — your notes.

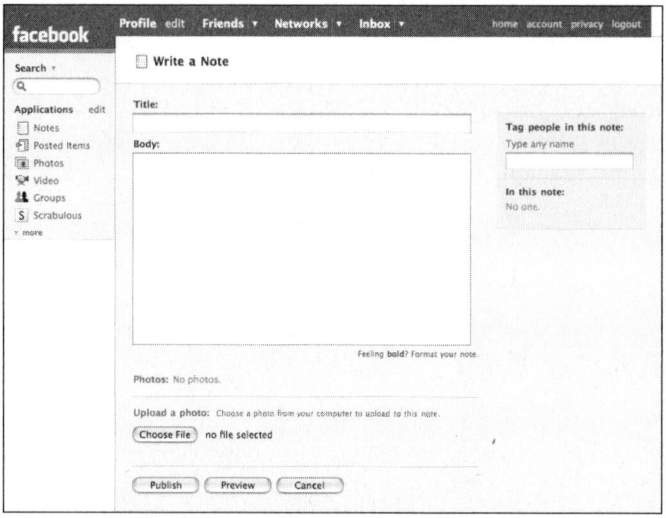

Figure 8-1:
The startling white canvas of a blank note staring at you.

Formatting a note

Formatting is one of the more annoying parts of Facebook Notes. Unfortunately, Facebook does not have a rich-text editor that enables you to press a large B, I, or U to have your text come out bold, italicized, or underlined. Instead, Notes uses HTML tags for formatting purposes. To make a word bold, you need to surround the text you want bold with the tags for that. For example, if you type

    this phrase

you get

    this **phrase**

For a list of HTML tags that can be used in notes, click the Format Your Note link (next to the words Feeling **bold?**) below the Body field. Doing so opens a new browser window with a cheat sheet of HTML tags, as shown in Figure 8-2.

The preview function within notes is a good way to figure whether your formatting is working how you want it to. Toggle between the Preview and Edit screens to figure out quickly whether your HTML tags are working.

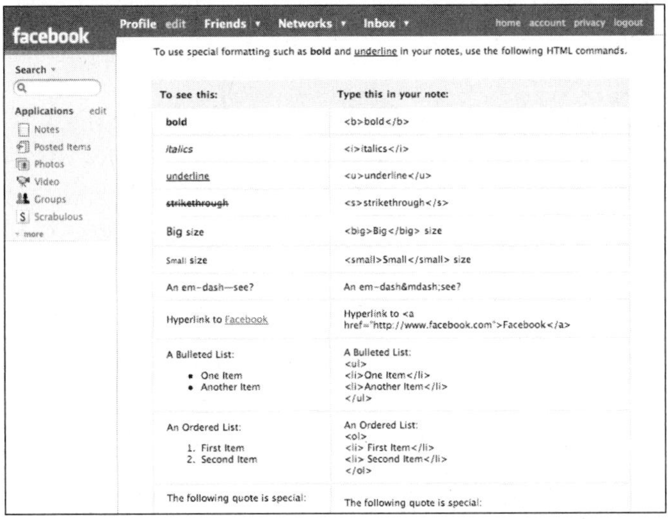

Figure 8-2: Use the HTML cheat sheet to format your notes.

Adding photos to a note

They say a picture is worth a thousand words. One could contend that it depends on the picture, which is why it is completely optional to include photos within your notes. However, if you do feel that slashing 1,000 words would help, add photos to your note. This also requires HTML tags.

1. **At the bottom of the Write a Note page, click the Choose File (on Safari) or Browse (on Firefox or Internet Explorer) button to find on your computer the photos that you want.**

   You can add only one photo at a time; therefore, repeat as necessary until you upload all the photos that you want.

   Each photo is given an HTML tag, usually numbered from <Photo 1> to <Photo X>.

2. **For each photo, add a caption and select how you want the photo to appear.**

   The photo can cover the full width of the note, or be resized and aligned to the left, right, or center as shown in Figure 8-3.

   The photo tags are put (by default) at the bottom of your note.

3. **Move the tags (just as you would move text) to where you want the photos to appear.**

4. **Use the Preview button to see how your note looks.**

5. **To change the look, click Edit, make your changes, and then click Publish.**

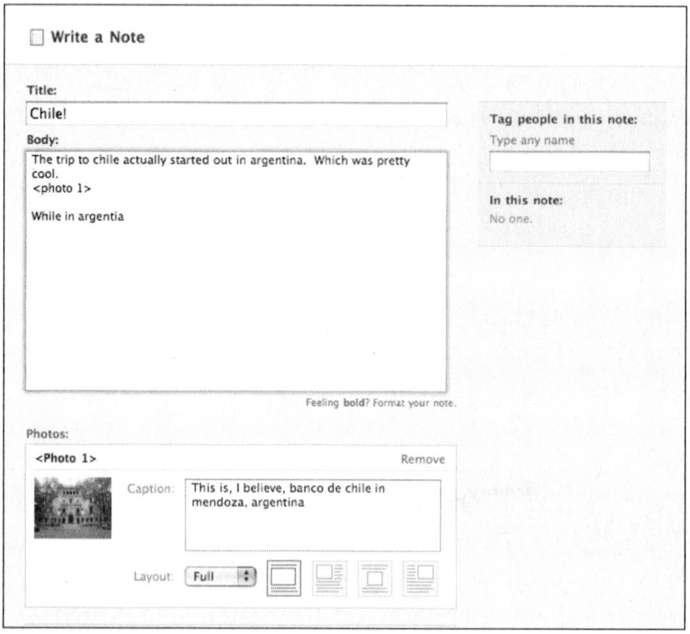

Figure 8-3:
Photo options for a note.

Tagging friends in your note

Sometimes your stories may involve your friends. Imagine that every time you tell a story about a friend in real life, she's notified of it. Yeah, maybe that doesn't sound so great for the real world, so imagine that every time you tell an awesome story about a friend, you also say to that friend, "Hey, I told that story about the time you laid out in the endzone of an Ultimate Frisbee game and nearly dislocated your shoulder." Your friend would feel pretty warm and fuzzy on the inside knowing that she was worth talking about (in a good way).

Tagging your friends in a note accomplishes this goal. You can write a whole note about the most epic night of your life, and all your friends are notified that they were part of it. Similar to a photo tag, people's profiles are linked to your note, and people reading the note are able to see who's tagged.

On the right side of the Tag People in This Note box, type the name of the person you're tagging; repeat as necessary. Facebook might offer some suggestions if it sees certain words that match names on your Friend List. Your tagged friends are now famous.

Importing a blog into Notes

Maybe you've already been keeping a blog, and the thought of moving everything over to Facebook sounds like a nightmare. Maybe you don't want to exclude your friends who haven't joined Facebook from reading all about you. Maybe you like the formatting and photo upload options of a different blogging platform better. Not to worry, Facebook is ready for you.

Importing a blog into Facebook is easy using the following steps:

1. **Open the Notes page.**

2. **In the gray column on the right, click Import a Blog underneath Notes Settings.**

3. **Enter the URL for your blog, certify that it's yours, and click Start Importing.**

   The next page displays a preview of all the existing entries that will be imported into your notes.

4. **Click Confirm Import on the right side.**

   Your entries are imported, and Facebook checks the feed of your blog every few hours to see whether there are any new entries.

When blogs are imported into notes, they frequently lose certain formatting or photos that were included in the original. Check your preview to see if these things happen to your blog.

Reading and commenting on your friends' notes

When you click on the Notes link in the left-hand Applications menu, a big aggregate view of all your friends' notes appears. Depending on how frequently your friends write notes, and what they write about, this can be an interesting way to catch up on at one time what different friends are doing. Entries are ordered chronologically. However, from this page, you can easily jump to a particular friend's notes by clicking on the Notes link in parentheses next to his name. It usually looks something like this: Carolyn Abram (<u>notes</u>).

When you just have to comment on something you read, look for the Add a Comment link at the bottom of the note. Click Add a Comment to open a comment box so that you can easily say your piece. When you're done, click the Add Your Comment button to submit it.

Posted Items

Posted Items is like a bulletin board of interesting information, articles, photos, and memorabilia that you carry around with you. You only get one bulletin board, so the new things you post simply stack on top of the old. It's another way that you reflect to the world what's important to you and what's interesting to you.

On Facebook (instead of a bulletin board), your Posted Items, photos, memorabilia, and articles are in the form of links and URLs to various Web pages — both on and off Facebook.

When you post something to your profile, it appears in your Mini-Feed and Posted Items box on your profile. It might also appear in your friends' News Feed and Posted Items page. Posted Items is a great way to circulate information. Moreover, if many of your friends use it, Posted Items is an excellent way for you to discover interesting things. Again, imagining a bulletin board, maybe you unpin an article and hand it to a friend, but wouldn't it be better if all your friends could see it?

The basics of posting an item

The most basic way to post a link to your profile is to do so from the Posted Items page. This isn't actually the easiest way to do so, but it helps you understand how Posted Items works.

1. **Click the Posted Items link in the left-hand Applications menu.**

2. **Under the Post a Link header, paste the link you want to post into this box and click Post.**

   You see a page similar to Figure 8-4. The blank box is for your comment, say, to explain why you're posting or to direct people to a certain part. Additionally, you can edit the excerpt and photo that accompany the post.

3. **(Optional) Write a comment.**

4. **Click Post.**

When you post something to your profile, it appears in your Mini-Feed and Posted Items box on your profile. It may also appear in your friends' News Feed, and will show in their Posted Items page. Posted Items are a great way to spread something and, if many of your friends use it, can be a great way to discover things that you never knew about but are interested in. Posted Items enable you to look at all your friends' bulletin boards, and have them look at yours, without needing to be in a one-on-one environment.

Figure 8-4:
The Post
dialog.

Using Share to post items

Posted Items works with the Share functionality to spread cool articles, links, blogs, and photos — "stuff" from around the Web and Facebook — in a public way. Share is also used to spread these things to individual people via message attachments. We talk about that side of Share in Chapter 10. For the purpose of Posted Items, look for Share links in the following places:

✓ **Around Facebook:** On many Facebook pages, you see Share buttons that have a plus sign. Pressing Share opens a dialog similar to the one when you copy and paste a link into the Posted Items page. Share might open the dialog with the Send a Message tab instead of the Post to Profile tab. Click on the Post to Profile tab to post the link to your profile.

Anything you share that's housed on Facebook (like profiles or photos) is still subject to Facebook's privacy settings. If Leah posts one of Carolyn's photo albums and that album is visible Only to Friends, only Carolyn's friends can see Leah's post.

✓ **On other Web sites:** Many Web sites, including NYTimes.com, Time. com, CollegeHumor.com, and hundreds more, have small links to Share on Facebook discretely located someplace next to each article. Clicking these links opens a Share dialog box similar to the Post to My Profile dialog box shown in Figure 8-4. You can then post the article to your profile without ever leaving the Web site you're looking at.

✓ **Anywhere if you install the Share bookmarklet:** The Share bookmarklet is a small link you place in your bookmark bar. Whenever you click it, it grabs whatever page you're currently viewing on the Internet and generates a preview for it that you post to your profile. Installing the bookmarklet takes only a minute, as we describe here:

For Firefox and Safari:

1. **Click the Posted Items link in your Applications menu.**

2. **In the right column, drag and drop the Share on Facebook button to the bookmark bar in your browser.**

   Now, wherever you're at on the Internet, simply look up to that bookmark bar and click Share on Facebook whenever you want to post something to your profile.

For Internet Explorer:

1. **Click the Posted Items link in your Applications menu.**

2. **Right-click the Share on Facebook button and choose Add to Favorites.**

   You have added it here, too.

   Now, wherever you are on the Internet, open the Favorites window and click Share on Facebook whenever you want to post something to your profile.

Getting the news, filtered through your friends

Posted Items appear in one of two ways: through News Feed (where, depending on activity, your friends' Posted Items are delivered) or through the Posted Items page. This page aggregates all your friends' recently posted items in chronological order. This is possibly the best way to get news that you care about and expand what you read. In one day, you might see a political article, a funny video from YouTube, a parody of that funny video about YouTube, a blog about gadgets, and so on. When we found the listing of *Facebook For Dummies* on Amazon.com, we were quick to post it, so our friends would know what we were doing. Posted Items means you get recommended reading and viewing lists every day of your life.

As with almost everything else on Facebook, if something sparks an interest, thought, or idea, add your comment to the posted item. Click the Add a Comment link at the bottom of the posted item preview, type your comment in the box, and click the Add Your Comment button. You'd be surprised about the debates that take place only in comments after posting a controversial article. Let the free flow of ideas begin.

Marketplace

Marketplace is the Facebook version of classified ads. You get to the Marketplace area just as you access any of the Facebook apps: click its link in the Applications menu on the left. Like any marketplace, Facebook Marketplace is a place for people to buy and sell. However, instead of buying a tent and sitting out in the sweltering heat for a few hours yelling at everyone who passes by that you have the best deal, simply fill out a few online forms and wait for people to come to you. You can create free listings for things that you are in the market for as well as things you have to sell, rent, or give away.

Marketplaces are based around networks. If you haven't joined a network, the Marketplace link won't appear in your left-hand Applications menu. You need to add it from the Application Directory.

Creating a listing

Creating a listing for something on Facebook involves answering a series of questions about the thing you're looking to buy or sell. Go to the Marketplace page (by clicking Marketplace in the Applications menu), and then ask yourself these questions:

1. **Are you selling something?**

   • If yes, click the big Add a New Listing button.

   • If no, click the big List What You Want button.

   The pages you land on have similar categories, but from the perspective of either looking for it or having it. Figure 8-5 shows the options for listing what you have to sell; Figure 8-6 shows the options for looking for something you want to buy.

2. **What are you looking to buy or sell?**

   If you're selling something, clicking For Sale shows you the basic items you might be selling — that is, books, furniture, and so on. Comparatively, if you're itching to buy something, click Item Wanted.

3. **More detail, please.**

   If you answered the first question by clicking Add a New Listing and the second question by clicking For Sale, the third question is trying to figure out whether it's furniture, books, electronics, or a car.

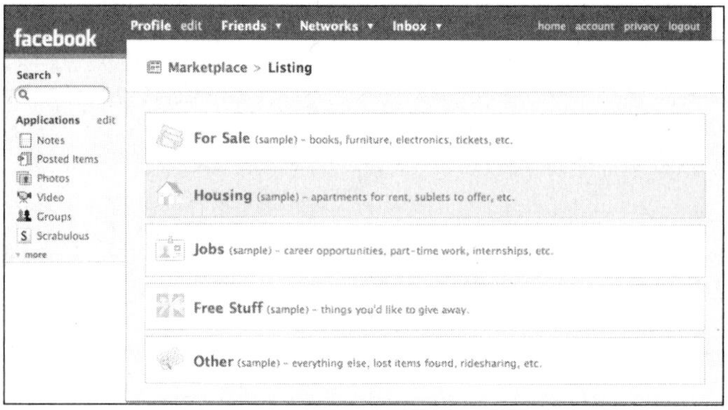

Figure 8-5:
Listing what
you have.

Figure 8-6:
Listing what
you want.

TIP

In case you get lost in the question trees, you can always see where you're located at the top of the page, represented like this:

Marketplace > Listing > For Sale > Tickets

If you find yourself here and say, "I didn't want tickets, I wanted electronics!" you can simply click For Sale to return to the options under that, which include both Tickets and Electronics.

When you've finished answering these questions, you see a form with a couple of blank fields. These fields may shift around depending on what category you're in. Figure 8-7 shows the form for Marketplace > Wanted > Housing > Sublets.

Despite some variation (housing has space for the number of bedrooms, a book has space for an ISBN number), the constant fields can help you understand who sees what:

- **Title:** The basics of what you're looking for or what you have to offer — job title, furniture item, book title, and so on. This should be short and to the point.

- **Description:** The description gives you a chance to elaborate on what exactly your item is, how you arrived at the pricing for it, and why your prized golden cookie jar is only going to someone who can truly appreciate it.

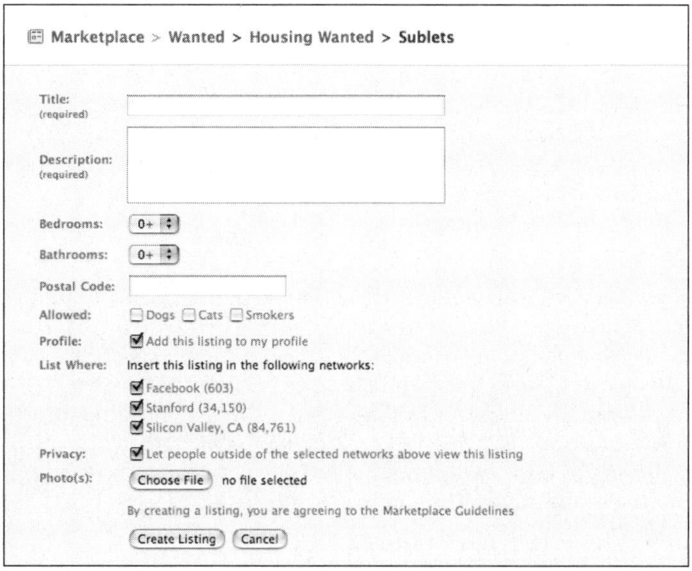

Marketplace > Wanted > Housing Wanted > **Sublets**

Title: (required)	
Description: (required)	
Bedrooms:	0+
Bathrooms:	0+
Postal Code:	
Allowed:	☐ Dogs ☐ Cats ☐ Smokers
Profile:	☑ Add this listing to my profile
List Where:	Insert this listing in the following networks:
	☑ Facebook (603)
	☑ Stanford (34,150)
	☑ Silicon Valley, CA (84,761)
Privacy:	☑ Let people outside of the selected networks above view this listing
Photo(s):	Choose File no file selected
	By creating a listing, you are agreeing to the Marketplace Guidelines
	Create Listing Cancel

Figure 8-7:
Marketplace
> Wanted >
Housing >
Sublets.

✔ **Price (only for Selling listings, not for Wanted listings):** This helps people sort for their budget when they're looking at listings.

✔ **List Where:** Marketplace is based around your networks. The assumption is that networks usually map to a geographic area or region, so making an item visible to your network is a great way to get it to people who are close by and who can pick up the item. You can select which networks you want a listing to be shown to. For example, you might not want your coworkers to know that you're in the market for a new job, so if you're listing a Wanted: New Job ad, you may want to uncheck your workplace network.

✔ **Privacy:** The privacy option is different from the List Where option. Although your listing is shown only to your selected networks, if people outside of those networks perform a search within that network for the keywords in your ad, you may or may not want them to see it. For example, if you're selling your car, someone who is moving to your area but hasn't joined your region network may want to buy it. Leaving the privacy option checked means that she can find your car and contact you in order to buy it.

✔ **Photos:** You can initially upload up to four photos of the item you're selling or looking to buy. To upload a photo, click the Browse button at the bottom of the listing, search your computer's files for the photo you want, select it, and then click Open. The photo is displayed with your listing, both as a thumbnail and as a full-size photo.

Browsing, searching, and viewing listings

When you want to buy something, you can go to a mall or you can go to a flea market. Both involve lots of walking, no guarantee that you'll find what you're looking for, and a whole lot of browsing. Marketplace also involves a lot of browsing and no guarantee — but walking is unnecessary — and you don't even have to get out of your pajamas.

Browsing

When you're not looking for anything in particular, you can just window shop in Marketplace, too. To browse, go to the Marketplace for each of your networks and look at the most recently added listings. Your default view when you click on the Marketplace link is your primary network's Marketplace. You can page through all the listings and see if there's anything interesting you might want to buy, or if people are looking for something that you happen to have. You never know when people are going to be looking for old speakers like the ones you have sitting in the basement waiting to be fixed for the last eight years.

Another great place for browsing is the Free Stuff category because you never know what people are going to give away — it might be something you never knew you needed.

Your friends' listings offer all sorts of browsing fun. You can get there by clicking on the Friends Listings link on the top of the page. Here, you get the real dirt on your friends, such as who's selling a house and who's posting a job listing for their own job.

Searching

Chances are, browsing only happens from time to time, whereas real shopping, with a direct intent to find something — whether it's a signed baseball, a signed lease, or a sign that reads *Duck Crossing* — happens frequently. For this reason, Facebook tries to make searching for listings as accurate and quick as possible. Do you remember some of the more unusual fields you filled out while creating a listing? This is so that people who are looking for an automatic car with less than 50,000 miles that costs less than $10,000 can find it quickly. Moreover, if you have a cat, you can quickly screen out apartments that won't allow pets. If you're looking for a book, you can find a direct ISBN match, so you don't have to spend hours looking through near misses and duplicate named books.

Start your search by entering a keyword in the search box in the upper right. You can select which category you want to search from the drop-down menu next to the search box. If keyword search doesn't get you the results you want, select a category from the main Marketplace page and see what crops up. You can enter extra information while you move through the various categories, eventually finding that near-mint condition Mr. Coffee for only ten bucks.

Marketplace listings are sorted by network. When you arrive on the Marketplace page, you're looking at your primary network's marketplace. Make sure to click the tab for the network that you want to search.

Viewing listings

After you've gotten some promising listings on the screen, you probably want more detail. Just how rusty is that rusty bike? Just how much repair is required for *some* body damage? Is there an evil gnome living under the floorboards of the apartment and that's why the rent is so low? When you click on a listing, it opens a pop-up window with all the information. You can scroll through the entire description, browse through photos by clicking the arrows underneath, and decide whether you want to contact the person who made the listing. If you don't like it, close the window. If you like it but don't want to commit, choose to View as Full Page (next to the Close button). This opens the ad in a new page, which you can come back to at any time.

Initiating contact

One of the cool parts about Marketplace is that you're not always buying from a complete stranger. Ever sold a car and thought, "I really don't want this random stranger coming over to my house to look at the car"? What if you could decide who gets to look at the car based on whether they knew someone who knew you or went to school with you? That's what Marketplace lets you do. Whenever you open an ad, in the bottom line, you see the name of the person who created the listing. If you know anyone he knows, it tells you the name of your mutual friend. If you belong to the same network, it tells you which one. Therefore, you can remove some of the creepy anonymity of online transactions without removing the privacy shields that Facebook provides.

After you decide that you are comfortable contacting that person, you can send him a message and work out the details of the transaction. Without ever leaving Facebook, you can find what you're looking for, contact the person who has it, and figure out the details of the transaction. All you have to do is put on some regular clothing, leave the house, and go pick it up.

When you receive a message from someone from your listing, you can automatically turn it into an FAQ. The person's name isn't included, just the question and your response. Thereafter, it's visible as part of your listing's description.

Video

Does your cell phone or digital camera also shoot video? Chances are the answer is, "Yes," and if we asked you where you put that video, you'd say, "On my computer." Probably hundreds of short video clips never make it past the camera that took them and wind up decayed and cobwebby on some hard drive somewhere. If you use a video Web site to upload your videos, you're faced with sending out e-mails to all the people that you want to see your video and making sure that the entire Internet doesn't have access to them.

Just like Photos, Facebook Video is a one-stop shop for uploading, recording, and sharing videos with your friends. It also enables really cool things like video messaging and video Wall posts. You can show all your friends that brilliant video that formerly languished on your computer. Whether it's a bunch of people saying, "Oh my gosh, is this video?" or your own indie film — there's a place for it on Facebook.

Uploading video

Uploading a video to a Web site includes going out into the world, recording something, and then moving it from your camera onto your computer. We're going to assume you've already done that part and are now back to being sedentary in front of your computer. To upload a video to Facebook:

1. Choose Video in your left-hand Applications menu.

If Video doesn't appear in your left-hand Applications menu, go to the Application Directory (click Edit next to the Apps menu and then click

Browse More Applications), click By Facebook in the right column, and then add the Video application.

2. **Click the big Upload button in the upper right.**

3. **Click the Browse button and select a video file from your computer.**

   After you select a video, Facebook starts uploading it. This might take a while. When it's finished, you see a yellow confirmation screen, similar to that in Figure 8-8. The information below the progress bar is part of the Edit Video screen that we discuss in the upcoming "Tagging and editing videos" section.

4. **Click Save Info.**

   We talk about saving information in the next section.

   Depending on the length and size of your video file, your video might need to be processed for a few minutes. Leaving the page when the screen displays *Your video is being processed* won't delete your video, so explore other parts of Facebook while you wait for the processing to finish.

5. **(Optional) Select to have an e-mail sent to you after processing is complete.**

   After processing is complete, your video displays in your Video box on your profile, and might show up in your friends' News Feeds.

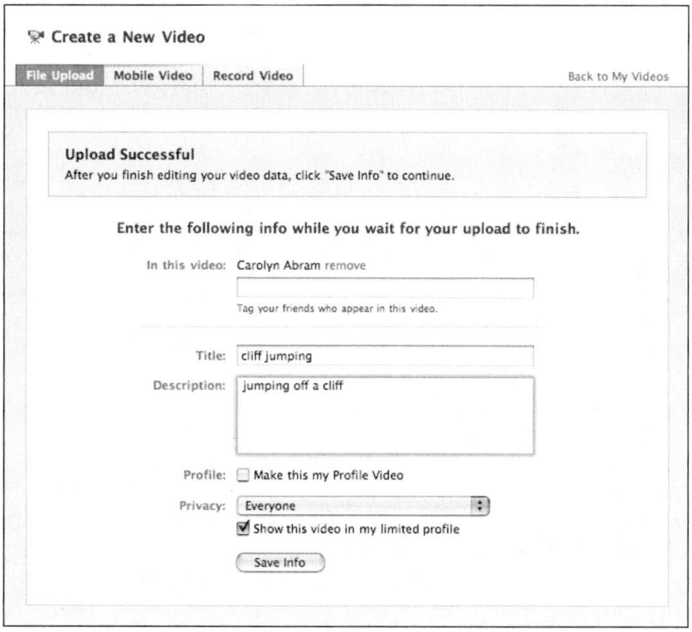

Figure 8-8:
Video
Upload
confir-
mation.

Recording video

If you have a Webcam either built in or attached to your computer, you can upload videos straight to Facebook.

1. Click the Record button in the upper right of the Video page.

You see your Webcam activate and the current input on the screen in front of you, as shown in Figure 8-9. Note that this is not yet recording.

Figure 8-9:
The Record
Video
screen.

2. Click the red button in the middle of the screen to start recording.

3. Click the button again when you're done.

4. Watch the preview of the clip to make sure you're happy with it.

5. Click Save when you're ready to continue.

The next screen (similar to Figure 8-10) involves video editing, which we cover in the next section.

Tagging and editing videos

In both uploading and recording videos, you see the Edit Video screen, which has fields similar to those shown in Figure 8-10. Facebook Video doesn't have many advanced video editing options, so add a soundtrack or cut the video prior to uploading it onto Facebook.

Figure 8-10:
The Edit
Video
screen.

The Edit Video screen has several fields to fill out; most of these are optional:

- ✔ **In This Video:** This option is similar to tagging a photo or a note. Simply start typing the names of all the friends that are in the video and then select the correct friends from the list that displays. Your friends are notified that they've been tagged in a video and can remove the tag if they decide they don't want to be forever remembered as *The one who got pied in the face.* You're automatically tagged when you record a video from a Webcam.

- ✔ **Title:** Name your video. You can be artsy and name it something like *Boston Cream Meets a Bitter End* or something descriptive like *Pie in the Face.* If you don't choose a title, the video is automatically titled with the timestamp of when you recorded or uploaded it.

- ✔ **Description:** This field is for you to describe what's happening in your video, though frequently, videos can speak for themselves.

- ✔ **Profile:** The Make This My Profile Video option relates to the order in which your videos display in your Video box on your profile. You can have only one profile video at a time; the profile video you choose stays at the top of your Video box in your profile. As long as you keep the Video box in the right column of your profile, your profile video can play from your profile, as opposed to going to another page.

- ✔ **Privacy:** Your privacy options for videos are on a per-video basis. Thus, you can choose that everyone sees *Pie in the Face,* but only certain friends (with strong stomachs) see *Pie-eating Contest.* For more about general privacy options, check out Chapter 4.

Viewing videos and leaving comments

Other than your News Feed, one of the best ways to see videos involving your friends is the Video page. The Video page displays a column of videos by your friends and another column of videos of your friends. Depending on how much your friends hang out with each other, you might see duplicates in the two columns. When you find a video you want to watch, click on the video thumbnail. A new page appears where you can watch the video in its entirety.

If you feel the need to respond to the video, leave a comment to let the owner of the video (and anyone in it) know what you think. Just type your text into the Add Your Comment box beneath the video and click Add Your Comment when you're done.

Video messages and Wall posts

In the same way that you can record videos onto your profile, you can record videos for your messages and Wall posts. When you're writing a message or Wall post, look for the Attach field and select Record Video to open the Record Video screen. Many applications plug into the Attach field, so you may see more options than on the Compose Message screen shown in Figure 8-11. Carolyn is preparing to send a message with a video attached.

Recording a video to attach to a message or Wall post is more or less the same as recording a video straight to Facebook. However, the two are slightly different from each other, so we give a set of steps for each.

To record a Video Wall post, follow these steps:

1. **Click Record Video.**

   The Record Video interface appears, as shown in Figure 8-12.

Figure 8-11:
Send a message with attachments.

Inbox	Sent Messages	Notifications		Compose Message

To:

Start typing a friend's name or email address

Subject:

Message:

Attach: 🎥 Record Video 🔗 Share Link

(Send) (Cancel)

2. **Click the red record button in the center of the screen to start recording your Wall post.**

3. **Click the same button again when you're done.**

4. **Preview it and click Attach.**

   The video becomes part of a preview for the entire Wall post, as shown in Figure 8-13. You can add text to your Wall post if you want, but it isn't required.

5. **Click Post.**

   Your video becomes an actual Wall post, as shown in Figure 8-14.

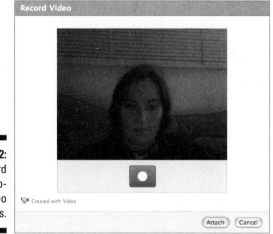

Figure 8-12:
The Record Video pop-up for Video Wall posts.

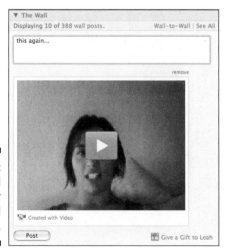

Figure 8-13:
The final preview for a Video Wall post.

To record a Video message, follow these steps:

1. **With a new message open, click Record Video.**

   The Record Video interface appears, as shown in Figure 8-15.

2. **Click the red button in the center of the screen to start recording; click it again to stop recording.**

Figure 8-14:
A Video
Wall post on
an actual
Wall.

Figure 8-15:
The Video
Message
recording
screen.

3. **Click Attach.**

   Finish writing your message, if necessary.

4. **Click Send and you're done!**

Gifts

The Gifts application offers *virtual gifts* — small tokens of appreciation that you can purchase to give to your friends. Gifts works with the Wall, so a Wall post that explains it accompanies your gift. New gifts are added every day, so you can express a wide variety of things via gifts. Did someone have a sweet lay-out at Ultimate Frisbee last night? Nothing says, "Congrats!" like the Laying out Ultimate Player gift. Is your friend always unable to get out because she works all the time? Virtual Handcuffs can be one way to ask, "Are you chained to your desk?" Gifts cost $1 each, unless you're buying bulk orders, in which case they're only $.50. Don't worry, your friends won't know whether you spent fifty cents or a whole dollar on them; they probably assume you went all out for the dollar.

The Gift Shop adds a new gift every day, so over time, the inventory has grown. You might feel a bit like a child told to pick one toy out of the entire toy store. Fortunately, you can always give more than one gift, and the vast inventory helps you always find the right gift to give to your friend. For example, if Dave Fisch is complaining about eating take-out alone every Saturday night, the Chinese Take-out Box gift might be the best way to say, "Hang in there." If it's Ami's birthday, pick from a plethora of birthday cakes, cupcakes, balloons, and banners all of which say, "Have a good birthday." If Leah makes her first ever lay-out catch in the endzone for Ultimate, the Get the Disc gift says, "Congrats!"

Giving gifts

Gifts is one of the few Facebook applications that doesn't have (by default) a left-hand Applications menu link. Because of this, there are a bunch of ways to get to the Gift Shop to give a gift. You can type **www.facebook.com/gift shop.php** into your browser or follow the links that sometimes pop up in the New Stuff box on your Home page. The most reliable way that we recommend, however, is to go to the profile of the person you want to give a gift to, scroll down to his Wall, and find the small link underneath the Wall post field that reads *Give a Gift to <Name>*.

1. **Click the Give a Gift to *<Name>* link to go to the Gift Shop, shown in Figure 8-16.**

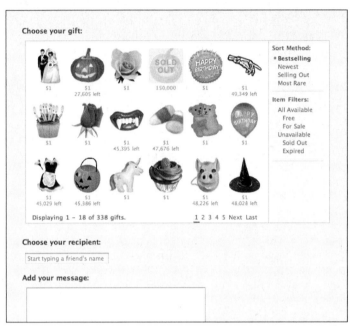

Choose your gift:

Sort Method:
• Bestselling
  Newest
  Selling Out
  Most Rare

Item Filters:
  All Available
  Free
  For Sale
  Unavailable
  Sold Out
  Expired

Displaying 1 – 18 of 338 gifts.   1 2 3 4 5 Next Last

Choose your recipient:
Start typing a friend's name

Add your message:

Figure 8-16:
The front
page of the
Gift Shop.

2. **Page through the Gift Shop using either the filters on the right or the page numbers on the bottom; Click the gift you want to give.**

   The gift appears below the Gift Shop.

   The name of your friend is pre-filled in the Choose Your Recipient field because you came from your friend's profile. If you don't come from a friend's profile, start typing a friend's name and select her from the drop-down list.

3. **Enter a message to accompany your gift.**

   Some gifts may require explanation, such as, "Here is a pair of pink underwear, not because I want to see you in your underwear, but because I thought it would make you laugh," or maybe, "Here is a pair of virtual handcuffs. They are weird, like you," or even, "Here are some cute teddy bears that are hugging each other. They make me smile, like you."

4. **Select your delivery method from one of the following:**

   • *Public:* Everyone who can see your friend's profile can see that you gave that particular gift as well as the message that accompanies your gift.

   • *Private:* People can see the gift but not the message that accompanied it or that you were the one who gave the gift.

- *Anonymous:* People can see the gift but not the message or that you were the one who gave it. In addition, the recipient will see the message, but not know who gave it.

5. **Click Continue.**

   The payment confirmation screen appears. The first time here, you have to enter your credit card info. Facebook has secure servers for storing this information, so you can be as confident entering your credit card number as you are on any Web site.

6. **After everything is entered, click Purchase and Send Gift.**

   Congrats, you just brightened someone's day!

Receiving gifts

Receiving gifts, as in real life, doesn't involve much more than sitting around, smiling, and reveling in the attention. Saying "Thanks," whether in a Thank You note, Wall post, or message, is often appreciated. The only things you really need to know as a virtual gift recipient are how to get to all your gifts and that you can control the gifts you receive.

The first, getting to your gifts, involves going to your profile and finding your Gifts box. The Gifts box is usually located right above your Wall, unless you moved it. After you find it, click See All to see all your gifts. Assuming you have received a gift, the My Received Gifts screen appears, as shown in Figure 8-17.

You might go to this page to swim in your gifts like Scrooge McDuck and revel in how much people love you. However, this is also the place where you control the gifts you receive. Do the cuddly teddy bears with the message, "I love you more than the air I breathe" make you blush? Are the virtual boxing gloves more of an inside joke? You can turn public gifts into private ones — or delete gifts entirely — if you don't want folks seeing what someone said to you or what someone gave you. From the My Received Gifts page:

1. **Scroll to the gift you want to manage.**

   Gifts that are public have two options: Make It Private? and Delete It? Gifts that are private have only the Delete It? option.

2. **Decide what you want to do with the gift and click that option.**

   You won't be able to undo these choices.

My Received Gifts | My Sent Gifts | Send a Gift | Back to My Profile

From: ▓▓▓▓▓▓▓▓▓ (gifts)

This is a public gift. Make it Private? | Delete it?
Others will see the gift, the message, and who sent it.

❝ better? ❞

From: ▓▓▓▓▓▓▓▓▓ (gifts)

This is a private gift. Delete it?
Others will see the gift, but not the message or who sent it.

From: ▓▓▓▓▓▓ (gifts)

This is a public gift. Make it Private? | Delete it?
Others will see the gift, the message, and who sent it.

❝ I saw this and thought of you, obvi. Thanks for the daily coffee dates. :) ❞

Figure 8-17:
Gifts you've
received.

Mobile

The Mobile application is added to your account automatically when you activate Facebook Mobile. The whole purpose of Facebook Mobile is for you to use Facebook while on the go. Nevertheless, when you're at your computer, the Mobile application offers some nifty functionality as well as a shortcut to editing your mobile settings. To learn more about using Facebook while on the go, check out Chapter 14.

Mobile uploads

When you select the Mobile link in the left-hand Applications menu, the Mobile Uploads page displays the most recent mobile uploads that your friends have made. Figure 8-18 shows a sampling of mobile uploads. These photos and notes offer great insight into what your friends have been doing most recently when they were out and about. You might see a few photos from a party, a few from a family outing, or maybe even a mobile note written from the airport.

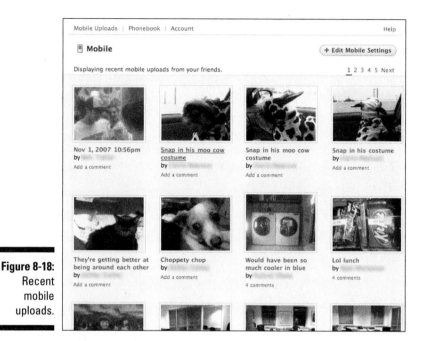

Nov 1, 2007 10:56pm
by
Add a comment

Snap in his moo cow
costume
by
Add a comment

Snap in his moo cow
costume
by
Add a comment

Snap in his costume
by
Add a comment

They're getting better at
being around each other
by
Add a comment

Choppety chop
by
Add a comment

Would have been so
much cooler in blue
by
4 comments

Lol lunch
by
4 comments

Figure 8-18:
Recent
mobile
uploads.

Phonebook

Click the Phonebook link at the top of the Mobile page to get to your online
phonebook. Using the information your friends provide on their profiles, the
Mobile application pulls all the phone numbers that you're allowed to see
into one convenient page, alphabetized by first name. You should know that
Phonebook is one of the most useful pages on Facebook as well as one of the
more hidden gems. With a self-updating phone book, you never forget to add
your friend's new number, and they never forget to add yours. You can access
this information directly from your cell phone, should you ever need to get in
touch with someone and realize you don't have her number. Don't forget to
read Chapter 14 to find out how.

Edit settings

On the Mobile Uploads page is a button in the upper right that reads *Edit
Mobile Settings*. Selecting this button opens the Edit Mobile Settings page,
shown in Figure 8-19. This page lets you edit your current options for
Facebook Mobile, including what text messages you receive, and how often
you receive them. You can also edit these settings from your phone.

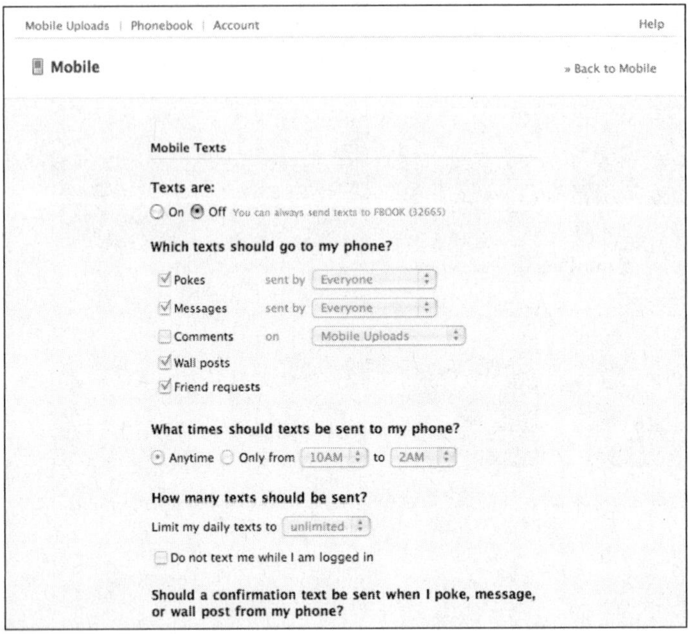

Figure 8-19:
The Edit
Mobile
Settings
page.

Politics

The Facebook Politics application is only truly available for users in the United States and Canada. Even then, the application is primarily for U.S. users and geared toward the 2008 elections. Most of the information in this section is going to be relative to U.S. voters interested in using Facebook to express their political affiliations, opinions, and choices.

Adding the Politics application

Politics is one of the few Facebook applications that you must first *add* to your account. The idea of adding an application is based on there being thousands of applications in the Application Directory — built by both Facebook and third parties. Most of these applications won't be used by each of the millions of users on Facebook. Appropriately, an application is added to the account of someone who wants to use that application for whatever reason. Not everyone on Facebook is interested in U.S. politics; therefore, you must add it to your account. To do this:

1. **Open the Application Directory by clicking the Applications link in the left-hand navigation menu and then clicking the Browse More Applications button.**

2. **Search for Politics in the upper-right search box.**

   Alternatively, you can click By Facebook in the right column of the Application Directory and then scroll down to find the application you want.

3. **Click on the US (or Canadian) Politics option.**

   The application's About page appears, as shown in Figure 8-20.

4. **Click Add Application in the upper right.**

5. **Agree to the Terms of Service on the Add Application page (Figure 8-21) and then click Add US Politics.**

   The US Politics front page appears, as shown in Figure 8-22. From here, you're able to access all parts of the US Politics application.

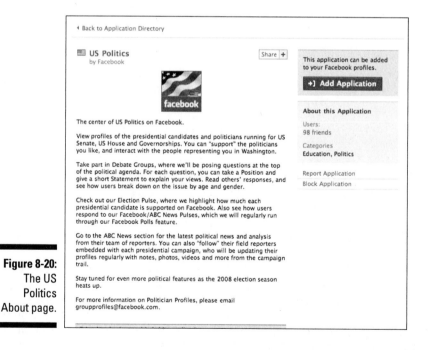

Figure 8-20: The US Politics About page.

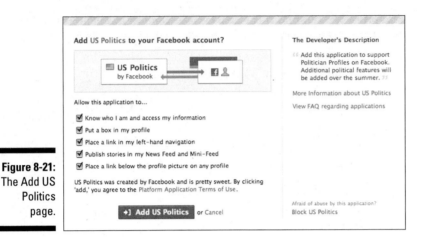

Figure 8-21:
The Add US Politics page.

Figure 8-22:
US Politics front page.

Supporting politicians

After you add the US Politics application, you can do many things to represent your political views to the world. First, you can add politicians you support to your profile. To do this:

1. **Open the US Politics page from the link in your left-hand Applications menu.**

2. **Using the Search box (in the upper-right corner), search for any politician you support.**

3. **Explore the profile of your search results.**

4. **Click Support This Politician to add this affiliation to your profile.**

Supporting a politician adds that person to the Politicians box in your profile, gives you the ability to write on your chosen candidate's Wall, and facilitates interaction with other supporters.

Debate groups

Debate groups allow you to take a stand on an issue, and debate that stand with everyone in the group. Debate groups are powered in part by a partnership with ABC News (see the next section). Debate groups pose a question, allow you to take one of a few predetermined viewpoints, and give you space to elaborate on your position. For those of you who just love debating, the discussion boards in the debate groups are for more involved discourse.

Taking part in a debate is pretty easy. Everyday until the 2008 election, when you go to the US Politics front page, you'll see a poll asking a question of the day (refer to Figure 8-22).

To participate, simply press Take a Position and submit your position. To get more in-depth, click the link for the question to view the full group, where you can see other people's positions and take part in the discussions.

ABC Partnership for US Politics

The ABC Partnership for US politics enables a couple of cool things, especially "On the trail" information from ABC reporters across the country. You can follow a reporter who's following a particular candidate and that reporter's Mini-Feed and profile serves as a constant source of news. To find a reporter you want to follow:

1. **From the US Politics Home page, scroll to the ABC Reporters You're Following box.**

2. **Click Browse Reporters.**

3. **Browse through the list.**

4. **If you find a reporter you want updates from, click Follow This Reporter.**

Other perks from ABC include ABC News content (both articles and videos), and an election pulse, which brings data from Facebook Polls into the US Politics application.

Chapter 9

Adding Third-Party Applications

*I*n Chapter 8, we talk about how the core of Facebook — your profile and your friendships — enables all sorts of applications to do highly interactive and interesting things with that information. Photos enables communal photo albums as well as a sort of indexing of who is in what album. Before you purchase a used item, Marketplace enables you to see whom you're buying from and whether you know any people in common. Chapter 8 talks about the applications built by Facebook, most of which are waiting for you when you create your account.

However, that's not all that the Facebook core can be used for — the functionality is limitless. Therefore, Facebook opened its core through *Facebook Platform,* which enables third-party developers anywhere in the world to build and integrate the same sort of applications that Facebook could build. Platform means that more people can get more from Facebook.

This chapter covers the additional parts of Facebook that are a result of its platform, including adding and finding applications. Additionally, we explore some of the applications you might decide to add to your account.

Why Add an Application?

Like everything else on Facebook, applications are all about options. You choose what information to put on your profile; an application box is another form of information. You add or use an application because you like the aesthetics. For example, leaving the Photos box on your profile displays your most recent photo albums. You also add or use an application because it makes your life easier; the mobile application keeps an easy-to-use phone-book of your friends' numbers.

Adding an application is another way of outfitting your profile. When you express yourself to the world, do you want them to see more photos of you? Do you want them to see that you're fighting a war of pirates and ninjas, and you're a ninja? Do you want them to see that you're taking classes and looking for study partners? Perhaps we're getting ahead of ourselves. All these options and more are available through the third-party applications built on top of Facebook's platform.

Finding Third-Party Applications

You find applications in two ways. The most common way is through your friends, which includes seeing something on your friends' profiles or them sending you a request or invitation from an application. The other way is through the Application Directory. Most of the instructions here involve having you go through the Application Directory to find certain applications.

Requests, notifications, and profiles

Facebook has this great concept of *viral* being a good thing. Instead of the bitter, "Thanks for spreading your cold, Katie," it's a cheerful, "Thanks for spreading the word, Katie." Facebook's viral is how things spread without people having to find it. Instead of you coming to an application, it comes to you. For example, when Meredith decides to quote Carolyn using the Quotes application, Carolyn is notified. If she likes the application, Carolyn can add it to her profile, and when Carolyn quotes someone else (say, Natalie), Natalie finds out about it.

When you receive a request, it usually appears in the right column of your Home page (where you receive friend requests and event invitations). When you receive a notification, it appears on your Notifications page, and a flag appears in your right column. If you have many notifications, only one notification flag appears. Notifications and requests are both generated by the application sending them, which is why it might be hard to predict what the content might be. Good applications send requests when you need to confirm something and notifications when you don't. For example, if some-one requires you to confirm a game of Roshambo before you start playing, it takes the form of a request. After the first move is made, you find out that it's your turn in the form of a notification.

If you haven't added the application when you interact with its notification or request, the application asks you to add it. We discuss the Add Application screen in the next section.

Applications also come to you while you use the site and browse your friends' profiles. Imagine that you just landed on Naomi's profile and she has a profile box displaying various slideshows made with her Facebook photos. You might think, "I, too, have photos that could be displayed in slideshows." Clicking the Add link in the upper right of the box you're looking at takes you to the Add Application screen.

If you want more information about the application before you add it, click the blue bar for that application to be taken to its About page, which we talk about later in this section. After you click Add on that page, the Add Application screen appears.

The Application Directory

Getting to the Application Directory is a two-step process. Go to your Applications page by clicking Applications in the left-hand menu. Then, on the Edit My Applications page (shown in Figure 9-1), click Browse More Applications in the upper-right corner.

Figure 9-2 shows the Application Directory where you just landed. This page is incredibly busy, so we take a minute to break it down.

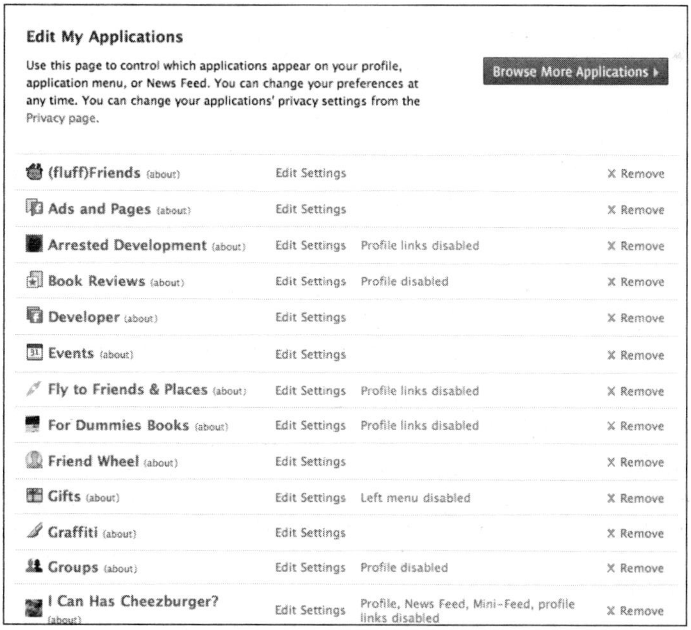

Figure 9-1:
The Edit My
Applications
page.

Edit My Applications

Use this page to control which applications appear on your profile, application menu, or News Feed. You can change your preferences at any time. You can change your applications' privacy settings from the Privacy page.

Browse More Applications ▸

(fluff)Friends (about)	Edit Settings	X Remove
Ads and Pages (about)	Edit Settings	X Remove
Arrested Development (about)	Edit Settings Profile links disabled	X Remove
Book Reviews (about)	Edit Settings Profile disabled	X Remove
Developer (about)	Edit Settings	X Remove
Events (about)	Edit Settings	X Remove
Fly to Friends & Places (about)	Edit Settings Profile links disabled	X Remove
For Dummies Books (about)	Edit Settings Profile links disabled	X Remove
Friend Wheel (about)	Edit Settings	X Remove
Gifts (about)	Edit Settings Left menu disabled	X Remove
Graffiti (about)	Edit Settings	X Remove
Groups (about)	Edit Settings Profile disabled	X Remove
I Can Has Cheezburger? (about)	Edit Settings Profile, News Feed, Mini-Feed, profile links disabled	X Remove

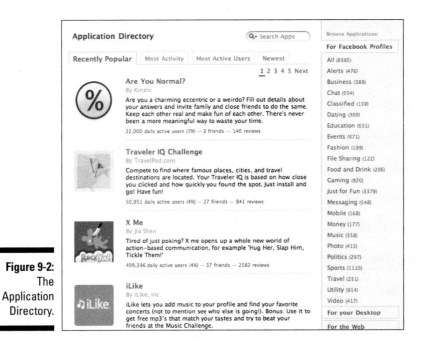

Figure 9-2:
The
Application
Directory.

✔ **Search Apps:** Use this search box on the top of the page to search for applications by keyword or name. Sometimes, applications that have funny names do exactly what you want, so searching by keyword is one of the best ways to find the functionality you're looking for.

✔ **Tabs:** The Recently Popular page of the Application Directory sorts applications based on *engagement.* The engagement algorithm is a combination of how many people have added an application as well as how many people are active users, which usually is the number of people who have used it that day. The four tabs behind this front page also represent the following metrics:

- Recently Popular

- Most Activity

- Most Active Users

- Newest

When you use the filters on the right, you still see these same tabs, although a smaller number of applications are being sorted.

✓ **Filters:** The Application Directory has four high-level filters and many lower-level filters. The highest possible setting is For Facebook Profiles, which lists all the Facebook applications by application type. (The All link appears at the top of the list.) You can also filter applications that are For Your Desktop, For the Web, and For Facebook Pages. By Facebook are the applications that Facebook has built and maintains.

✓ **Applications:** The most important part of the page is the *content* — the applications that you might be interested in adding. The big, long, dynamic list with all sorts of thumbnail pictures changes when you select different tabs and filters.

After you arrive on the Application Directory, explore the various applications. Clicking an application's thumbnail takes you to its About page.

About pages

Application About pages are exactly that — all about the Application. An About page includes relevant information from the developers, such as who they are, a description of the application, and screenshots of how it looks. The About page also has a space for reviews of the application and a discussion board for talking about the application. An About page is shown in Figure 9-3.

About pages play a big role in your decision to add an application or not, which is convenient because we've arrived at. . . .

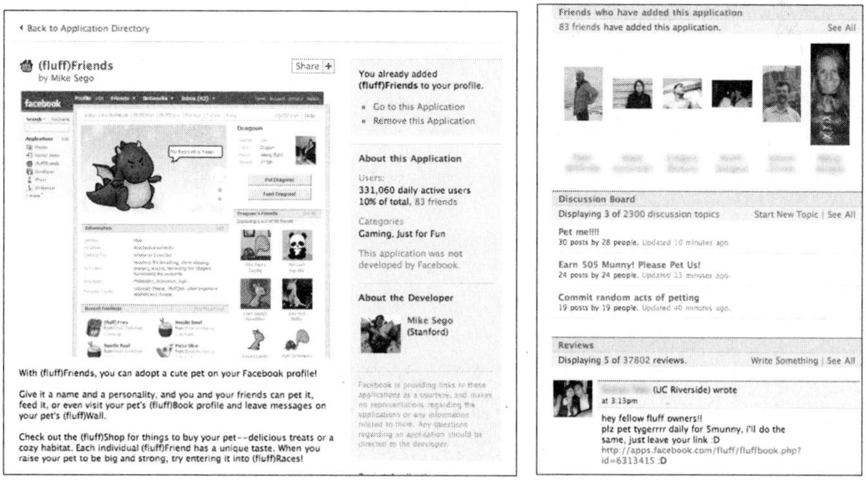

Figure 9-3:
A sample
About page.

Understanding the Add Application Page

When you perform the actions described in this chapter, you might get to a page that asks you to add an application. For the most part, when you add an application, you're adding something that wasn't built by Facebook, which is why Facebook makes you go through the Add Application page — a confirmation page where you have the opportunity to back out if you don't want to add the app. You need to certify that you understand the following when you add an application:

- ✔ **Applications can access your information in order to work.** That is, if an application is measuring how similar you are to your friends, it pulls the interests listed in your profile and your friends' lists and compares the two. If you draw on someone's Graffiti Wall, that application knows who you are and puts your thumbnail profile picture next to the drawing. Keep in mind that profile information doesn't include your contact information.

- ✔ **Applications can make additions to your account.** That is, applications add a box to your profile or a link to your left-hand Applications menu.

The Add *<Application Name>* to Your Facebook Account? page looks something like what is shown in Figure 9-4. Notice the check boxes: The first is most relevant to the first bullet in the preceding list; the others are more relevant to the second bullet.

The check boxes provide a sense of how and where you want to see this application in use. For example, if you want easy access to its Canvas page but don't want it taking space on your profile, check Place a Link in My Left-hand Navigation and uncheck Add a Box to My Profile. These settings are not permanent; you can always change them from your Edit Applications page. To get there, simply click the Edit link next to Applications in the left-hand menu.

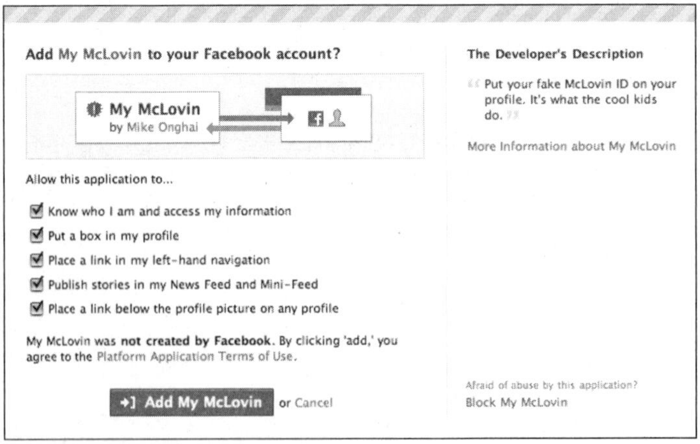

Figure 9-4: Determine whether you really want to add an application.

Add My McLovin to your Facebook account?

🏵 **My McLovin**
by Mike Onghai

The Developer's Description

Put your fake McLovin ID on your profile. It's what the cool kids do.

More Information about My McLovin

Allow this application to...

- ☑ Know who I am and access my information
- ☑ Put a box in my profile
- ☑ Place a link in my left-hand navigation
- ☑ Publish stories in my News Feed and Mini-Feed
- ☑ Place a link below the profile picture on any profile

My McLovin was **not created by Facebook**. By clicking 'add,' you agree to the Platform Application Terms of Use.

+] Add My McLovin or Cancel

Afraid of abuse by this application?
Block My McLovin

The most important thing you're doing on this page is agreeing to let the application access your profile and profile information. If you don't trust the application enough to do that, then you can't add that application.

You decide whom to trust the same way you decide whether a profile is trustworthy or real — you look at the data available. When on an application's About page in the Application Directory, look for who built the application. Was it a company you've heard of and trust, such as Amazon.com? Check out the reviews and the discussion boards. Are people reporting problems with the application, such as spam or inappropriate content? Feel comfortable before adding the application and allowing it to access your information.

Exploring a Trio of Third-Party Applications

You can add thousands of applications to your profile. As much as we love discussing how to use each of these in depth, we simply don't have the space to cover them all. Instead, we pick a few examples of applications that represent the variety of things that applications can do for you. Applications make your life better, stronger, and faster while providing entertainment and connecting you with an extended community. In these examples, we focus on why it's important that the application exists on Facebook as opposed to just being a Web site. In Chapter 19, we highlight ten more applications that we love.

Movies, by Flixter

Movies is an application that offers a variety of functionality related to movies. You can take trivia quizzes, build trivia quizzes, display your favorite movie posters in your profile, see how compatible you are with your friends' movie tastes, write reviews for movies you've seen, and see what movies your friends have reviewed.

Movies is a one-stop shop for anything movie-related. More importantly, aspects of movie viewing, such as getting a friend to recommend a movie or reading a review before you waste your money on a ticket, are built into Movies because of the friendship connections you have on Facebook.

Additionally, Movies is an example of an application that you might want people to see. The movies you like can be incredibly informative in expressing who you are to people. For example, you like action movies, movies that take place in high school, movies that involve copious amounts of dancing, and mysteries. Display those favorite movie posters in a profile box and proclaim it to your friends. They don't even need the Movies application added to their profiles.

Imagine if Movies was a separate Web site from Facebook. You could still go there and do most of these actions. However, on Facebook, your review of *Braveheart* might influence a friend to rent it, finally. Reading a friend's review of *Titanic* might cause you to send them a message saying, "Really? You watch that every week?" By gathering this movie-related data about you and your friends, Movies becomes an interactive and useful tool for all your film-viewing pleasure. Elsewhere, it's simply a destination for some fooling around.

Files, by Box.net

Files is fairly self-explanatory: You upload files from your computer to the Files application and then share these files with friends. This sort of application is one that we consider a pure utility. The profile box for Files isn't particularly flashy or emblematic of you as a person, but it offers huge value. Files enables you to access your files anywhere you go — simply log into Facebook whenever you need to them.

The social aspect of Files is that it allows you to share files easily with friends through Facebook. Much like Share, you don't have to remember people's e-mail addresses or constantly upload the same file into several separate e-mails. Additionally, if you have files that don't quite fit into the sort of functionality that other applications offer (for example, your dissertation on Agricultural Symbolism in Early Reconstructionist Fiction), add that file to the Profile Files folder, and your friends can access it from your profile.

Box.net has a Web site; however, the Facebook application merely gives people another way of accessing existing file-storing functionality. In doing so, however, Facebook turns a site for storing stuff into a convenient way for you to store and share things with your friends.

Dogbook, by Poolhouse

Dogbook (there's also Catbook and Babybook) is an application that answered a real need that niche groups had. People wanted to represent these members of their families on Facebook to tag them in photos and show their affections through the connection.

Dogbook allows people to create a sort of sub-profile for their pet, which can attach to more than one profile on Facebook. Each dog has a network of friends — the dogs of your friends. Dogbook also allows people to connect with other dogs in the area. Dogbook is the perfect application for people who love their dogs.

Again, Dogbook would be an excellent site, but it would require a certain amount of time and drive to create your profile, create your pet's profile, and keep up with all the other pets in the area. On Facebook, this one aspect of your life is integrated into all the other aspects.

Accessing Facebook outside Facebook

Although this chapter and Chapter 8 focus mostly on applications within Facebook, Facebook Platform enables all sorts of applications that exist outside of Facebook. That is, something might be more useful with information from your friends, but it needs to be enabled either somewhere else on the Web or on your desktop.

- **Desktop:** Desktop applications require you to download things to your desktop that enable some nifty things, such as screensavers displaying your friends' photos, desktop notifications when someone sends you a message or Poke, and exporting your desktop photos directly into Facebook. To see some of these options, select the For Your Desktop tab in the right column of the Application Directory.

- **Web:** Web applications live on other Web sites. Logging in with your Facebook credentials enables certain functionality on that Web site. A good example is MoochSpot. You build virtual piggy banks to keep track of who owes you what, which is great for the casual lender. MoochSpot accesses your Friend List through Facebook Platform and allows you to select who owes you money and to whom you owe money. Many other sorts of Web applications can be built on Facebook's platform.

- **Mobile:** While phones get more powerful, and Facebook Mobile improves, Facebook can better integrate with communication devices. The Facebook for BlackBerry Smartphones application is a great example of an application whose only goal is to make it easier to access Facebook on the go. See Chapter 14 for more on that topic.

- **Toolbars:** In a cross between Web and desktop applications, Facebook toolbars use Facebook Platform to keep you updated no matter where you are on the Web. For example, if you're logged into the Firefox

Toolbar for Facebook and don't have a Facebook page open, you're still notified of incoming friend requests, Pokes, and messages. Additionally, adding a toolbar to your browser incorporates a convenient Share button in your browser at all times; therefore, sharing a Web page is never more than a click away.

Managing Your Applications

Adding applications is the best thing since sliced bread, and we understand that you might have, well, gorged on the sliced bread and are regretting it just a little. Don't worry; here are several easy ways to manage your applications so that you maintain control over your Facebook experience.

The Edit Applications page

When your left-hand menu grows longer, you might forget that the Applications and Edit links at the top take you to the Edit My Applications page. An Edit My Applications page is shown in Figure 9-5.

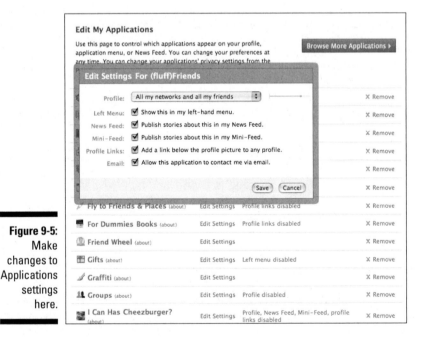

Figure 9-5: Make changes to Applications settings here.

All of your applications are listed here. Before you start moving them and changing settings, think about what is bothering you or what you want to accomplish. Ask yourself these questions:

- ✓ Are you getting too many News Feed stories from a particular application?
- ✓ Are you annoyed by a certain box looking ugly or not really doing anything on your profile?
- ✓ Are you unhappy that your Mini-Feed is getting overwhelmed by stories from a certain application?
- ✓ Is your left-hand menu making it difficult to navigate to where you want to go?
- ✓ Are you not seeing enough information from one of your favorite applications?

As much as these questions might sound like a magazine quiz (your answers clearly indicate that you're a Libra, by the way), they're extremely important in directing what, exactly, you wind up doing on the Edit My Applications page.

Remember: When you add an application, it asks where it's allowed to interact with your account, including

- ✓ News Feed and Mini-Feed
- ✓ Profile boxes
- ✓ Profile action links
- ✓ Application menu links

The settings that you select when you add the application are reflected on the Edit My Applications page. Depending on what problems you're dealing with, change them accordingly with the following steps:

1. **Click Edit Settings next to the application you want to change.**

2. **Select which options you want to change in the pop-up window that appears (refer to Figure 9-5).**

3. **Click Save when you're done.**

Your Applications menu

An easy way to find a particular application is through its link in your left-hand Application menu. Seven application links fit above the More link and as many as you want fit below; drag and drop these items into any order you choose. When you add an application, its left-hand menu link (provided it has one) usually appears underneath the More link.

A little known fact about the More link at the bottom of the Applications menu: You don't have to click it to get the menu to expand. Simply hover over More with your mouse and the rest of your Application menu appears.

Profile layout

Having too many applications can really clutter your profile and confuse you. After you've expressed yourself by adding a million applications, getting your friends to see the ones that best express you is easy with Facebook's drag-and-drop interface. Perform the following steps to adjust your profile's layout and organize your profile boxes:

1. **Hover your mouse over the blue bar of the box you wish to move.**

   The mouse changes into a little, grabby hand. Additionally, a symbol appears on the right side of the blue bar. It's either a little compass, as you'd see on a map, or two arrows, one pointing up and one pointing down. The compass indicates that the box you're holding can move between columns; the up and down lines indicate that it needs to stay in a particular column.

2. **Click and hold the blue bar and then move the box to where you want it.**

   Other boxes jump out of the way when you position your box where you want it.

   Pay attention to error messages that appear while you move your box around the page. Some boxes can be moved only so high on the page or can't be moved at all (like the Friends box). These little messages tell you what you need to know.

3. **After you get your box where you want it, let go of your mouse.**

   This drops the box into place.

If you ever feel a little bored with your profile but aren't sure what to change, a change in layout can feel like a mini-makeover — the same you, just a little different looking.

Part III
Keeping Connected and Staying in Touch

The 5th Wave   By Rich Tennant

"I know it's a short profile, but I thought 'King of the Jungle' sort of said it all."

In this part . . .

Back in the day, people stayed connected by writing letters or listening through the grapevine. While there might still be an occasion for the old quill and ink or a good game of telephone, one of the primary reasons people come to Facebook (and stay) is to connect with other people and form deeper, enhanced relationships.

In this part, we show you how people use Facebook to communicate and interact with other people, emphasizing the ways in which interactions online can enhance interactions offline. You discover how close friends communicate through messaging, sharing, and public displays of online affection. We show you how people with similar interests and affiliations connect with one another via Facebook Networks, Groups, and Events. Finally, you find out how to take all this (and more) on the go with Facebook Mobile.

Chapter 10

Keeping Up with Your Friends

. . . .

In This Chapter

▶ Messaging your friends

▶ Discovering how to share interesting content from the Web

▶ Increasing communication with open (Facebook) relationships

▶ Keeping in touch without even trying

. . . .

The art of communication is defined by subtlety and finesse. Some people coordinate plans over text messages; others use phones. Some lovers write their letters on paper; others use e-mail. Gossip might happen over instant messages or in low whispers. Friends might catch up over coffee, others over beer, and still others over Webcam. People often get fired in person yet are hired over the phone. A hug might mean, "I love you" in one context, but "I missed you" in another. How humans communicate in any given situation has everything to do with the specific message, context, personalities, and relationships.

Because Facebook is all about connecting people, enabling everyone to communicate with one another in whatever complicated and precise way they want is a top priority. This chapter explains the modes of communication on Facebook, including private conversations in the Inbox, public back-and-forth on the Profile Wall, Pokes, Shares, Comments, and more.

No matter how you use Facebook to reach out to people, you can be confident that they're notified that you're trying to reach them. Whether they sign into Facebook often — or not at all, but they check their e-mail — all communications through Facebook generate a notification delivered to the recipients e-mail or mobile phone (for those who choose to be notified that way). Don't worry about bothering any one because they can opt out of any kind of notification.

Just between You and Me

Often, people interact with one another on Facebook in a semi-public way, which allows other friends to join the conversations. Later, we talk about the different forms of open communication and the general benefits of an open environment. Sometimes, however, people are in need of more private, personal, or intimate communication. This section details the different one-to-one or one-to-few methods of communication on Facebook.

Messages

You can think of Facebook messages pretty much the same way you think of personal e-mail, but with a few subtle differences.

For one thing, no one can message more than 20 people at a time. Twenty is somewhat arbitrary, but imposing a limit is a deliberate way to preserve *the sanctity of the Inbox*. To understand what that means, take a minute to think about the last few e-mails you've received, which likely include

- An e-mail from a close friend.

- A newsletter containing featured deals from a store you sometimes frequent.

- A notice from your bank, if you do that kind of thing online.

- A monthly communiqué from an old acquaintance detailing for you and everyone else she knows her recent travels.

- At least one e-mail from an unrecognizable address, requesting that DEAR SIR OR MADAM take advantage of a deal you can't refuse. ***Note:*** Send this last one straight to your spam folder; do not click any links in the e-mail, do not pass go, do not collect (or pay) $200.

E-mail has become so universal and all-purpose that just about anything can show up there. You never really know what you're getting until you open a particular e-mail. In the introduction to this chapter, we explain that Facebook offers a number of alternative methods of communication that help people reach out (and be reached) in a way appropriate for the particular content and the particular people. Facebook messages are meant to be private communications between people who either know each other personally, or want to know each other. They're specifically designed to prevent the general mass-communiqués. *The sanctity of the Inbox* refers to the fact that when you see that you have a new message on Facebook, nine times out of ten it will be something personal. There are a few exceptions, which we cover later in this chapter.

Another difference between Facebook messaging and e-mail is the lack of a Forward feature. Again, in the name of intimacy, when you send a message to someone, you can feel confident that it won't end up in the Inbox of someone you didn't intend, provided your recipient doesn't get sneaky with a picture of his screen.

The other differences between Facebook messaging and e-mail stem from the fact that messaging is designed to mimic a simple real-world conversation, whereas e-mail can be a complex communication tool. You won't find folders, starring, or flagging, and you can't sort or filter your Facebook messages. At its core, Facebook messaging is all about the simple back-and-forth.

Sending a message

Sending messages through the Facebook Inbox is simple stuff. The most straightforward way to send a message on Facebook is to follow these steps:

1. **Sign in (if you aren't already) and then click Inbox on the blue bar at the top.**

2. **Click Compose Message in the upper right of the screen.**

   A blank box that looks similar to a blank e-mail (with a few subtle exceptions) appears, as shown in Figure 10-1.

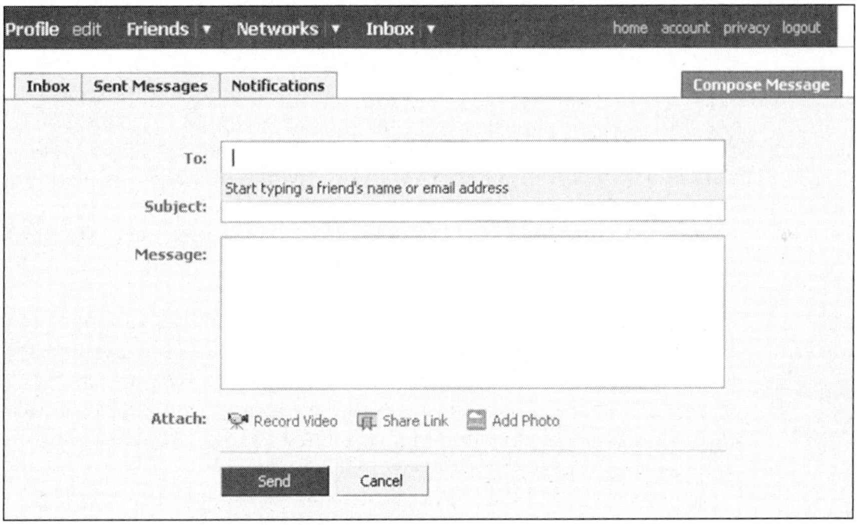

Figure 10-1: Composing a message from the Facebook Inbox.

3. **Start typing a friend's first name.**

   While you type, you see a drop-down box listing possible matches. When you see the name you're after, you can either click it with your mouse, press the down arrow until the name is selected, or keep typing until the correct name is highlighted in dark blue; then press Enter. If you accidentally select the wrong name, press the Backspace key twice or click 'X' next to the name you're trying to delete.

   To send a message to a friend who isn't a Facebook user, type the full e-mail address (copy and paste won't work here) and then press Enter.

4. **(Optional) To add another recipient, just start typing the next name or e-mail address; you don't need commas, semi-colons, or anything else to separate the names.**

5. **Fill in the Subject line just as you would in an e-mail.**

    Some people choose to leave this field blank, but we don't recommend it. Blank subjects make it hard for your recipients to find your message after reading it the first time.

6. **Fill in the Message box with whatever you want to say.**

    Before you send it, we recommend rereading what you've written — Facebook doesn't offer a spell checker on the site. Beneath the Message box, you see the Attach options, which you can ignore for now; we explain those in the upcoming "Sharing is caring" section.

7. **Click the Send button (beneath the Attach options) when your message is complete.**

    If you ever change your mind about sending the message, click Cancel.

To reply to a message that is just between you and one other person, simply fill in the box underneath Reply and click Send. To reply to a message between you and more than one other person, you have two options. To reply to everybody, fill in the box at the bottom of the message labeled Reply All, and click Send. If you want to reply to only a particular person in the conversation, click Reply underneath her profile picture, which opens a Compose Message window addressed to that particular person and with the subject already filled in. Again, you just have to fill in the Message box and click Send.

Some Internet browsers have a built-in spell checker to scan any text that you enter into a Web site. Firefox, for example, puts a dotted red line under any word you enter that its spell checker doesn't recognize. If you happen to be someone who is, what we politely refer to as, *spelling impaired,* you might want to find a browser you like with spell check functionality. Carolyn and Leah both use and recommend Firefox.

Receiving a message

If you find sending a message on Facebook exciting, you should try receiving one. Remember that you can navigate to your Inbox from any page by clicking Inbox on the blue bar at the top. Before you find anything interesting there, you have to inspire one of your friends to send you something.

Set your status (see Chapter 3) to something inquisitive or provocative, as long as you have enough friends who are active on Facebook. Writing a good status usually triggers a message or two. When Leah set her status to *Leah is anticipation incarnate,* she received several messages from friends taking wild guesses about what she was so excited about, including, "You're psyched for the weekend?" and "You can't wait for our Frisbee game?" One friend told her flat out, "The anticipation is over, here's the message you were waiting for."

Before we walk through the particular experience of receiving a message, it helps to understand how the Inbox is arranged. While you receive Facebook messages, your Inbox fills with rows; each row corresponds to a particular thread. You might be asking, "What do you mean by thread? What does thread have to do with messages? Do I have to sew a button onto one? No one said anything about sewing on Facebook." *Message threads* are best explained by examples.

Say your sister sends you a message on Facebook, then you reply, and then she replies. All three of these messages are considered part of the same thread because they're spawned from the same initial message and between the same people: you and your sister. When you look at your Inbox, you don't see two separate rows for each message your sister sent; you see one row encapsulating the entire thread. When you click that thread's subject, you see, from oldest to newest, all the messages exchanged on that thread: her first one, your reply, and then her reply.

The point of collapsing messages into a thread is to help keep your Inbox clean and easy to read. If you and your sister keep on messaging each other, your Inbox eventually fills with messages from your sister. To find older messages, you have to keep paging back through the Inbox. Your mousing finger doesn't appreciate such abuse. By collapsing messages, whole conversations are kept together, allowing you to see more conversations at one time in your Inbox.

To get a little more complicated, say, Leah, Holly, and Carolyn are friends trying to make plans. The exchange might go something like this:

1. Leah writes a message to Holly and Carolyn.

2. Holly replies to Leah and Carolyn, and then Carolyn replies to all in response.

   All three of these messages, Leah's initial one and Holly and Carolyn's subsequent replies, are considered part of the same thread — a single row in the inbox — because they're all in response to the same initial message and the participants (Leah, Holly, and Carolyn) are the same. By clicking the Subject line of the thread from the Inbox, each person sees all three messages from oldest to newest, as shown in Figure 10-2.

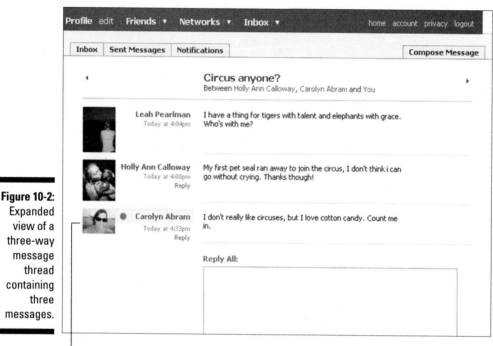

Figure 10-2:
Expanded
view of a
three-way
message
thread
containing
three
messages.

Leah hasn't read this message yet.

3. Holly wants to say something privately to Leah about Carolyn's response, so she clicks Reply under Leah's profile picture and sends only Leah a message.

Although this message was a response to the thread, a new thread is created in Leah's Inbox because it has a different set of participants: only Leah and Holly. Separating threads when the audience changes helps you keep track of who *exactly* received which messages. See Figure 10-3.

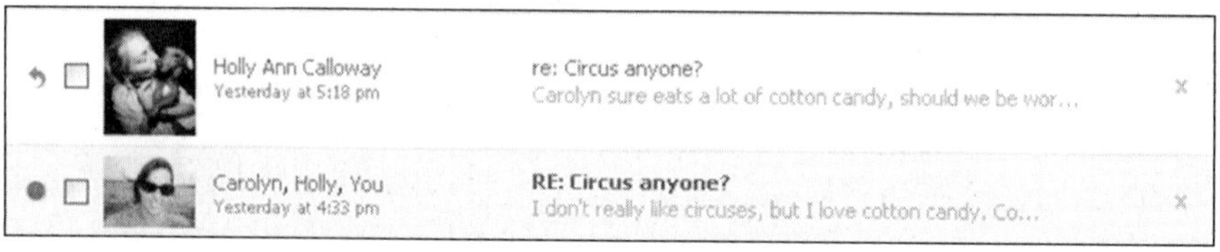

Figure 10-3:
A collapsed
view of two
thread
examples
on
Facebook.

When you sign into Facebook, you know you have a message waiting for you if you see a number in parentheses next to Inbox on the blue bar at the top. The number corresponds to the number of unread threads you have. In the second example, where both Carolyn and Holly replied to all, Leah would sign in and see *Inbox (1)*. Even though she received two new messages, when she navigates to her Inbox, only one thread has unread messages in it, hence the Inbox (1).

Unread threads have light blue backgrounds and a dark blue dot on the far left (refer to Figure 10-3). Click the subject of the thread to open and read the messages. Messages that are new since the last time you opened the thread have the same dark blue dot next to the new sender's name, which is also highlighted. In this case, both Carolyn and Holly's replies to the thread are marked as unread (refer to Figure 10-2).

Anatomy of a thread

In this section, we define a thread in the context of Facebook messaging, demonstrate how they work, and illustrate why they make your messaging life less complicated. Here, we deconstruct a thread:

- ✔ **Thread Status:** On the far left of a thread, you might see a little circular arrow, a blue dot, or nothing. An arrow means you were the last person to add a message to that thread. A blue dot means the thread has unread messages on it. No symbol means you've opened the thread at least once since the last message was sent.

- ✔ **Action Check Box:** At the top of the Inbox, you see three links: Mark as Unread, Mark as Read, and Delete. To use these links, first select a check box at the left of any thread. You can mark types of thread by using the Select box at the top of the Inbox. Choosing Read, for example, marks the check box next to every thread and places them in a "read" state. Clicking Delete removes all the selected threads.

- ✔ **Profile Picture:** The picture on the left of a row in the Inbox is that of the person who most recently sent a message on that thread. However, if you're the last person to send a message on the thread, you see the person who wrote before you. The reason for that is to save you from looking at your beautiful face on every other thread in the Inbox. Having your face on every thread you've recently responded to doesn't help to differentiate the threads from one another at a glance.

- ✔ **Sender Names:** The names next to the profile picture are the authors of the most recent messages (up to four) on that thread. Again, if the very last message came from you, then you don't show up on this list — the arrow before the picture is the give-away that you were the last to reply. The last name in this list always matches the picture.

- ✔ **Date and Time:** Shows when the last message on the thread was sent.

✔ **Attachment Icon:** Some threads will have an attachment icon just to the right of the Subject line. This icon indicates that one of the senders shared a photo, a video, or some other linked media with a message. (The icon isn't pictured in Figure 10-3.) We explain Attachments (also known as Shares) in more detail in just a bit.

✔ **Subject:** The subject is entered by the first person to send a message on a particular thread. If *RE:* or *re* is appended to the subject, then more than one message is on the thread. *RE:* is a visual indication that the message is to more than one person, and *re* means the thread is just between two people.

✔ **x:** Click this to delete the entire thread. Note that you can't delete a thread permanently. If someone sends a message in reply to the thread, it returns to your Inbox in full. When you open the thread, however, only the new message shows, and you have to click the Show Deleted Messages on This Thread link to see previously deleted messages.

Messaging non-friends

In the "Sending a message" section, earlier in the chapter, we mention that you can share with friends on Facebook or people not on Facebook via their e-mail addresses. You can also message a person who is on Facebook but not a friend. This is particularly helpful when you encounter someone on Facebook whom you'd like to say something to, but you're not sure whether you want to add her as a friend yet, or ever. Here are a few examples:

✔ **Identification:** You search for an old friend and find three people with the same name. One profile has a clear picture of someone who is definitely not your friend. The second person has a profile picture of someone in the distance climbing a mountain, which could be your friend, except that you notice that person is in the Dallas network and you're sure your friend has never lived in Dallas. The third profile doesn't have a picture, just a question mark. (If that turns out to be your friend, you should recommend they read this book, especially the section in Chapter 2 about setting up a profile.) From the search results page, you can click Send Message next to the person with the question mark profile picture and ask whether you know each other.

✔ **Friend of a Friend:** Here's a story: "Last week my friend had a birthday, and I wanted to send him a present. He was about to move into a new house, and I didn't know the address. I knew the name of the girl he was moving in with, so I found her on Facebook and sent her a message; she sent me the address." For most features on Facebook, you need to be someone's friend or at least in someone's network in order to interact with them in any meaningful way. However, sometimes you have legitimate reasons to contact someone who really doesn't belong in your Friend List. For these interactions, Facebook messaging is perfect.

✔ **Getting to Know You:** Pretend you've just moved to a new city, and you know very few people. You can use the Browse page (click Search on the left of the Frame, and then click Browse in the bottom left) to message someone in your network in a particular demographic whom you'd like to get to know or ask a question.

You should keep in mind three things when messaging non-friends:

✔ **You can message only one non-friend at a time.** You have two ways to do it:

- By navigating to that person's profile and clicking Send <*so-and-so*> a Message from underneath his profile picture.

- From the search results page, by clicking Send Message next to the person you want to message.

In the earlier "Messages" section, we said you could message up to 20 people — that applies to only your Facebook Friends and people whose e-mail addresses you already have.

✔ **Some people message non-friends to get a date.** If you're successful here, congratulations! We hope you lovebirds have fun — be safe and invite us to the wedding. Generally, though, we don't recommend using Facebook for this purpose. Unlike some other Web sites, most people aren't on Facebook to find dates. Before you message someone for this purpose, be sure that the Looking For field on that person's profile strongly indicates openness to romantic inquiries.

Messaging a non-friend should be treated with caution. If you message non-friends too often or too many people report your message as solicitous or unwanted, your account is automatically flagged in the Facebook system. You receive a warning first, but if you continue to repeat the offence, your account may be disabled. Remember earlier in this chapter when we mentioned the sanctity of the Inbox? If every person on Facebook could message everyone else, Inboxes would start to fill with impersonal or unwanted messages, eventually making the Inbox too messy to be functional.

✔ **When you message non-friends, those people automatically receive access to some of your profile.** You can adjust what they see by going to the privacy page and clicking Poke, Message, and Friend Request Settings. This works for you in two ways:

- Remember the case when you're trying to message an old friend? By default, that person isn't in your Network and, therefore, can't see your profile. When you send the message saying, "Are you the <*so-and-so*> I went to school with?" part of your profile opens to that person who can then verify whether you two know each other by looking around your profile.

- When someone sends *you* an unexpected message, you can check out his profile to see whether he's a person you know or care to respond to.

Sharing is caring

Have you ever read something on the Web that reminded you of a friend? Or that you thought would appeal to someone in particular? Or that related to a conversation you were *just* having? Or that made you laugh so hard you couldn't wait to find someone to tell? If you're any kind of Internet user, then the answer to those question are "Yes," "Yes," "Yes," and "Oh my gosh, yes." (If you answered them aloud in a public place, you might have caused some head-turning.)

For all those times, Facebook offers Share. *Share* allows you to send a link, a preview, or sometimes a whole piece of content easily to any friend — on Facebook or not. If you're thinking e-mail is effective enough for sending this kind of Web content, we're willing to bet you've never tried Share.

In this section, we detail several different ways to share on Facebook. In most cases, clicking one button opens a Compose Message window (see the earlier section, "Sending a message") with the photo, video, or link of the Web page you're currently looking at automatically included in the body of the message.

Sharing from the Inbox

In some ways, sharing from the Inbox is the hardest way to share because it requires more clicks and some copy and paste action, but it's most similar to what you're probably used to in e-mail:

1. **Copy a link to the page you want to share with someone.**

2. **Click Inbox on Facebook.**

3. **Click the Compose Message button in the upper right.**

4. **Paste the link into the Message box.**

   You can also click the Attach button and put the link in the field that opens.

Although this is just as much work as sharing a link via e-mail, it's way cooler. When you paste the link into the Compose Message window, the window expands to show a preview of the page you're about to share. The preview includes the title of the page you're sharing and a snippet of text swiped from that page. If the page you're sharing has any images on it, you'll see one of those, too. This is exactly the preview of the page your recipients see when you send the message.

You can change any element of the preview that isn't accurately descriptive of the page you're sharing. You can select a different image by clicking the arrows underneath Choose a Thumbnail. (***Note:*** A *thumbnail* in computer-speak refers to a little version of a larger picture. In this case, Facebook grabs the biggest image from the page you're trying to share, shrinks it, and uses that thumbnail for the preview.) If no picture is actually representative of the content, you can check the No Picture box. You can also edit the title or the snippet of text in the preview by clicking right on the text itself.

If the page you're sharing features a video, a page on YouTube (www.youtube.com), for example, then the actual video shows up in the preview. Here, *preview* is an understatement because you and your recipient can actually play the video straight from the preview without leaving Facebook.

Share buttons on Facebook

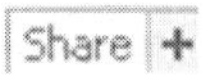

Share +

Perhaps you've already noticed the little Share buttons all over Facebook. They show up on albums, individual photos, notes, events, groups, market-place listings, News Feed stories, user profiles, and more. They help you share content quickly without having to copy and paste. You don't even have to go into the Inbox.

If you're looking at content on Facebook that you want to show someone, simply click the Share button next to it. The Share button actually serves two separate purposes. When you click the button, you see two tabs: Send a Message and Post to Profile. Here, we cover the Send a Message tab. You can read about the Post to Profile tab in Chapter 8.

After you click the Share button, a small Share window opens. Click the Send a Message tab and the Share preview appears with the subject, description, and thumbnail image already filled in for you. All you have to do is fill in the To line. Again, these can be friends on Facebook or the e-mail addresses of those not on Facebook (yet). Optionally, fill in the Message box, and click Send. In Figure 10-4, Leah is preparing to share a photo with Carolyn.

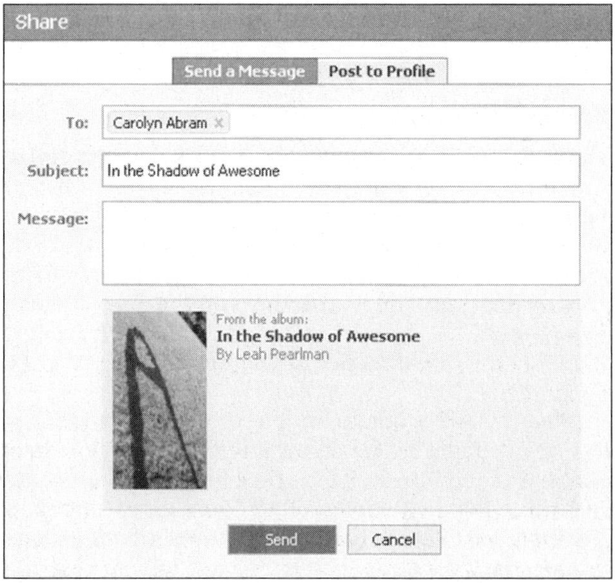

Figure 10-4: Sharing a photo through Facebook.

Sometimes you share something with someone on Facebook and he can't see it because of the privacy settings of the content you're sharing. Here's an example: Say you see some photos a friend posted of her recent trip to India. You have another friend (they don't know each other) who is traveling to India soon, so you click the Share button on the album and send it to him. If the first friend has set the privacy of the album so that only her friends can see it, your second friend won't be able to see the album. The second friend receives the message, but instead of the preview, there's a note that the content isn't visible because of privacy settings.

You can't really know beforehand whether someone will be able to see the content you're sharing, but if the two aren't friends with each other and aren't in the same network, be prepared for your second friend to write back asking you to describe what you were trying to share. While this can be frustrating at times, especially because there's no good way to work around it, it's helpful to remember the rules are in place to help everyone maintain control over their own content, which ultimately is a good thing.

The Share buttons on the Web

Share ⊹ Facebook offers plenty of interesting stuff, but the rest of the Web presents a lot of engaging material as well. Facebook allows (and encourages) Web sites to add Facebook Share buttons near interesting content. For example, next to every article on www.nytimes.com is a Share link; clicking it lists a few Web sites' sharing capabilities, including Facebook's. If you click Facebook, you get the same Share pop-up (refer to Figure 10-4) that you do when you click Share buttons on Facebook. More than 15,000 Web sites have placed Facebook Share buttons on their content to make it easier for you to spread the information love.

The Share bookmarklet

Although it's convenient that many Web sites have Share buttons built right in, you don't actually need any of them for super-simple, one-click sharing. You can add a special Share link to your browser's bookmarks folder, and no matter where you are on the Internet, you can share the page just by clicking that Share bookmarklet. The easiest way to add the Share bookmarklet to your browser is by following the instructions on the Share Bookmarklet page (located at www.facebook.com/share_options.php). (We give you more details about adding the bookmarklet in Chapter 8.)

After you've added the Share bookmarklet, try it out. Head to any Web page you like, and click the Share on Facebook link from your bookmark list. (On Internet Explorer, you need to click Favorites first, and then Share on Facebook. On Firefox, you just need to click Share on Facebook from your Bookmarks Toolbar.) Just like all the Share buttons, the bookmarklet recognizes when you're sharing videos or music to make them easy to play directly from the recipient's Inbox.

Poke

From any search result or profile, you see the option to "Poke *<so-and-so>*!" As Facebook employees, probably one of the most frequent questions we're asked is, "What is *Poke?*" We're happy to tell you what it *does*, but we can't tell you what it *is*, other than to say Poke is the interpretive dance of the Internet; it can mean something different to everyone. In some cases, Poke is a form of flirtation. Other times, Poke might mean a genuine *thinking-of-you*. Some people do it just to say, "Hi." Leah's mother pokes her when she hasn't called home in a while.

Pokes

You were poked by
Leah Pearlman.
poke back | remove poke

Say your wife pokes you (maybe her Poke means *take out the trash, honey*). The next time you log into Facebook, on the right side of your Home page, you'll see You Have Been Poked by *<your wife's name>* and a little picture of a poking finger. You have the following options: Poke Back and Hide Poke. *Poke Back* means she'll see the same notice you got the next time she logs in (except with your name instead of hers). *Hide Poke* simply removes the notice from your Home page. If you sense the potential for an endless loop, you sense right.

Requests

Requests

1 friend request

The last kind of private communication is a request. The most common type of request is a friend request. When someone finds you on Facebook and clicks Add *<your name>* as a Friend, the next time you log in, you'll see (on the right side of your Home page) that you have a request waiting for you. Other types of requests are invitations to attend events and join groups, or to tag your photos (see Chapter 7). Whenever you have a request waiting for you, it shows in this same location on your Home page. If you don't see the Requests box on your Home page, then you have no pending requests.

Although sending a request is a private affair, often the response to the request is public. For example, if you request that someone add you as a friend, only that person will ever know about that request, until that person accepts your friend request; then others will see in their News Feed that you two are now friends. Similarly, no one sees your invitations to join a particular group, but if you act on that request by joining, this information will generate a News Feed story to your friends.

Unlike a message, you can't explicitly send a request. Requests are only generated in the context of other actions. For example, if you invite someone to an event (see Chapter 13), a request is automatically sent to that person. If you tag people in someone else's photo (see Chapter 7), a request is sent to the photo owner. If you specify that you're in a relationship with someone in particular, a request is sent to that person to confirm your claim. You also receive a request if someone wishes to join a closed group or event you administer. (For more about groups and administrators, see Chapter 12.)

Public Displays of Affection

So far, we've been talking about the kind of communication that takes place between specific people, in private. Private conversations are perfect for discussing topics relevant to only a few people, confiding in friends, or getting to know (and spending time with) someone specific. This section talks about a different kind of conversation; the kind you have among friends at a party where anyone may jump in or at a restaurant or bar where others may overhear. These conversations cover topics of potential general interest, unspecific to a particular group of people within the bounds of one's friends or networks. In the real world, we tend to have more conversations that are private. This is not because we're all gossips and secret-keepers, it's because the existing modes of communication, until now, have only facilitated private conversations. A phone call, e-mail, post card, or instant message, for example, always engages a specific set of participants. Facebook supports the aforementioned private conversations, but also offers new ways to communicate to enable the open conversation.

In this section, you read how Facebook allows you to have conversations in a public way that encourages any of your friends to jump in if the mood strikes. Facebook encourages openness for the way it allows more information to flow to more people, which deepens and strengthens relationships.

The writing's on the Wall

Have you ever thought someone was so great that you wanted to look at him and say, "You are *so* great," and then turn to the world and say, "World, isn't he *so* great?" That's the spirit of the Wall. Every user, you included, has a Wall on their Profile page where friends (and only friends) can write things to you or about you that the whole world can see. To write on someone else's Wall, simply navigate to that person's profile, click the Wall icon under the profile picture, write your message in the box, and then click Post. When you write on someone's Wall, remember that this generates a News Feed story that any one of your friends might see.

The spirit of posting on someone's Wall is to say nice things about that person in public. In practice, different people in different situations do Wall-writing for different reasons. Some people use the Wall to have basic back-and-forth conversations similar to how other people use messaging. Others use the Wall as a place to comment on a change to someone's profile. If you change your status to something intriguing like *<Your Name> is keeping a secret,* expect a friend or two to ask about it on your Wall. If you change your relationship status, add new favorite bands, or update your profile picture, you'll probably get feedback on your Wall as well.

A Wall practice that is nearly universal among Facebook users is the "Happy Birthday!" Wall post. Assuming you leave your privacy set so that your friends can see your birthday on your profile (you can hide the year), they will also see a reminder on their Home page as your big day approaches. On the actual day, you can expect to receive Wall posts all day long wishing you a happy birthday. If this doesn't happen, either you need more Facebook friends or you need to buy this book for some of the friends you do have.

When you look at your Wall, you see a few different links and buttons (as shown in Figure 10-5). Here's how they work:

✔ **Share Link** works just like the Attach button in the Inbox. (See the earlier "Sharing from the Inbox" section.) Click Share Link and then paste a link into the box. This puts a Share preview directly on your friend's Wall, along with any comments you add.

Figure 10-5: The anatomy of a Wall on a Profile

✔ **Give a Gift** takes you to a virtual gift shop where you can choose a fun or personal picture to have pasted on your friend's Wall. Gifts cost $1 each, so if you receive one, someone cares about you at least $1 worth. (Actually, you can purchase 10 gifts for $5, so someone might only care about you 50 cents worth, but still.)

✔ **Post** is simply how you submit the text you wrote in the box on the Wall. If you change your mind after you've posted, click Delete right next to your Wall post.

✔ **Wall-to-Wall** is another way that Facebook makes communicating easy. Say you're looking at Friend A's profile. On his Wall, you see a post from Friend B that doesn't make sense: "And what did she say after that?" This usually happens because B's post is a response to something A wrote on B's Wall first. In order to see the full flow of the conversation, click Wall-to-Wall. It shows you the recent Wall posts, in order, between A and B. Note that you only see this option when you can see the profiles of A and B.

✔ **Write on <*so-and-so's*> Wall** allows you to jump straight to the Wall of the person who wrote the post you're looking at. That way, if Friend A wrote "Want to go to skiing?" on Friend B's wall, you can jump straight to Friend A's wall and ask, "Can I go skiing, too?"

✔ **Message** lets you compose a message to the person who wrote the post you're looking at. Therefore, in the scenario above, you can message Friend A and privately say, "You shouldn't go skiing with B. He's nice, but he's a terrible skier."

✔ **Delete** (not pictured in Figure 10-5) is an option you see only next to Wall posts you've written or ones that appear on your Wall. Note that if you write on someone's Wall and then delete it, by default she will still get an e-mail notification informing her that you've written on her Wall. She won't see what it said, but she might ask about it. So if it was something you regret having posted, be prepared to make up something up when she asks.

Care to comment?

Leaving comments is another form of public communication. You can leave a comment on a photo, a video, a note, or various other things just by writing in the Add a Comment box beneath the object (some objects have an Add a Comment link that you have to click first to see the box). Leaving comments has the double-nice property of informing the content author something about their work *and* attracting other's attention to the content when the comment shows in other people's News Feed.

Status symbol

Sometimes you have something to say, but no one in particular to say it to. For those times, meet Facebook Status Updates.

Holly Ann Calloway

Holly is [   ] ▾   Clear Status | Cancel

Set your status by going to your Profile and clicking Update Your Status just beneath your name. You can also click this link next to your profile picture on your Home page. (If you have a current status, you see an Edit link instead.) Note that the form is *<Your name>* _____. Facebook encourages you to use your status to tell the world what you're doing right now. Leah's status is *Leah is writing about statuses.* Your status should probably read *<Your name> is reading a book about Facebook.* (It's your choice whether to include that the book you're reading is *For Dummies.*)

Sometimes people use their status to help connect: *Leah is at Starbucks if you want to join.* Sometimes, they use it to keep people informed of things they need to know: *Carolyn is off to Chile — don't expect her to reply to anything.* Often, it's a reflection of mood: *Blake is happy it's Friday.* And sometimes, people ignore the motivation for the suggested *is* structure entirely and write whatever they want, such as the following:

> *Dustin loves comics about dinosaurs.*
>
> *Katie does breakfast for dinner.*
>
> *Ezra says pay attention to politics, people.*

When you update your status, it shows on your profile and in your friends' News Feed, so remember: If you write something intriguing like *<Your name> is about to pop the question,* you'll probably hear about it from your friends.

To see what your friends are up to, you can either go to their profiles directly (hard way), or you can click the arrow next to Friends on the Frame and choose Status Updates from the drop-down list that appears. On that page, notice Mobile Status Updates on the right. If you care a lot about a particular person's status, such as a husband or best friend, you can enter his name here. Any time he changes his status, you'll get a text message about it.

Heard It through the Grapevine

So far, in this chapter, we've focused on *active communication*. That is, communication you have with people by reaching out to them. Although this kind of communication is essential to human relationships, one unique and powerful aspect of Facebook is how it enables *passive communication,* or communicating without even having to try.

News Feed

To reach out to all the friends you care about all the time to find out what's going on in their lives, it's a lot of work; in fact, it's too much. Similarly, it's a lot of *repetitive* work to have to tell everyone you know about what *you* are up to. In Chapter 3, you read about News Feed. We discuss it here because it's important to understand how News Feed is more than just a bulleted list of he did this and she did that. It's a powerful communication tool. Here's how one user describes her experience with News Feed:

> After I graduated from school, whenever I moved to a new city or changed jobs, I met new people and left others behind. Each of these transitions would either mean completely letting go of friends or racking up the number of people I'd have to call or e-mail periodically until those relationships felt like a chore rather than friendships.

> Facebook has changed things for me. I might not talk to an old friend for a year, but through News Feed I see pictures from her travels, news of her relationships, and other updates about her life. Similarly, she can see what I'm up to as I change my status, RSVP to events, or write on a mutual friend's Wall. Occasionally, I might see a photo of hers I like, and I'll leave a comment about it for her. She might see that I'm attending a mutual friend's birthday party and ask me to say, "Hi!" from her.

> With my friends on Facebook, I no longer have to ask the broad and impersonal question, "What have you been up to?" Instead, my friends and I can skip the small talk and head straight to the specific, "I read on Facebook that you're training for a marathon. I've wanted to do the same. Can you tell me about it?"

Leah explains how Facebook has improved her relationship with her family:

> I've lived away from home for seven years now, calling home about once a week. Sometimes it's hard for me to remember all the details of my life that might interest my family. Now that we're all on Facebook, my parents and siblings see when I'm attending a company party, heading to the mountains, or having a girls' night out. When we talk at the end of the

week, I don't have to flip back through my brain's calendar to remember what I've been up to; my family can help remind me. Although we still talk about once a week, we also interact frequently by sharing articles, poking, and playing Scrabble. (See Chapter 19 for details about the Scrabulous application.)

Notifications

Sometimes rather than reach out *to* you on Facebook, your friends reach out *about* you. For example, say you attend a U2 concert with a friend. The next day, your friend might write a note about how mind-blowing he found the concert, and because you were there next to him having your own mind blown, he tags you in the note. (See Chapter 8 for details on Note tagging.) Your friend wrote the note about you, but he doesn't have to tell you he wrote the note about you because Facebook notifies you when you're tagged in a note or photo. It's a way of letting you know that someone's thinking or talking about you. When you have a tagging notification, you see it on the right of your Home page as soon as you log in.

Notifications

1 new notification

Clicking this flag takes you to the Notifications tab in your Inbox, where you see all the notifications you've received for the last seven days.

Here are examples of other kinds of useful notifications:

- When someone tags other people in a photo you uploaded, tags you in note, or tags you in a photo.
- When someone has written on your Wall or on the Wall of a group or event that you admin.
- When someone leaves a comment right after you've commented on a photo, note, or posted item.
- When someone replies to a post that you made on a discussion board.
- When someone comments on one of your notes, posted items, photos that you've taken, or photos that you're tagged in.

You can actually receive an unbounded number of different kinds of notifications, thanks to a rich array of applications. Even if you don't have the Video application added to your profile, you receive a notification when someone tags you in a video. If someone quotes you using the Quotes application, the notification shows here.

You can stop receiving notifications from any application. Just do this:

1. **Go to the Notifications page by clicking the arrow next to Inbox on the Frame and selecting Notifications.**

2. **Deselect the check box next to the application from which you no longer want to receive messages.**

3. **To receive these notifications again (and see any you've received in the last seven days from that particular application), simply reselect the check box.**

Notifications is kind of an overloaded term on Facebook. The kinds of notifications we describe in this section are those you receive on Facebook when someone talks about you. (They all show on the Notifications tab in your Inbox when you log in.)

Email Notifications, however, refer to the e-mails you receive when anyone is talking about you or to you, as in all the preceding examples, including messages, pokes, and requests. These notifications ensure you know when something of interest is going down on Facebook — even when you're not logged in. To see the full set of notifications and to select which types of e-mail notifications you want to receive, click Account on the blue bar and then click the Notifications tab. Select all check boxes you find relevant to you, and click Save Changes when you're done.

Facebook in an emergency

Communicating on Facebook can be a lot of fun. It can also be useful, emotional, and enriching. However, sometimes, the ability to communicate on a wide scale with those you know can be critical.

On April 29, 2007, at Virginia Polytechnic Institute and State University (Virginia Tech), a lone gunman killed 32 students and wounded many more. While the story broke over television and radio, those with loved ones on the campus scrambled for information. Students across Virginia Tech who were not involved in the attack, logged into Facebook. To help reassure their friends and family that they were okay, the students set their statuses to something similar to *<so-and-so> is safe.* Thanks to reporters and word-of-mouth, news spread quickly that Facebook was the fastest way to confirm the safety of any particular Virginia Tech student.

Chapter 11

Defining Your Outer Circle
with Networks

*F*acebook strives to reflect your real-world connections, and let's face it: In the real world, not *everyone* you communicate with is your friend. And if they are, stop bragging. Nobody likes a bragger.

You probably know many people with whom you'd like to connect online even if you choose not to add them as a personal friend. Perhaps you want to write notes intended for anyone who works at your company or create an event and invite anyone who goes to your school. To help you stay in touch with these "outer circles," Facebook offers networks.

Introducing Networks

A *network* is a community of Facebook users who attend the same school (school network), work at the same company (workplace network) or live in the same region (region network). Joining a network is a great way to find other people you know on Facebook.

After you join a school or workplace network, you see the profiles, photos, notes, and so forth of anyone in the network — and they can see yours. If you're uncomfortable with that, tweak your privacy settings to restrict all or part of your information to your friends. See Chapter 4 for more information.

To ensure that online networks accurately reflect their real-world counterparts, Facebook put some restrictions in place. We walk you through the three types of networks and discuss these restrictions.

School networks

Facebook offers both college and high school networks.

College networks

When Facebook began, college networks were the only option available to its members. These networks are like virtual college campuses. When you browse them, you're sure to stumble across people you know — if not directly, then at least through a few degrees of separation.

Of course, you might spend your days on campus even if you're not a student. After you join a college network, specify whether you're a current student, alumni, faculty, or staff. This enables more granular privacy settings, so if you're a Stanford professor, you can show your profile to only other Stanford faculty but not students.

Even if you're no longer hanging out at the ol' campus anymore, you can still join a college network as alumni and reconnect with former classmates.

Restrictions: You must have an e-mail address supplied by a college to join its network. For example, to verify that you're affiliated with Stanford — and to join this network — you must have an `@stanford.edu` or `@stanford alumni.org` e-mail address.

High school networks

Three guesses as to what these are.

Restrictions: Facebook has stringent rules in place to protect young Facebook users.

- ✔ You can join a high school network only if you're currently a high school student.
- ✔ If your high school offers e-mail addresses, you must have one to join the network.
- ✔ Otherwise, you can participate in *social authentication*. After joining a high school network, your Facebook account is placed in pending status until a friend in the network confirms that you go to school with them. To obtain this confirmation, add the person as a Facebook friend. If your account is pending for too long, it's disabled.

Workplace networks

Join a workplace network to connect with your co-workers after business hours, as if you don't see enough of them already. Facebook offers tens of thousands of workplace networks representing the most popular companies in the world.

Listing a workplace on your profile isn't the same thing as joining a workplace network. The first has implications on search because people can search for anyone who lists Pierce & Pierce Executers on their profiles. Joining the Pierce & Pierce Executers network, however, means that your co-workers have access to your profile and you have access to theirs.

Restrictions: You must have a corporate e-mail address to join a workplace network. For instance, to join the Microsoft workplace network, you need an `@microsoft.com` address.

Region networks

Region networks correspond to geographic regions of the world. Joining a region network is a great way to access some interesting content, either by seeing more profiles or by checking out a Network page for some cool, posted items, groups, and more.

Restrictions:

- ✔ You can be in only one region network at a time.
- ✔ You can change region networks only twice every 60 days.

Joining a Network

Now that your appetite is whetted, go ahead and join some networks. Keep in mind that you can be in (at most) only five networks at one time. This shouldn't be a problem unless you live in two places and attend two schools while going to work — you don't, or you wouldn't have time to read this.

You might have joined a network in the Facebook Welcome Wizard when you first joined Facebook. If not — or to join another network — click the arrow next to Networks on the blue bar at the top of every Facebook page and then click Join a Network.

The appearance of the resulting page depends on whether or not you're in at least one network. If you are, you see the page shown in Figure 11-1, with your current networks listed down the left side and a box on the right side for joining a new network. You use this box to join any of the three network types: school, workplace, or region. If you aren't in any networks, you see the page shown in Figure 11-2. To make it easier to get started, this page offers three separate boxes, one for each network type. It also includes a brief video about the benefits of joining a network.

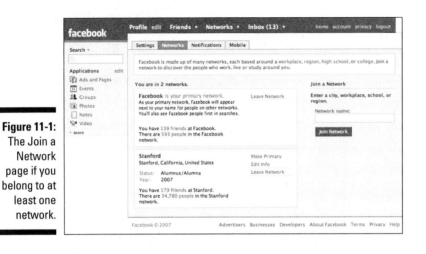

Figure 11-1:
The Join a
Network
page if you
belong to at
least one
network.

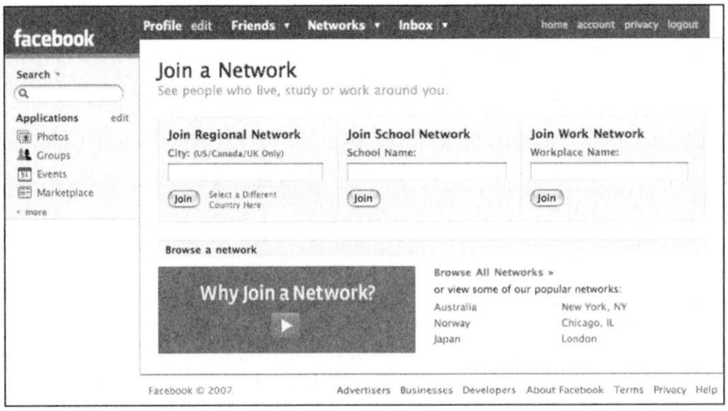

Figure 11-2:
The Join a
Network
page if you
don't belong
to any
networks.

When you join a school or workplace network, your profile, photos, and other information is visible to other network members by default. You can change this behavior via the Privacy Overview page. See Chapter 4 for more information and instructions.

Pretend you're in at least one network and using the second page so that the following steps for joining a network remain useful:

1. **Start typing the name of the network you want to join, such as** Stanford University, Los Angeles, **or** Procter & Gamble.

   The field auto-completes while you type.

   Facebook supports tens of thousands of networks, all of which are listed at www.facebook.com/networks/networks.php. If Facebook doesn't support your school, company, or region, request that they do via the Suggestions form at www.facebook.com/help.php?tab=suggest.

2. **If you choose a region network, simply click Join and then confirm that you want to join that network.**

   You're done!

   If you chose a school or workplace network, you need to enter your work or school e-mail address and then click Join.

3. **If you're joining a school or workplace network, check your e-mail. Click the link in the confirmation e-mail that Facebook sent you to verify that you own the school or work e-mail address that you entered.**

   After you click that link, you officially join the school or workplace network.

If you wish to leave a network, simply return to the Join a Network page and click the Leave Network link next to the network in the left column.

Designating a primary network

If you join more than one network, designate the network that you most identify with as your primary network. For instance, if you graduated Stanford 25 years ago, you're probably much closer to your current co-workers than to your classmates, so you would choose your workplace network as your primary network.

Your primary network appears next to your name in many places on Facebook, such as when you write on a friend's Wall or comment in a group's discussion board. Members of your primary network appear first when you search for people on Facebook. Additionally, when you click the Networks button on the blue bar at the top of Facebook, you're taken to your primary network's Home page. (See the "Keeping Up with Your Networks" section later in this chapter for more information on network Home pages.)

To specify your primary network, click the Make Primary link next to the network on the Networks page (refer to Figure 11-1). If no such link is available, that network is your primary network. If you're a member of only one network, that network is automatically your primary network.

Indicating your school affiliation

If you join a school network, Facebook enables you to specify your relationship with the school. Are you a current student, professor or other faculty member, or alumni? Think of these groups as mini-networks within the larger school network. As outlined in Chapter 4, use your privacy settings to restrict access to members of certain mini-networks. For instance, if you're a professor, you can choose to show your profile to only other school faculty members. Moreover, if you're alumni, you can decide that only other alumni (and not current students) see your profile.

To specify your school affiliation:

1. **Click the Edit Info link next to the school network on the Networks page.**

   The dialog box shown in Figure 11-3 appears.

2. **Choose your affiliation from the School Status drop-down menu.**

3. **Click Save Settings.**

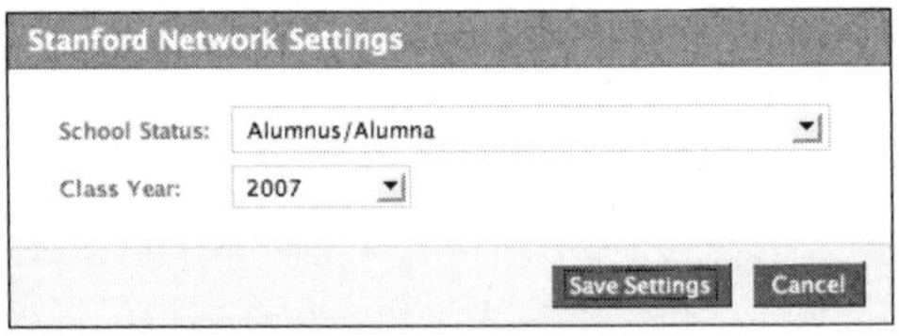

Figure 11-3:
Use the
Network
Settings
dialog box
to indicate
how you're
affiliated
with a
particular
school.

Browsing Your Networks

Imagine spending an entire day at work just walking around meeting your co-workers and discovering their interests. The Facebook Browse tool allows you to do that — without being fired for slacking off.

1. **Click Search in the left-hand navigation menu.**

2. **Click the Browse link in the Basic Search page that appears.**

   The Browse page displays (by default) ten random people from across your networks, as shown in Figure 11-4.

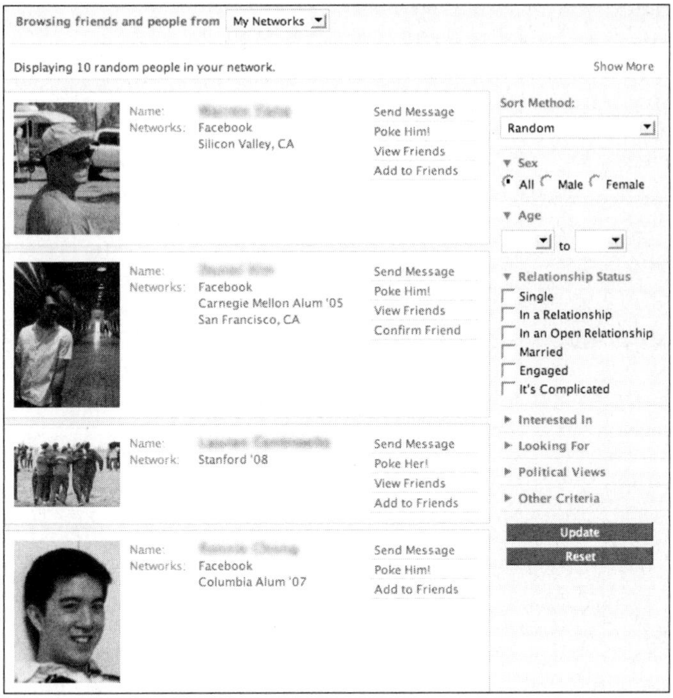

Figure 11-4:
Browse
your
networks to
find your
classmates,
co-workers,
and
neighbors
on
Facebook.

3. **Click their names to see their profiles unless they have restricted their privacy settings.**

4. **To see ten more random network members, click the Show More link at the top right of the page.**

5. **To view an alphabetical list of all network members, change the Sort Method drop-down list at the upper right of the page from Random to Alphabetical.**

6. **To browse people from a particular network, choose the network from the Networks drop-down list at the very top of the page.**

7. **To further filter the list of people displayed, change the criteria on the right sidebar and click Update.**

   For example, you can choose to browse people who are your age and share your religious views.

Keeping Up with Your Networks

Your News Feed shows you what's going on among your friends, but what if you want to see what's going on in your networks? Just like your profile gives your friends a quick summary of you, each network has a Home page that gives you a brief summary of what's happening in that community — from upcoming events to recent Marketplace listings. The Stanford Home page is shown in Figure 11-5. Nobody maintains a network's Home page; Facebook generates it automatically based on the activities of the network's members.

To access a network's Home page, click the arrow next to Networks on the blue bar at the top of Facebook; then choose the network you want to see. If you're a member of only one network, click Networks to visit that network's Home page.

If you're a member of multiple networks, the tabs at the top offer quick access to the Home page of your other networks. You may also browse the Home page of networks that you're not a member of by typing a network name into the Browse Other Networks box in the upper-right and pressing Enter. Note that these Home pages are restricted because you aren't a member. For example, you might view only basic network information about a workplace network, and you can't write on the discussion board or Wall of other school or region networks.

Figure 11-5: A network Home page offers a snapshot of the network's latest activity.

A network's Home page is divided into two columns. The wide, left column offers the following sections:

- ✔ **Network Info:** Shows basic information, such as the number of people that belong to the network, the number of friends you have in the network, and the network type.

- ✔ **Action links (which appear just below Network Info):** Offers quick access to the following popular network features:

  - *Browse All Networks:* A list of all the networks that Facebook supports.

  - *See What's Popular:* Web sites, groups, events, and notes people in this network enjoyed recently.

  - *Find Classmates or Find Coworkers:* A search available to school or workplace networks.

  - *View Discussion Board:* The network-wide discussion board that any network member may participate in.

- ✔ **Upcoming Events:** Shows events created within the current network that are occurring within the next month. Click See All for the complete list of events. See Chapter 13 for more information about network-specific events.

- ✔ **Popular in *<Name of Network>*:** Lists content, such as Web sites and Facebook groups, that many people within the current network enjoyed recently.

- ✔ **Discussion Board:** Displays recent topics from the network-wide discussion board, in which any network member may participate. The topics vary widely depending on the network type. Members of a school network might discuss this weekend's football game, whereas, members of a workplace network might strategize for next week's presentation. Click See All for the complete list of discussion board topics.

- ✔ **The Wall** is the same feature you find on your profile, Facebook Groups, and Facebook Event Home page — a place for casual chitchat among members.

The narrow, right column contains these sections:

- ✔ **People in *<Name of Network>*:** Displays the name and profile picture thumbnails of (at most) six random people who belong to the current network. Click the member's name or picture to be taken to their profile.

- ✔ **Marketplace:** Offers a snapshot of recent Marketplace listings (for example, job postings or furniture for sale) that originate from this network. Click See All for the complete list.

✔ **Network Statistics:** Provides tasty insights into the preferences or composition of the network, such as the top ten movies or books enjoyed by its members (based on their profile information), their gender, or political makeup. A new statistic is shown at random each time you visit the network's Home page. Click See More Stats to see all the available statistics on one screen.

✔ **Nearby Networks:** Displays a list of Facebook networks that are located near this network geographically, along with the number of people in each network. The network's name is a link that you can click on to visit its Home page. This box is only displayed on college and region network Home pages if there are networks nearby.

Chapter 12

Creating and Joining Groups on Facebook

*H*umans are social animals. Although you spend plenty of time tweaking and massaging your profile, the real value of Facebook lies at the intersections of its massive network: more than 100 million people in 75 countries meeting up for a virtual cup of coffee. Can you foot this bill? We'll get the next one.

The coffeehouses on Facebook are known as *groups*. Every 30 seconds, a new discussion is started in one of over 10 million groups on Facebook, on topics ranging from The Beatles to global warming to Ottawa University's Class of 1958 reunion. If you can't find the group you're looking for, you can create and host it yourself. Like everything on Facebook, you decide who can participate — from ten of your closest friends to everyone in the world.

Getting Going with Groups

Like Photos, *Groups* is a pre-installed application built for you by Facebook. You can access the application's Home page (Figure 12-1) by choosing Groups in your Applications menu on the left-hand navigation bar. This page shows you what's new in the Groups scene on Facebook, in terms of which groups your friends have joined recently and which of the groups that you participate in have been updated. You can also browse and search groups or even create your own.

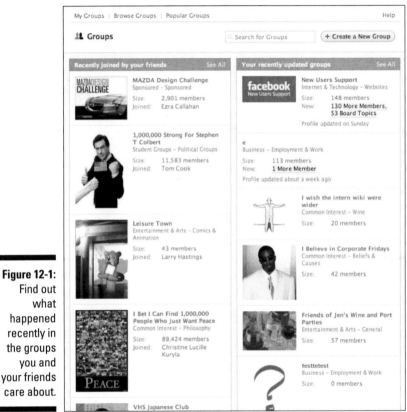

Figure 12-1:
Find out what happened recently in the groups you and your friends care about.

Joining a group

The best way to understand a Facebook group is to look at one from a member's perspective. We're using the Beatles Fans Around the World group, where over 8,000 fans congregate, as an example. To find this group, just follow these steps:

1. **Type** Beatles Fans Around the World **into the Search box and press Enter.**

   Note that groups on Facebook might share similar or even identical names. If you're having trouble finding it, the address is `www.facebook.com/group.php?gid=2204708817`. The group is shown in Figure 12-2. (More information about searching for groups comes later in the chapter.)

Figure 12-2:
Over 8,000
fans relive
good music
and
memories in
the Beatles
Fans
Around the
World
group.

2. **Click the Join This Group link under the picture at the top right of the page and become an insider.**

   If you don't want to frolic in strawberry fields forever, don't worry; we show you how to leave the group when we finish.

   When you join a group, your fellow members can't see your profile unless they're your friends or in your networks (depending on your privacy settings). In other words, standard Facebook privacy rules apply; groups don't influence them in any manner. The only indirect consequence of joining a group is that the group appears in the Groups section of your profile (unless you've hidden that section) and in your Mini-Feed. Furthermore, a story about your joining the group might appear in your friends' News Feed. None of these consequences occurs if the group you join is secret, which is a concept we discuss in the upcoming section, "Creating Your Own Groups."

Anatomy of a group

The first thing you see when you visit a group is its Home page. Just as your profile provides a summary of you (not to say that *you* could ever be summarized), this page provides an overview of what's happened in the group recently, including snapshots of the most recent photos, videos, and member comments.

At the top of every group's Home page sits a gray bar with two important bits of information: the group name and the group network. Just as you might decide to restrict your profile to some of your networks, you might also decide that only people in certain networks should be able to join a group that you create. In this case, you see that the creator of Beatles Fans Around the World has chosen to place the group in the Global network, which means that anyone on Facebook — regardless of the networks they belong to — may become a member of this group. This makes sense given the group's mission to bring together Beatles fans from all over. However, if you decide to create a group for your company's basketball team, you would probably choose to limit group membership to people in your company.

Depending on privacy settings (see the later "Creating Your Own Groups" section), you might be able to see all of a group's contents before joining it even though you can't post new content. That's the case with the Beatles Fans Around the World group because the administrator has chosen the most flexible settings.

In many ways, a group is similar to a profile shared among its members. Like your profile, a group's Home page is divided into a wide, left column and a thin, right column; each column contains a number of different sections. Each section is delineated by a blue title bar and contains the most recent content posted in that section, such as the last few photos or discussion topics. To see everything posted to a section, click See All on its title bar. A group administrator might decide to hide certain sections for his group, although we purposely chose this group because it contains all the possible sections.

From top to bottom, the left column offers the following sections:

✔ **Information:** This section contains the basic details of the group, such as a description that outlines its purpose as well as its type and subtype, which must be standard Facebook categories (see the upcoming section, "Creating Your Own Groups"). The type of Beatles Fans Around the World is *Music,* and its subtype is *Rock*; you can click either word to see other groups belonging to the selected type.

If the group represents a real-world group (for example, the National Breast Cancer Foundation), the Information section might also contain the organization's contact information, such as a physical address or an Internet address. Because the administrator of this group isn't an official representative of the band and has no public presence, he has decided to jokingly specify the address as *151 E. Broad St.* in homage to Paul McCartney's album, *Give My Regards to Broad Street.*

✔ **Recent News:** This section discusses recent events, such as a new re-release of a classic Beatles album. This section appears only when the group administrator provides recent news.

✔ **Photos:** As you might guess, this section contains photos that are of relevance to the group. In this case, fans of The Beatles have posted over 180 of their favorite photos of their beloved band. Only the four most recent photos are shown on the group's Home page, but you can click See All to view the rest of them.

In some instances, these photos are of group members posing with the band long ago. Such photo sharing is a staple of many Facebook groups. For instance, visit Facebook hiking groups and you see members sharing pictures of their most recent conquests. Group members can leave comments on these photos just as your friends can comment on the pictures you post to your profile.

✔ **Videos:** Like photos, videos enrich groups by moving them beyond mere discussion. Here, fans of The Beatles tickle their memories with clips from the band's golden years. Viewing videos is very similar to viewing photos. The most recent videos are shown on the group's Home page, and you can click See All to view the rest. To watch a video, click it. Group members can also leave comments on videos.

✔ **Posted Items:** This section contains links to types of content that don't belong under Photos or Videos. For example, a member named Michelle posts a link to a funny article that explains how to persuade your friends to like The Beatles, while another member named Daniel posts a link to his favorite video of The Beatles. (You might be wondering why he put that video in Posted Items rather than in Videos. He did that because he found the video on another popular video Web site called YouTube. He doesn't have the right to copy the video into Facebook Video, so he just points members to its original home.) Like virtually everything else in a Facebook group, you and other members can comment on the items that people post.

✔ **Discussion Board:** The home of lively conversations and debates between members, the discussion board is the nexus of a group. Each topic in a discussion board represents a new area of the broader group dialogue where particularly insightful or provocative topics can garner hundreds or thousands of responses. For instance, as you can imagine, the "What's your favorite song by The Beatles?" topic has kicked off quite a heated debate. We can't imagine why because the answer is *Hey Jude*.

✔ **Members:** This section shows you other Facebook members that are part of the group. If any of your friends are in the group, they're listed first, followed by other people who belong to your networks. This is similar to how friends and network neighbors appear first in Facebook search results, which reflects our belief that the people close to you are always more interesting than strangers. *Remember:* Groups don't influence the basic Facebook privacy model, so you're not able to see the profile of a fellow group member unless they're already your friend or belong to one of your networks.

Beatles Fans Around the World has more than 8,000 members, which is impressive but far from the size of the largest Facebook groups that boast more than a million members (such as "When I was your age, Pluto was a planet"). Of course, more than 500 distinct groups about The Beatles exist throughout Facebook, each with their own member base and personality. That's a prime benefit of it being so easy to create a group on Facebook: one size need not fit all.

✔ **The Wall:** You've probably noticed that Facebook loves the Wall — and constructs one just about anywhere there's space. Why not? Although discussion boards do a great job of facilitating structured, hierarchical conversation, the Wall is the perfect mechanism for casual, free-form commenting. In Beatles Fans Around the World, members often use the Wall to verbalize passionately their gratitude for 50 years of great music. They aren't trying to start discussions.

Whew. You'd think that'd be enough, but settle down: We've got another column to go! The right column contains information that might be interesting to members but is probably less important than the things we just discussed. It includes:

✔ **A picture:** Group administrators can choose any picture they like to represent the group on the Home page, but they have to be picky: They get only one.

✔ **Action links:** Just as your profile contains a set of important actions (such as View Photos) underneath your picture, a series of action links follows the group picture. These include View Discussion Board (which is a shortcut to the See All link of the Discussion Board section), and either Join This Group or Leave Group depending on whether you're already a member of the group. If the group is *closed* (see the later "Creating Your Own Groups" section), you may join only with a group administrator's approval, in which case the link reads, Request to Join Group. If you're the administrator of a group, you see additional administrative options here.

If the group administrator chooses to allow it (the administrator of Beatles Fans Around the World has), you also see a link to Invite People to Join.

✔ **Share:** The Share links scattered throughout Facebook allow you to quickly share with your friends interesting content that you find, either by sending it to them in a message or by posting it onto your profile. This Share button allows you to share a link to the group (along with a preview containing the group's name, description, and picture).

If the group is *open*, you might want to use the Invite People to Join link to send an invitation to join rather than a mere link. If the group is *secret*, you can't share a link to the group with anyone who isn't already a member because the group's privacy settings don't permit it. (See the upcoming section, "Step 1: Group Info," for more information about open and secret groups.)

✔ **Officers:** If a group has any officers, the Officers section lists their names, primary networks, and titles. Because this concept doesn't really make sense in Beatles Fans Around the World (the administrator has not designated any officers), the section doesn't appear. However, check out the Istanbul Toastmasters (`www.facebook.com/group.php?gid= 11892850450`) for an example of officers in a group. Istanbul Toastmasters meets in Turkey to help each other with public speaking. See the upcoming "Managing your group" section for more information about officers.

✔ **Related Groups:** This section displays a list of other Facebook groups that you might be interested in based on the group you're currently looking at. *Related* is a bit of a misnomer; Facebook builds this list by looking at the other groups that members belong to, rather than looking for other groups that offer similar content. As a result, the list often contains quirky groups that are more reflective of the member's interests and personalities than of the group's topic.

✔ **Group Type:** This section displays information about the group's privacy settings. As we mentioned, the administrator of Beatles Fans Around the World chose the most flexible settings possible in his effort to attract fans of The Beatles. This means he exposes the existence of the group to the Global network and allows anyone in that network (which is everyone on Facebook) to see the group, join it, and invite others to join. This latter set of permissions constitutes an *open* group. A group might also be *closed* or *secret,* as we discuss in the "Step 1: Group Info" section, later in this chapter.

✔ **Admins:** The Admins section lists the names and primary networks of all the group's administrators. Whoever creates a group is automatically the administrator of that group, meaning they write the group's information, control its privacy settings, moderate its discussions, and generally keep the group running smoothly. They can also promote other members to administrators to grant them the same privileges. See the upcoming section, "Managing your group member list," for help with promoting members to administrators.

We've been referring to the administrator of the Beatles Fans Around the World group throughout this chapter. Thanks to the Admins section, we can finally give him a name! It's Matt, and as you see from the parenthetical note after his name, at the time of this writing, he hails from the University of Georgia (UGA is his primary network). If the group had other administrators or officers, they would be listed here as well.

A group's Home page ends how it began: with a gray bar. The bottom bar contains a Report Group option that you can use whenever you encounter a group you consider offensive. See the "Finding the Group for You" section, later in this chapter, for more information about reporting groups.

Adding your two cents (or more)

The best way to get started with a group is to contribute to the discussions that are already taking place among its members. Click a topic that sounds interesting in the Discussion Board section and dive in. **Remember:** You can click See All on the section title bar to see all the ongoing discussions for the group rather than just the most recent ones displayed on the group's Home page. If you don't see a topic that strikes your fancy, start your own by clicking Start New Topic.

After you reply to an existing topic or start your own, Facebook helps you keep up with the conversation in a number of ways:

✔ Facebook sends you a notification whenever someone replies to one of your discussion posts. By default, this notification arrives not just on Facebook but also via e-mail. You can turn this off if you don't want it; see Chapter 10 for more information on notifications.

✔ The Groups page (on the Applications menu) displays a list of your recently updated groups in its right column. The yellow-highlighted text indicates the group's content that changed.

✔ As always, your News Feed is a great way to keep up with what's happening in your Facebook universe.

Finding the Group for You

Groucho Marx once said that he wouldn't want to be part of any club that would have him as a member. He probably wouldn't be happy about Facebook, which has millions of public groups that would readily accept him, you, or anyone else who'd like to join. This section helps you pinpoint the groups that cover your interests, whether you search for specific groups, browse groups, or check out groups that your friends like.

Regardless of which method you use to find interesting groups, the outcome is always the same: a list of results, such as that shown in Figure 12-3. Each result contains information to help you decide whether the group is for you before you click through to it, including the group's picture, network, size, and type. If the group has changed recently, the information that changed is highlighted in the result. When you find a group that looks interesting, click its name to see its Home page and whether you have the option of joining.

Figure 12-3:
A group
search
result
displays
basic
information
as well as
recent
changes.

Group:	**Hiking For A Cure**	View Group
Network:	**Global**	Join Group
Size:	207 members	
Type:	Organizations – Philanthropic Organizations	
New:	1 More Member	
Matches:	Name	

Searching groups

If you already have a topic in mind, the following is the fastest way to find groups that cover it:

1. **Click within the Search box.**

   The Search box sits on the left-hand navigation bar of every Facebook page, right above the Applications menu.

2. **Enter the name of a group you wish to find, such as Cat Lovers, and press Enter.**

   The search results contain content from all over Facebook, such as profiles, groups, and events.

3. **Click the Groups tab at the top to filter to group results.**

To search only groups and thus avoid Step 3, use the Search box at the top of the Groups page. The search results are the same in each case. To navigate to the Groups page, choose Groups from the Applications menu on the left-hand navigation bar that resides on every Facebook page.

When an administrator creates a group, she decides who may see and join the group by assigning it to a network. If everyone should be able to see it and join, the group can be assigned the Global network. The administrator may further restrict privileges within that network by changing the group access type to *closed* or *secret*, as we discuss in the upcoming section, "Creating Your Own Groups." Facebook displays only the groups that you have permission to see in the list of search results.

Narrowing your search

If you're having trouble finding the group you're looking for, you can try refining your search by group network or type.

By default, Facebook displays groups that are accessible to all of your networks. For instance, if you belong to the Proctor & Gamble workplace network, the Stanford college network, and the San Francisco region network, you see all the groups that match your search phrase that belong to any of those three networks or the Global network. If you're looking for a group that pertains to your job, school, or region, you can filter the search results to just the relevant groups by selecting the desired network from the drop-down list next to *within* on the gray bar at the top of the search results page (see Figure 12-4). By default, the My Networks option is selected.

Figure 12-4:
The networks drop-down list helps you narrow your groups search.

| Searching for | hiking | within | My Networks | ▼ | Advanced \| Filter Results |

| All results | 500+ Groups | 1 2 3 Next |

Alternatively, you may find that the default Facebook search is *too* narrow because Facebook puts additional emphasis on groups belonging to your networks by ranking them higher in the search results. For instance, you might be trying to find a hiking group that brings together hikers from all over the world but end up with hiking groups that are local to your city. To instruct Facebook to de-prioritize groups in your networks, select Global from the network drop-down list.

You can also filter your search results by group type and subtype. Say you search for *Cats* and end up with many groups about furry felines when you really wanted groups about the not-quite-as-furry Andrew Lloyd Weber and his iconic show. When looking at a list of group search results, just follow these steps:

1. **Click the Filter Results link on the gray bar above the search results.**

2. **When the filter sidebar appears on the right, choose the appropriate type from the drop-down list.**

   In this case, you'd choose Entertainment & Arts. After you choose the type, Facebook instantly filters your results.

3. **To filter your results further, choose the appropriate subtype.**

   In this case, you'd choose Performing Arts.

You can also narrow your search more quickly by adding words to your search phrase to make it more specific. For instance, in this case, searching for *Cats the musical* rather than *Cats* returns results that are more relevant.

Whether the search filters help, you can clear them and return to the original results list by clicking the Clear Filters link, which appears in place of the Filter Results link on the gray bar at the top.

Browsing groups

If you don't have a particular topic in mind and would rather get a sense of what Facebook groups have to offer, you can browse them at your leisure by following these steps:

1. **Choose Groups in the Applications menu on the left-hand navigation bar to navigate to the Groups page.**

2. **Click the Browse Groups link at the top of the page.**

   By default, Facebook displays a random list of interesting groups that you have permission to see, beginning with those that belong to your networks.

3. **Use the options on the right-hand sidebar to filter the displayed list by group network or type.**

   For more information about these options, see "Narrowing your search," earlier in this chapter; these options filter browsing results just as they filter search results.

You can also browse groups that are popular among your friends and networks. See the next section for more information about that.

Checking out popular groups

When you go to the bookstore to find an interesting book, you're not at the mercy of the staff. Your friends, co-workers, classmates, and neighbors — who know you better than anyone — can guide your search by telling you which books *they* enjoyed. Groups are no different, so don't worry if you're having trouble finding good ones; your friends and networks are here to help.

Whenever you visit the Groups page, you see a running list of groups recently joined by your friends in the left column. Your friends don't manually suggest these groups to you; Facebook assumes that your friends join groups that interest them and automatically pushes those groups to you. To see all groups recently joined by your friends, click the See All link on the column's title bar or the See All Recent Groups Joined by Friends link at the bottom of the list.

If you want a broader look at what's hot among groups, click the Popular Groups link at the top of the Groups page to see a list of recently active groups within your primary network. You can also see which groups are popular in your secondary networks by viewing the Groups sections of those Home pages. See Chapter 11 for more information about network Home pages.

Reporting offensive groups

If you stumble upon an offensive group in your travels, you should report it to Facebook so that the company can take appropriate actions. To report a group:

1. **Click the Report Group link on the gray bar at the bottom of its Home page.**

   You see a form like that shown in Figure 12-5.

2. **Fill out the report by choosing a reason for the report and include a comment that explains why you feel the group should be removed.**

3. **Click Report.**

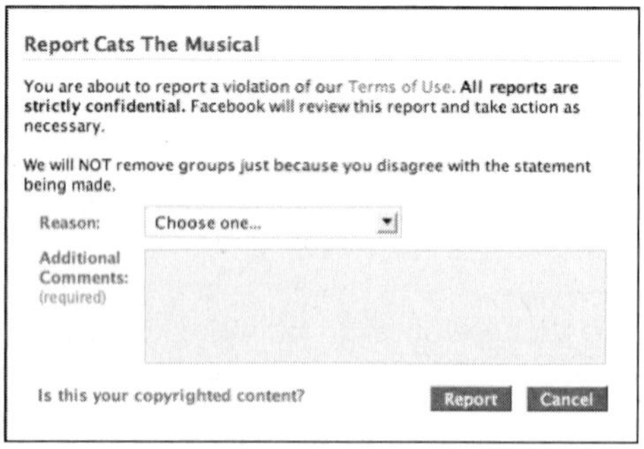

Figure 12-5:
If you find a
group is
offensive,
Facebook is
here to help.

Report Cats The Musical

You are about to report a violation of our Terms of Use. **All reports are strictly confidential.** Facebook will review this report and take action as necessary.

We will NOT remove groups just because you disagree with the statement being made.

Reason: Choose one...

Additional
Comments:
(required)

Is this your copyrighted content?   Report Cancel

Facebook removes all groups that

- ✔ Contain pornographic material or inappropriate nudity.
- ✔ Attack an individual or group.
- ✔ Advocate the use of illicit drugs.
- ✔ Advocate violence.
- ✔ Serve as advertisements or are otherwise deemed to be spam by Facebook.

Many groups on Facebook take strong stands on controversial issues, such as the legalization of abortion or gun control. In an effort to remain neutral and promote debate, Facebook won't remove a group because you disagree with its statements.

Creating Your Own Groups

If you can't find the group you're looking for on Facebook, or even if you can but you just want one with a different personality or member list, you're welcome to create your own. As a group's creator, you're by default the *group administrator*, which means that you write the group's information, control its privacy settings, moderate its discussions, and generally keep it running smoothly. You can also promote other members of the group to administrators to grant them the same privileges, and then they can help you with these responsibilities.

To begin creating a group:

1. **Choose Groups from the Applications menu on the left-hand navigation bar to navigate to the Groups page.**

2. **Click the Create a New Group button at the top right of the page.**

Creating a group entails at least one step — specifying the group's name and other basic information — and you have the option of completing two additional steps: specifying a group picture or a member list. Facebook divides the process into three screens, one for each step, and highlights the current step at the top of the page. We discuss each step in depth here. You can edit any property of a group except for its name at any time after its creation, so don't fret too much about getting things just right your first time around.

Although you can't manually delete a group that you create, Facebook automatically deletes groups that have no members. If you're the only member, simply leave the group and poof — the group is gone. If there are other members, you (as administrator) can remove them from your group using the Members dashboard. See "Managing your group" later in this chapter.

Step 1: Group Info

The Group Info step asks you for the following information about the group. Some information might not be relevant or desirable for the group you have in mind. You must enter the information designated as *required*, as shown in Figure 12-6.

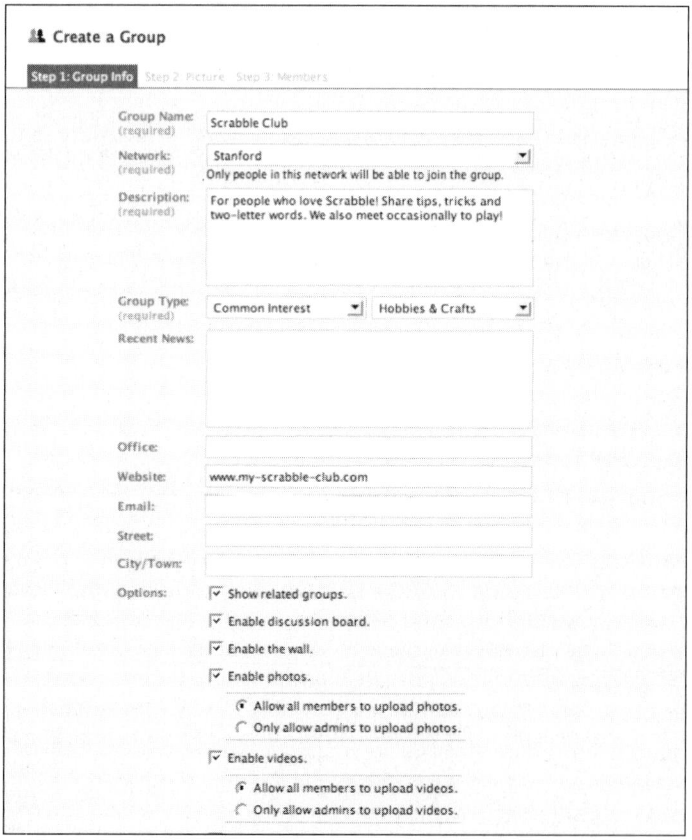

Figure 12-6:
You need to enter only four basic bits of information to get your group up and running.

✔ **Group Name (required):** The name of the group you wish to create, such as Beatles Fans Around the World. If you want people that you don't know to join your group, choose longer, more specific names to help them locate it through a search.

✔ **Network (required):** The network to which the group belongs. Only Facebook users who belong to the network you choose can see and join your group. To make the group available to everyone on Facebook, choose Global. Otherwise, choose another network that you belong to. Regardless of what you choose, you have the option to restrict further access to your group via the Access option outlined below.

✔ **Description (required):** A brief overview of the purpose or mission of the group. This is similar to an organization's charter and is one of the first things a user sees when looking at your group and determining whether to join.

✔ **Group Type (required):** A broad category that describes the focus of your group, such as Music. You must also choose a subtype that further narrows the focus, such as Rock.

✔ **Recent News:** Anything that's happened recently that might be of interest to the group's members. For groups reflecting real-world organizations, this might be information about recent organizational activities posted for the benefit of members who didn't participate (say, the outcome of a blood drive). For groups uniting people with a shared hobby or interest, such as hiking, this might be pertinent news about the activity, such as the temporary closure of a popular hiking trail. *Remember:* You can update this information at any time.

✔ **Office:** If your group represents an organization that operates on a work or school campus, you can enter the colloquial location of the organization's office here, such as Tressider Building, Second Floor. If your group has a broader audience for whom such an intimate description would not be helpful, you can enter a more precise physical address in the Street and City/Town fields, as described later in this list.

✔ **Website:** The address of a Web site that's pertinent to the group. If the group represents a real-world organization, such as the National Breast Cancer Foundation, this would typically be the organization's official Web address, such as `www.nationalbreastcancer.org`. If the group brings together fans of a particular television show, this would often point to the television show's official home on the Web.

✔ **Email:** The e-mail address of a person or organization that's pertinent to the group. It isn't necessary (and might be undesirable) to list your own e-mail address here. As the administrator, your name is listed under the Admins section of the group's Home page, and members have the option to send you a Facebook message.

✔ **Street:** If the group represents a real-world organization that has a physical office, you can enter its street address here.

✔ **City/Town:** If the group represents a real-world organization that has a physical office, you can enter the city or town of the office here. Combined with the Street field discussed above, these constitute the most important parts of a physical address.

✔ **Options:** A mixture of options control which sections appear on your group's Home page and, where applicable, which members can add content to them. We explain these sections in "Anatomy of a Group" earlier in this chapter.

- *Show Related Groups:* Shows a section that displays a list of other Facebook groups related to yours. This is largely determined by looking at which other groups your group's members are likely to belong, so the listed groups might not necessarily relate to your group's topic. You cannot control what appears in this list, and the contents can change at any time.

- *Enable Discussion Board:* Shows the discussion board. Groups are typically used to host discussions among members, so you probably want to keep this enabled.

- *Enable the Wall:* Shows the Wall, which is typically used for informal, casual remarks from members. If you'd rather encourage the more structured, in-depth discussion usually found in the discussion board, you might want to hide the Wall.

- *Enable Photos:* Shows the photos section. If you decide to show this section, you might also decide who may add photos to it. By default, all members of the group may add photos, but you can restrict this to administrators by selecting Only Allow Admins to Upload Photos.

- *Enable Videos:* Shows the videos section. If you decide to show this section, you might also decide who may add videos to it. By default, all members of the group may add videos, but you can restrict this to administrators by selecting Only Allow Admins to Upload Videos.

- *Enable Posted Items:* Shows the posted items section. If you decide to show this section, you might also decide who may post items to it. By default, all members of the group may post items, but you can restrict this to administrators by selecting Only Allow Admins to Post Items.

✓ **Access:** When you designate a network for your group, you indicate the broadest set of people that are allowed to join it. You can further restrict this set via one of the three access settings that Facebook offers:

- *This Group Is Open:* This default setting allows that anyone can view the group's content. Only members in the group's network (which is everyone if the network is Global) can join the group. Group members can also invite members of the network to join.

- *This Group Is Closed:* Anyone in the chosen network can see the basic group information, but only members can see the photos, discussions, and so forth. People who want to join must request membership, and you, or another administrator, have the opportunity to approve or deny these requests.

- *This Group Is Secret:* People can join the group only if you or another administrator invites them. They cannot request membership; they won't even know of the group's existence because it won't appear in search results or on the profiles of its current members. Therefore, only members can see the group description, discussions, photos, and so forth. The group's network has little effect here given these additional restrictions on membership.

✔ **Publicize:** By default, open and closed groups are listed on their respective network's Home page as well as in relevant search results. If you don't want this exposure, deselect this check box. The group might still appear in the Groups section of its members' Home pages as well as in Mini-Feed and News Feed stories. This option isn't relevant and thus not available for secret groups because such groups already prevent this exposure by their very nature.

When you finish filling out the group's information, click the Create Group button at the bottom of the screen to create the group and move to Step 2: Picture. If you left any required fields empty or otherwise made an error, you remain on the first step, and a red box appears at the top explaining how to proceed.

Step 2: Picture

In the earlier section, "Anatomy of a Group," we explain that group administrators can choose a single picture to appear prominently at the top of their group's Home page. If no picture is chosen, the question mark shown in Figure 12-7 is displayed.

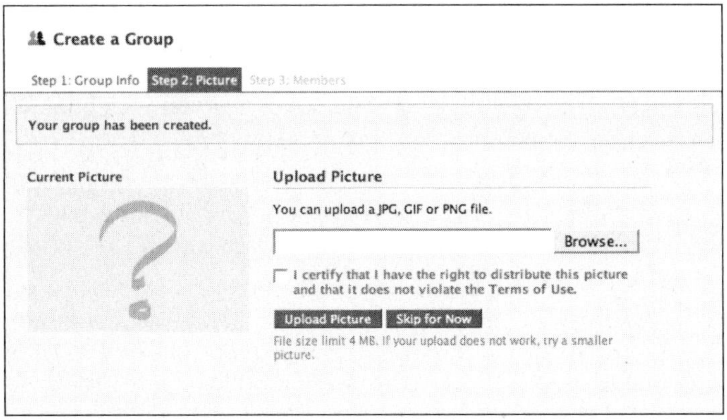

Figure 12-7: You may upload a picture for your group in Step 2.

To specify a picture:

1. **Click the Browse button to open your computer's standard interface for finding a file.**

2. **Navigate to and select the picture on your computer that you wish to use.**

The picture you choose must meet the file size and type requirements outlined on the page. If you're not sure whether your desired picture meets the requirements, select the picture and continue with these steps. Facebook notifies you if the picture you choose can't be used.

3. **Select the check box to certify that you have the right to distribute the picture (it isn't copyrighted), and that it doesn't violate the Facebook terms of use (it isn't pornographic or otherwise offensive).**

4. **Click Upload Picture.**

5. **Click Continue.**

If you don't want to choose a picture yet, click Skip for Now to move to Step 3: Members. You can always return to this step later to add a picture (or to change it if you do select one now).

Step 3: Members

This final step enables you to invite people to join your group (in the right column) as well as manage its current members (in the left column), as shown in Figure 12-8. Because your group is new, this step is useful to you only for its inviting capabilities.

Figure 12-8: Get the party started by inviting your friends to join your group in Step 3.

Remember that if you designated your group as open or closed, it's not necessary for you to invite people; they might discover the group on their own via the News Feed, the search feature, the Groups section on their friends' profiles, or many other sources. However, if you chose to create a secret group, these invitations are the only means through which someone can discover and join your group.

If you decide to invite people to your group, it takes just a few seconds:

1. **Invite your friends who are already on Facebook by checking them in the list at the top of the right column.**

   If you have a lot of friends (congratulations!), you can type part of a name in the box above the list to filter the list quickly. When you invite a Facebook member to join your group, they receive a Facebook request from you. Depending on their notification settings, they might also receive an e-mail from Facebook regarding your invitation. Note that Facebook doesn't send the invitation to your friend as soon as you select him in the list. Keep reading for instructions on actually sending the invitation.

2. **Invite friends who aren't yet on Facebook to join the group by typing their e-mail addresses (separated by commas) into the box in the bottom of the right column and click Add.**

   Can't remember their addresses? No problem. Click the Import Email Addresses link to open a window that enables you to select their addresses from your e-mail address book, assuming Facebook supports your e-mail provider (it supports the most popular ones). This process is very similar to that outlined in Chapter 6. Forgot some folks? Enter more addresses into the box and click Add again.

   The complete list of Facebook and non-Facebook users you've invited appears in a new list at the top of the left column.

3. **If you accidentally add someone to the list that you don't want to invite, click Remove to delete them from the list of people to be invited.**

4. **(Optional) Include a message with your invitation by typing it in the box below the invitee list.**

   Although optional, this adds a personal touch and makes your invitation more persuasive.

5. **Click Send Invitations.**

   The invitations are sent to the people on the list. Forgot some people? You can repeat these steps at any time.

6. **When you're all done, click Finish in the upper right to complete the group creation process and then click the View button to see the Home page of your new baby.**

Managing your group

When you finish creating your group, you might want to do a number of things as people start to join. Many of these steps appear as action links under the picture on your group's Home page. These actions are visible and available only to you and other administrators; if you recall, you did not see these special links when viewing the Beatles Fans Around the World group earlier in this chapter. This section outlines the additional power (and responsibility) you wield as a group administrator.

Designating group officers

Many groups reflect real-life groups or clubs that have members serving in various leadership roles. Administrators can mirror these positions in a Facebook group by designating members as officers and assigning titles, such as Secretary or Treasurer. To promote members to administrators, see the "Managing your group member list" section later in this chapter.

When your group has officers, an Officers section appears on its Home page listing their names, primary networks, and titles. Group officers don't have the same privileges as administrators or any more administrative rights than regular members do.

To designate officers of your group:

1. **Click the Edit Group link under the picture in the right column of your group's Home page.**

2. **Click the Officers tab at the top of the Edit Group page.**

   You see two lists: a list of the officers (and their positions), followed by a list of non-officers.

3. **Promote a non-officer to an officer by clicking the Make Officer link next to her name.**

4. **When Facebook prompts you, enter a position (such as Secretary) for the officer-to-be.**

   You can enter any position you want, so it can be as silly or serious as your personality (and your group's personality) dictates.

5. **Click Add to promote the member to officer or Cancel if you changed your mind.**

   A notification is sent to the member letting her know about the change.

6. **To change the position of an existing officer, click Edit next to his name in the Officers list. To demote an existing officer back to a regular member, click Remove Officer.**

Managing your group member list

After you have members in your group, you can use the group member list to remove (and even permanently ban) undesirable members, promote your most trusted members to administrators, or demote your existing administrators (if any) back to regular members:

1. **Click the Edit Members action link under the picture in the right column of your group's Home page.**

2. **Use the link to the right of each member name that corresponds to the action you wish to take: Remove, Ban, Promote, or Demote.**

If you choose to remove a member from your group, you can also ban him permanently so he may not rejoin the group in the future. This is useful if the person is posting offensive content or otherwise starting trouble. Click Remove next to the member's name and then select the Ban Permanently check box in the confirmation window that appears.

Messaging your group members

Although you can use your group's discussion board and its Wall to communicate with your members, there might be times when you want to guarantee that members read your message. Facebook messages are just the ticket because they appear in your members' Facebook Inbox, and (depending on notification settings) your members might receive an e-mail notification about them. Because of Facebook restrictions on spam, this option might not be available to you if your group has a very large number of members.

To send a message to all members, click the Message All Members action link under the picture in the right column of your group's Home page. You're taken to the standard Facebook Compose Message window. Complete the rest of the process as if you were sending a message to a single friend of yours, as outlined in Chapter 10. To your members, the message appears to originate from the group rather than from you personally, and they're not able to respond to it.

Creating a group event

Your group is open around the clock, but what if you want to gather your members in one place — either online or offline — at one time? For instance, you might wish to convene your Scrabble Lovers group for a friendly tournament. In such cases, you might create a Facebook event to host the details of the gathering and send the invitation to your members.

Although Facebook offers the Events feature to all of its users, it gives special capabilities to group administrators for scenarios like this. By clicking the Create Related Event action link under your group's Home page picture, you can create an event that has the group — rather than you personally — listed as the host in the event and its invitation. Furthermore, you can easily add all of your group members to the event's invitation list by clicking the Invite Members button in the upper right of the event's Edit Guest List page. See Chapter 13 for more information about Events.

Chapter 13

Scheduling Your Life with Facebook

*T*hink about the worst birthday party that you ever had — the big kickball party during the hurricane when the clown was three hours late (and a little drunk) and none of your friends showed up because your mom (hands full with a torrential downpour and drunken clown) forgot to invite them.

Facebook can't do anything about clowns or the weather (as of publication time), but the invites would've happened if your mother used Facebook Events to plan the party. Facebook removes the hassle of hosting an event — creating and sending the invites; managing the guest list — and allows you to focus on preparing the event itself.

Not much of a party planner? No worries. Hundreds of events in your area are on Facebook every week. This chapter shows you how to find the best of the best for this weekend.

Getting Going with Events

Like Photos and Groups, Events is an application built by Facebook and pre-installed by default. To access its dashboard, click the Events link in the Applications menu of your left-hand navigation bar. The Events page (shown in Figure 13-1) displays everything that's happening in the world of events on Facebook. It's divided into the following three tabs:

▌ **Upcoming Events:** Lists upcoming Facebook events that have you on their guest list. This includes events you were invited to and events that you joined.

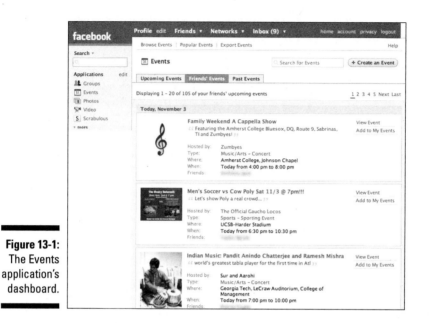

Just in case you change your mind, even events you said you aren't attending appear in the list. To change your RSVP, click the RSVP link on the right side of the event listing. Click Remove to remove an event permanently from your list (and yourself from the event's guest list). See the "Anatomy of an Event" section for more information about this feature.

To see more information about an event, click its title to view the event's Home page, which contains a detailed overview of the event just as your profile does about you. Facebook also embeds a summary of the most important information — the event's tagline, host, type, location, and date; your RSVP; and which friends (if any) are attending — directly into the event listing, as shown in Figure 13-2. Wherever you find an event listing on Facebook — say, the Events browsing tool or a list of search results — this information displays.

✔ **Friends' Events:** Lists the events that your friends are planning to attend. Each listing includes the names of the friends attending the event. As always, click the event title to view the event's Home page. Click Add to My Events to add yourself to the event's guest list and to your Upcoming Events tab. Doing so automatically specifies your RSVP status as Attending, although you can change this by visiting the event's Home page.

✔ **Past Events:** Lists Facebook events that had you on their guest list, regardless of whether or not you attended them. Facebook doesn't delete an event's Home page after the event occurs. Instead, the event's Home page, its photos, videos, and other media remain for posterity as a chronicle of what transpired.

Anatomy of an Event

Events are represented on Facebook through its Home page, such as the one shown in Figure 13-3. A Home page evolves throughout the lifecycle of an event. Before the event takes place, it serves as an invitation and offers critical information for attendees, such as the event's date and location. An event's Home page also tracks who will or might attend the event so that its host can plan accordingly. After the event is over, the Home page serves as a water cooler for attendees to share their experiences in the form of photos, videos, and discussions.

Like many pages on Facebook, an event's Home page is divided into two columns, and each column is further divided into boxes. Some boxes, such as photos and videos, contain only a snapshot of the most recently shared media; click See All in the title bar of these boxes to view a comprehensive list.

While we walk through each box, keep in mind that certain boxes might not appear on a certain event's Home page, at the administrator's discretion.

The left column on the event's Home page contains the following boxes:

✔ **Information:** The Information box displays basic event information, such as the name of the event and the names of the individuals or organizations hosting it. It also contains the event's *tagline* — a brief, catchy slogan, such as *A devil of a good time* for a Halloween costume party (but usually catchier). Most importantly, it contains the time and place for the event. If the administrator specifies a street address, Facebook automatically displays a View Map link that provides directions.

✔ **Description:** A paragraph or two about the event, courtesy of its administrator.

✔ **Photos:** Photos of interest to the event's guests. The Photos box often remains empty until the event takes place, after which attendees fill it quickly with photos from the event. However, a Sweet 16 event might include a series of photos showing the guest of honor growing up throughout the years. A wedding event might include a picture of the real wedding invitation.

✔ **Videos:** As with photos, this box usually displays videos taken at the event, but it might also contain related videos. For instance, a band hosting a concert might decide to share videos of their past performances.

✔ **Posted Items:** Links to Web sites, photos, videos, and other content that exists outside of Facebook that is relevant to the event. For instance, if a museum curator was showcasing an exhibit, he might include a link to his museum's Web site.

✔ **Confirmed Guests:** The list of people who RSVP as Attending the event. The Confirmed Guests box lists your friends and people in your networks before anyone else. Standard Facebook privacy rules apply, so you may not be able to view the profiles of some guests.

✔ **Wall:** No page on Facebook would be complete without the Wall, a forum for casual discussion. Event guests usually leave well wishes here (for example, *Happy birthday!*) or their regrets if they can't attend.

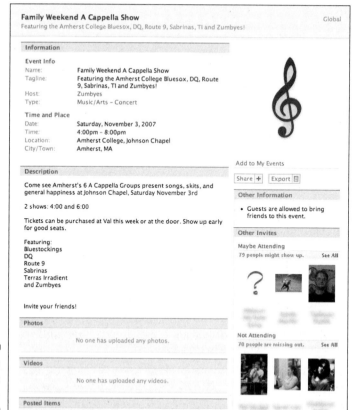

Figure 13-3:
An event's
Home page.

The right column of the event's Home page contains the following:

- ✔ **Event picture:** An event administrator can choose a single picture that best represents his event and display it prominently here.

- ✔ **Action links:** A series of important options kicks off the right column, including Add to My Events (if you aren't on the event guest list), Invite People to Come, and Remove from My Events (if you're on the guest list). Unless you're an event administrator, you have only the option of inviting other people if the event is Open; see the "Creating Your Own Events" section for more information. If you're an event administrator, this section includes additional options to edit the event information, the guest list, or to cancel the event.

- ✔ **Share:** The Share link scattered throughout Facebook allows you to share interesting content quickly with your friends, either by sending it to them in a message or by posting it on your profile. The Share button allows you to share an event link along with a preview containing the event's name, description, and picture.

  If the event is Open, you might want to use the Invite People to Come action link to send an invitation rather than a link. (See the upcoming "Creating Your Own Events" section for more information on Open events.) If the event is Secret, you can't share a link to the event with anyone who isn't a member because the event's privacy settings don't permit it.

- ✔ **Export:** Facebook enables you to export an event in ICS file format. Many popular calendaring programs, such as Microsoft Outlook, import ICS files; therefore, you can add your Facebook events to your regular calendar.

- ✔ **Your RSVP:** Displays whether you're planning to attend the event. Your RSVP can be Attending, Maybe Attending, or Not Attending. Your RSVP can be changed at any time by selecting a new option and choosing RSVP.

- ✔ **Other Information:** Displays other relevant information about the event not important enough to include in the main column, such as whether guests may bring friends. The Other Information box doesn't appear if there's no additional information to display.

- ✔ **Other Invites:** Displays the people on the guest list who might attend, aren't attending, or who haven't responded (Awaiting Reply). The Other Invites section is shown in Figure 13-4.

- ✔ **Event Type:** Displays the type of the event chosen by its administrator. Event types are Open, Closed, or Secret. See the "Creating Your Own Events" section for a description of these types.

- ✔ **Admins:** A list of the people who serve as administrators of the event; therefore, they're in charge of writing the event information and keeping guests up to date. Admins are usually (but not always) the hosts of the event.

Figure 13-4:
The Other
Invites box
shows
everyone on
the guest
list who
hasn't
responded.

Going to the After Party

When you get home from that birthday party or reading club, return to the event page to post any photos or videos you shot. Click the Add link in the photo or video boxes and you're taken to the standard Facebook media selection interface. Note that these features are only available if the event administrator has turned them on. Keep an eye on your News Feed to see when other guests post their photos and videos, which usually happens in one big flurry of activity a day or two after the event. After all, there's nothing more rousing than a video of your reading club.

Finding the Event for You

With more than 100 million people on Facebook, it's no surprise that, at any given time, there are hundreds of events in your area. Facebook gives you a number of tools to help you find the best ways to spend your weekend.

Searching events

If you have an event in mind, the fastest way to find it is to search.

1. **Click within the Search box.**

   The *Search box* is the textbox in the left-hand navigation bar of every Facebook page that sits right above the Applications menu.

2. **Enter the topic of an event you want to find, such as** Dave Matthews Band**, and press Enter to begin your search.**

   The search results contain content from all over Facebook, such as profiles, groups, and events.

3. **Click the Events tab at the top to retrieve only event results.**

To search only events and avoid Step 3, use the Search for Events box at the top of the Events page. The search results are the same in each case. To navigate to the Events page, click the Events link in the Applications menu of the left-hand navigation bar.

If you're having trouble finding the event you're looking for, try refining your search by network.

By default, Facebook displays events that are located within your networks. For instance, if you belong to the Proctor & Gamble workplace network, the Stanford college network, and the San Francisco region network, you see events that match your search phrase from those three networks and the Global network. Additionally, you can look for an event that pertains to your job, school, or region. Filter the search results to just the relevant events by selecting the desired network from the drop-down list next to *within* on the gray bar above the search results. By default, the My Networks option is selected. You may also search events in networks that you don't belong to by choosing Other from the drop-down list and typing the name of a different network.

To filter your search results by date or type:

1. **Click the Show More Filters link next to the gray bar above the search results.**

2. **When the filter sidebar appears on the right, use the Date drop-down list to change the range of events displayed.**

   You can show events occurring on the present day, from now until tomorrow, within the next week, or within the next month.

3. **You can also use the Type drop-down list to filter the list to parties, sporting events, and so forth.**

If the search filters don't help, clear them and return to the original results list by clicking the Hide Filters link, which appears in place of the Show More Filters link on the gray bar at the top.

Browsing events

If you don't have a particular event in mind, browse them at your leisure.

1. **Click the Events link in the Applications menu of the left-hand navigation bar to navigate to the Events page.**

2. **Click the Browse Events link at the top of the page.**

   Facebook displays (by default) a list of events taking place within the next month that belong to your networks and that you have permission to attend, as shown in Figure 13-5.

3. **Use the options on the right sidebar to filter the displayed list by network, date, or type.**

   The sidebar also includes a calendar of the current month; click a day on the calendar to view events occurring on that day.

Figure 13-5: Browse events to find one that suits your fancy.

To browse events that are popular among your friends and networks, see the next section, "Checking out popular events."

Checking out popular events

Face it — nobody wants to go to *That Party*. The one where nobody shows up but you and you're stuck reassuring the host that, "It's probably the weather, because, you know, who wants to go to a party when it's partly cloudy out, anyway?"

Fortunately, Facebook gives you an easy way to see which events are popular among your friends and networks. The Friends' Events tab on the Events page shows you events that your friends are attending soon that you can attend. Your friends didn't manually suggest these events to you; Facebook simply assumes that your friends join events that interest them and automatically pushes those events to you.

If you want a broader look at what's hot among events, click Popular Events at the top of the Events page to view a list of upcoming events that are being attended by many people in your primary network. To view which events are popular in your secondary networks, click the Events section of their Home page. See Chapter 11 for more information about a network's Home page.

Creating Your Own Events

Tired of being a *guest*? Ready to be in charge? Want to host your own event, have complete control over the guest list, and almost single-handedly decide who among us is *in* and *out*? Follow these simple steps:

 1. **Take a cold shower.**

Now that that's out of your system, get down to business — the business of organizing and hosting fun events.

To begin creating an event, do the following steps:

 1. **Click the Events link in the Applications menu of the left-hand navigation bar to navigate to the Events page.**

 2. **Click the Create an Event button at the top right of the page.**

Creating an event entails at least one step: specifying the event's name and other basic information. You have the option of completing two additional steps if you want to specify an event picture or guest list. (If you don't invite anyone to your event but make it public, people can still stumble upon it, although it might be pretty lonely.) Facebook divides the process into three screens — one for each step — and highlights the current step's tab at the top of the page. We discuss each step in depth here. Any property of an event (except for its name) can be edited at any time after its creation, so don't fret too much about getting things just right your first time through.

Step 1: Event Info

The Event Info step asks you for the following information about the event (see Figure 13-6). Some information might not be relevant or desirable for the event you have in mind. However, you must enter the information designated as *required*.

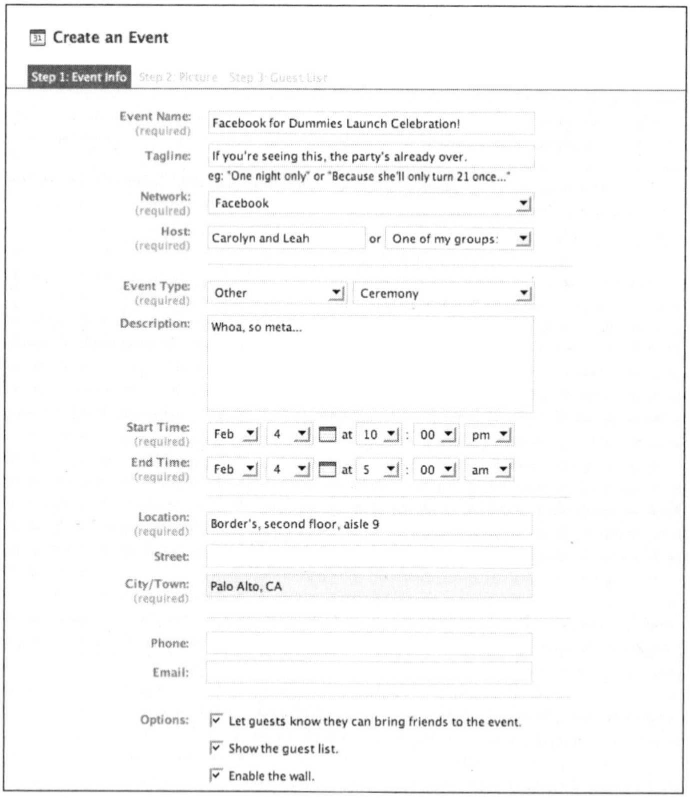

Figure 13-6:
Creating an
event takes
just a few
minutes.

✔ **Event Name (required):** The name of the event you want to create, such as *Jenny's 21st Birthday*.

✔ **Tagline:** A brief slogan for your event, such as *Because she'll only turn 21 once*.

✔ **Network (required):** The network to which the event belongs. Facebook users who belong to the network you choose are able to find your event easily, although you can invite people from other networks to attend. To make the event available to everyone on Facebook, choose Global. Otherwise, choose another network that you belong to. If you aren't a member of any networks, your event is automatically created within the Global network. Regardless of what you choose, access to your event can be restricted further via the Access option outlined below.

✔ **Host (required):** The name of the individual or organization hosting the event. This might just be your name, or it might be something similar to *The Rotary Club*. If you administer any groups, you can choose a group in the drop-down list to host the event. You then have the option to invite your group's members to the event in Step 3. See Chapter 12 for more information on events.

✔ **Event Type (required):** The category of the event, such as *Party* or *Meeting*. After you choose a type, you also need to pick a subtype, such as *Holiday Party* or *Business Meeting*. Facebook members create events for gatherings as small and casual as happy hour or as large and formal as a wedding.

✔ **Description:** A brief overview of the event, such as why you're holding it, what the attire is, and why to come. The description is one of the first things a guest sees when looking at your event and determining whether to attend.

✔ **Start Time / End Time (required):** The anticipated timeframe for your event, including date and time. Click the calendar icon to select a date more quickly.

✔ **Location (required):** The name of the venue where your event is taking place, such as Pete's Pizzaria. Some events are online gatherings, in which case this can be a Web site address.

✔ **Street:** The street address of the location where the event is taking place. If you specify this information, Facebook displays a View Map link that your guests can click to get directions.

✔ **City/Town (required):** The city or town where your event is taking place. While you type in the name, Facebook autocompletes it for your convenience.

✔ **Phone:** A phone number your guests can call when they have questions about the event or to RSVP (if you indicate in the event description that you prefer phone RSVPs). The phone number can be your number or the number of an organization hosting the event.

✔ **Email:** An e-mail address your guests can write to for more information about the event. Remember that your guests can always message you on Facebook, so you might not want to give out your e-mail address.

✔ **Options:** A mixture that controls which sections appear on your event's Home page and, where applicable, which guests can add content to them. We explain all of these sections in the earlier "Anatomy of an Event" section.

- *Let guests know they can bring friends to the event:* Shows the Other Information section that indicates to guests that they can bring other people. Don't have enough chicken for everyone? Holding a party in an 8 x 5 box? You might want to leave this unchecked, or things could get ugly.

- *Show the guest list:* Displays the guest list, which includes everyone invited not just the people who are planning to attend.

- *Enable the Wall:* Shows the Wall section, which is typically used for informal, casual remarks from guests.

- *Enable photos:* Shows the Photos section. If you decide to show it, decide who may add photos to this section. By default, guests of the event may add photos, but you can restrict this to administrators by selecting Only Allow Admins to Upload Photos.

- *Enable videos:* Shows the Videos section. If you decide to show it, decide who may add videos to this section. By default, guests of the event may add photos, but you can restrict this to administrators by selecting Only Allow Admins to Upload Videos.

- *Enable posted items:* Shows the Posted Items section. If you decide to show it, decide who may post items to this section. By default, guests of the event may post items, but you can restrict this to administrators by selecting Only Allow Admins to Post Items.

✔ **Access:** Access to your event may be restricted via one of the following settings:

- *This event is open:* The default setting; allows anyone to view the event's content. Guests can also invite other people to join.

- *This event is closed:* Anyone can view the basic event information, but only guests can see the photos, the Wall, and so forth. People who want to attend must request an invitation, and you or another administrator have to approve or deny these requests.

- *This event is secret:* People can join the event only if you or another administrator invites them. They can't request an invitation because it won't appear in the search results. Therefore, only guests can view the event's description, photos, and so forth. The event's network has little effect here given these additional restrictions.

✔ **Publicize:** Open and Closed events are (by default) listed on their respective network's Home page as well as in relevant search results. If you don't want this exposure, uncheck this box. The event might still appear in Mini-Feed and News Feed stories. The Publicize option isn't relevant or available for Secret events because such events (by their very nature) prevent this exposure.

When you finish filling out the event information, click the Create Event button at the bottom of the screen to create the event and move on to Step 2: Picture. If you left any required fields empty or otherwise made an error, you remain on the first step, and a red box appears at the top explaining how to proceed.

Step 2: Picture

In the earlier section, "Anatomy of an Event," we explain that event administrators can choose a single picture to appear prominently at the top of their event's Home page. If no picture is chosen, the question mark shown in Figure 13-7 displays. To specify a picture, do the following:

Figure 13-7:
If you don't specify a picture for your event, Facebook uses a question mark.

1. **Click the Browse button to open your computer's standard interface for finding a file.**

2. **Navigate to (and select) the picture on your computer that you want to use.**

   The picture you choose must meet the file size and type requirements outlined on the page. If you're not sure whether your desired picture meets the requirements, select the picture and continue with these steps. Facebook notifies you if the picture you choose can't be used.

3. **Check the box to certify that you have the right to distribute the picture (it isn't copyrighted) and that it doesn't violate the Facebook terms of use (it isn't pornographic or otherwise offensive).**

4. **Click Upload Picture.**

If you don't want to choose a picture, click Skip for Now to move on to Step 3: Guest List. Return to this step later to add a picture (or to change it if you do select one now).

Step 3: Guest List

The final step enables you to invite people (in the right column) to attend your event as well as manage its current guests (in the left column). When your event is new, this step is only useful to you for its inviting capabilities.

If you designate your event as Open or Closed, it's not absolutely necessary for you to invite people; they might discover the event on their News Feed, the Search feature, or many other sources. However, if you create a Secret event, these invitations are the only means through which someone can discover and attend your event.

If you decide to invite people to your event, it takes just a few seconds.

1. **To invite your friends who are on Facebook, check the box next to their name in the list at the top of the right column, as shown in Figure 13-8.**

   If you have several friends, type in part of a name in the box above the list to filter the list quickly. When you invite a Facebook member to attend your event, she receives a Facebook request from you. Depending on their notification settings, they might also receive an e-mail from Facebook regarding your invitation. Note that Facebook doesn't send the invitation to your friend as soon as you select her in the list.

Figure 13-8:
Inviting
Facebook
friends to
your event
is as simple
as checking
their names.

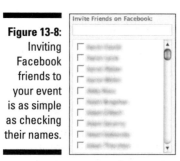

2. **To invite friends who aren't on Facebook to join the event, type their e-mail addresses (separated by commas) into the box in the bottom of the right column and click Add.**

   Can't remember their addresses? No problem. Click the Import E-Mail Addresses link to open a window that enables you to select their addresses from your e-mail address book, assuming Facebook supports your e-mail provider (it supports the most popular ones). This process is very similar to that outlined in Chapter 6. Forgot some folks? Enter more addresses into the box and click Add again.

   The complete list of people you've decided to invite, including Facebook and non-Facebook users, appears in a new list at the top of the left column.

3. **If you accidentally add someone to the list that you don't want to invite, click Remove to delete them from the list.**

4. **(Optional) To include a message with your invitation, type it in the box below the invitee list.**

   This step adds a personal touch and makes your invitation more persuasive.

5. **To send the invitations to the people on the list, click Send Invitations.**

   Forgot some people? You can repeat these steps at any time.

6. **When you're done, click Finish to complete the event creation process; click View to view your new event's Home page.**

Managing your event

You can do a number of things when you finish creating your event and people start to join. Many of these steps appear as action links under the picture on your event's Home page. These actions are visible and available only to you and other administrators. This section outlines the additional power you wield as an event administrator.

Messaging your event's guests

Rain delay? Halloween canceled? Keep your guests up to date about the event by sending them a Facebook message. These messages appear in your guests' Facebook Inbox, and depending on their notification settings, they might also receive an e-mail notification.

To send a message to guests, click the Message All Guests action link under the picture in the right column of your event's Home page. You're taken to the standard Compose Message form with one addition: an Attendees drop-down list that allows you to indicate which guest list segment you want to message (everyone, those who are attending, maybe attending, or haven't responded). Complete the rest of the process as if you were sending a message to a single friend. (If you need help with that process, see Chapter 10.)

Managing your event's guest list

After guests RSVP to your event, use the event guest list to remove (even permanently ban) undesirable guests, promote your most trusted guests to administrators, or demote your existing administrators (if any) to regular guests.

1. **Click the Edit Guest List link under the picture in the right column of your event's Home page.**

   The Guest List page is shown in Figure 13-9.

Figure 13-9: The Guest List page is your one-stop shop for keeping tabs on your current guests and inviting more.

2. **Use the link to the right of each guest name that corresponds to the action you want to take.** For instance, to make a member an administrator, click the Make Admin link. As an administrator, the member will have the same privileges discussed in this chapter as you do for this particular event.

   If you choose to remove a guest from your event, you can also ban him permanently so he may not rejoin the event in the future. Banning someone is useful if the person is posting offensive content or otherwise stirring trouble. Click Remove next to the guest's name and then check the Ban Permanently box in the confirmation window that appears.

Chapter 14

Facebook on the Go

*T*hroughout this book, we show you how Facebook enriches relationships and facilitates human interaction. Nevertheless, what can Facebook do to enrich your relationships while you're *not* sitting in front of a computer? Life is full of beach weekends, road trips, city evenings, movie nights, dinner parties, and so on. During these times, as long as you have a mobile phone, Facebook still provides you a ton of value.

We don't propose that you ignore a group of people you're actively spending time with to play with Facebook on the phone (unless of course you *want* to ignore them). Moreover, we don't think you should tune out in class or in a meeting to Poke your friends. We do suggest that knowing the ins and outs of Facebook Mobile actually enriches each particular experience you have — while you're having it. With Facebook Mobile, you can show off your kids' new photos to your friends, or broadcast where you're having drinks, in case any of your friends are in the neighborhood and want to drop by.

Facebook Mobile serves another function — making your life easier. Sometimes you need *something*, say, a phone number, an address, the start time of an event. Maybe you're heading out to have dinner with your friend and her boyfriend whose name you can't, for the life of you, remember. Perhaps you hit it off with someone new and would like to find out whether she's romantically available before committing yourself to an awkward conversation about exchanging phone numbers. (Just a heads up: This conversation could be awkward even *if* you find that person is single. Facebook can do a lot for you but not everything.)

In this chapter, we assume that you have a mobile phone and know how to use its features. If you don't have a phone, you might consider buying one after reading this chapter; this stuff is way cool. Mobile Texts simply requires a phone and an accompanying plan that enables you to send text messages. Facebook Mobile Web requires a mobile data plan (that is, access to the Internet on your phone).

Mobile Texts

You're out and about and realize you need the phone number of someone who isn't stored in your phone. What do you do? Call a mutual friend? What if they don't answer? 1-411? What if 15 Robert Johnson's live in your city? For this scenario and several others, you send an *SMS*, or text message, to 32665 (FBOOK) containing a code word that tells Facebook what kind of information you're trying to access. For example, the word *Cell* informs Facebook that you're trying to access a cell phone number. The results of your inquiry are sent to your phone via SMS.

To follow along with this section, head to the Mobile Tester:

1. **Click Help in the bottom right of the Frame.**

2. **On the Help Topics page that appears, click Mobile under Applications by Facebook.**

3. **Scroll down to Mobile Texts and then click the Mobile Tester link.**

Alternatively, you can type **http://www.facebook.com/mobile/?texts** into your browser. Either way, the tester appears, as shown in Figure 14-1.

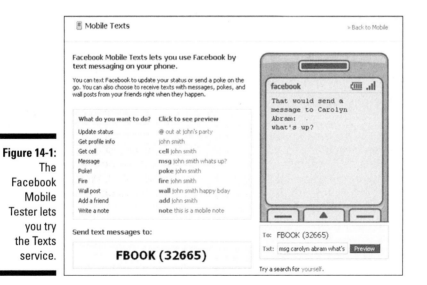

Figure 14-1: The Facebook Mobile Tester lets you try the Texts service.

The tester allows you to try various commands and see the result as if it were from a real phone. Mobile Tester is handy for two reasons: You can try commands without contacting your friends, and it's free. Typing **Poke Carolyn Abram** into the tester tells you that doing so from a mobile phone would actually Poke Carolyn, but doing so from the tester won't. The Mobile Text tester is free — Facebook Mobile never charges you for using any feature, although your mobile plan might charge you per text message. Here's the lowdown on what you see in Figure 14-1:

- **Update your status** by typing @ in the body of the SMS followed by whatever you want your status to be. For example, **@ on a ski lift** changes your status to *<Your Name> is on a ski lift*. You receive a text message from Facebook stating that your status has been updated.

- **Get Profile information** for a particular friend by sending the name of the person you're looking for. If Facebook finds an exact first and last name match, you receive the profile information that person has given you permission to see. For example, if Leah sends an SMS to 32665 containing **Carolyn Abram**, within seconds she receives a text from Facebook containing Carolyn's mobile phone number, e-mail address, status (she's at a party right now), relationship status, and networks.

  If you enter a name for which Facebook finds more than one match, such as **Carolyn**, you receive a text message asking, *Which Carolyn?* with a list of the four most-likely matches among your Friends and then your networks. Each result is accompanied by a number. (For Leah, Carolyn Abram is first.) When you see the result you're looking for in the list, reply to that text message with the number associated with the matching result. Facebook then sends you the profile information. If you don't see a match, reply with *n* to see the next set of results.

- **Get someone's cell phone number** by sending a text containing **Cell** followed by the name of the person whose number you're after. For example, **Cell Carolyn Abram** returns Carolyn's cell phone number (as long as you have access to it via her profile). This time though, if multiple matches appear for the name you entered, Facebook sends you the first four matches and their numbers (if they're listed and visible to you). Again, if the name you're looking for isn't in the list, simply reply with *n* for more results.

- **Message someone's** Facebook Inbox by typing **Msg** followed by the first and last name of the person you'd like to message and the body of the message. For example, Carolyn could send a text to 32665 that reads, **Msg Leah Pearlman Stop writing and come to this party**. Leah immediately receives the message in her Inbox.

✓ **Poke someone** by texting **Poke** followed by the person you'd like to Poke. If Carolyn sends a text message containing **Poke Leah Pearlman**, Leah is immediately poked. Just as with profile information, if Facebook finds multiple matches for people you might be trying to Poke, you receive a text message containing a list and a request that you clarify whom you're trying to Poke. Reply with the number associated with the right name.

✓ **Fire** is a feature of Facebook available only through Facebook Text. Send **Fire *<friend's first & last name>*** to 32665. Just beneath your friend's profile picture, everyone sees that you Fired your friend. You'd probably better try this out to see what that means. Think of Fire as the more aggressive Poke, whatever Poke means.

✓ **Post on a friend's Wall** by writing **Wall** followed by your friend's first and last name and the contents of the post. Leah could text **Wall Carolyn Abram I'll come to the party after writing about Facebook Mobile** to let Carolyn and everyone who looks at Carolyn's Wall know why she is late to the party.

✓ **Add a new Facebook friend** by sending **Add** and the person's name. While Carolyn waits for Leah to come to the party, she might make a new friend, named Blake Ross, say. Carolyn can text **Add Blake Ross**. She might have to choose from multiple Blake Ross's, but then the request is automatically sent. Blake can confirm when he's back at his computer. Using your phone to immediately *friend* a person you meet is less formal than exchanging business cards, less awkward (and more reliable) than exchanging phone numbers, and gives you more flexibility later for how you want to get in touch. However, remember that by *friending* someone, you give away access to your profile, so think twice before you Add.

✓ **Write a note** by texting **Note** followed by the contents of a note to 32665. We cover why Mobile Notes are awesome in the "Mobile uploads" section.

✓ **Check a friend's status** by texting **stat** and the person's full name to 32665. When Leah hasn't shown up some hours later, Carolyn can text **Stat Leah Pearlman** to receive a text message with Leah's status, something like, *Leah is about to put off work and put on party shoes*. See the most recent status updates from your friends by simply texting **stat** without specifying a name.

In Chapter 2, we recommend that you enter your mobile phone number to confirm your account, so you might already be set up to use Mobile Texts. If not, or to double-check, click Account in the upper right of the Frame, and select the Mobile tab. If you see your number listed, you're good to go. If not, enter your phone number to receive a confirmation code from Facebook. Enter the code into this Mobile Settings page, and you're all set up. Following this step automatically adds the Mobile application to your profile.

Mobile Texts is currently available only in the United States and Canada. Mobile Texts works on any mobile device as long as it can send and receive text messages. However, the only carriers that support Mobile Texts in the United States are Boost, Cingular, Nextel, Sprint, Virgin USA, and Verizon. Bell Mobility, Aliant, Solo, Fido, Rogers, TELUS, Virgin Mobile Canada, SaskTel, and MTS are supported in Canada. Facebook never charges you for any text messages sent but your carrier might — check your plan to know what to expect on your bill.

The Mobile Application

To participate in a number of the features described in this section, you must have added the Facebook Mobile application to your profile. You might have done this while you were setting up your account; if *Mobile* is listed under the Applications menu, skip ahead to the "Mobile notifications" section. If *Mobile* isn't there, follow these steps to get set up:

1. **Click the Edit link next to the Applications menu.**

2. **Click Browse More Applications at the top of the page.**

3. **Select the By Facebook tab on the right, scroll to Mobile, and then click Mobile.**

4. **Click Add Application in the upper right.**

5. **Click Add Mobile to confirm you want this application added to your profile.**

6. **To access the features of Facebook Mobile, click Mobile in the Applications menu of the left-hand navigation bar.**

The Mobile application provides a reliable way to receive notifications about activity on Facebook when you're not at your computer. The Mobile application also enables you to add content to Facebook from wherever you are. When you're at the computer, the Mobile application's Home page gives a filtered view of your friends' mobile content; some folks love the authenticity of mobile content because it's often less edited or censored than other types of information on Facebook.

Mobile notifications

An old wives' tale claims that when you feel your ears burn, someone is thinking about you. (Maybe it just means to back away from the campfire.) Here's a slight modification: Someone, somewhere, is thinking about you when your phone starts vibrating. Turning on Facebook Mobile Texts notifies you via SMS when someone Pokes you, sends you a Facebook message, comments on your photos and notes, writes on your Wall, or requests to be your friend.

To activate Facebook Mobile Texts, click Mobile in the Applications menu, click Edit Mobile settings, and then select Texts Are On (shown in Figure 14-2).

The Mobile Texts page offers a number of granular settings:

✔ You opt-in to most of the Mobile Text notifications. For messages and Pokes, you specify whether to receive notifications about all of them or just those from your friends.

✔ You can specify what time you prefer to receive Text Notifications, so that if someone Pokes you at 2 a.m., you don't have to wake up for it. (Maybe you *only* want to know who's trying to Poke you at 2 a.m. No judgment here.)

✔ If you have a mobile plan for which you're charged per text message (and you're exceedingly popular), use the settings that limit the number of messages Facebook sends you per day.

✔ You can select whether to receive confirmations about the success of the Pokes, messages, or Wall posts that you send from your mobile phone.

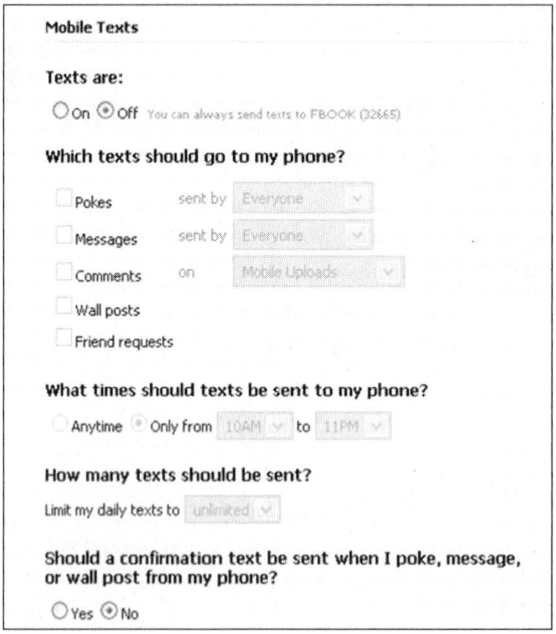

Figure 14-2:
Set up your preferences for receiving notifications on your mobile phone.

Mobile Texts

Texts are:

○ On ⦿ Off You can always send texts to FBOOK (32665)

Which texts should go to my phone?

☐ Pokes   sent by Everyone ∨

☐ Messages   sent by Everyone ∨

☐ Comments   on   Mobile Uploads ∨

☐ Wall posts

☐ Friend requests

What times should texts be sent to my phone?

○ Anytime ⦿ Only from 10AM ∨ to 11PM ∨

How many texts should be sent?

Limit my daily texts to unlimited ∨

Should a confirmation text be sent when I poke, message, or wall post from my phone?

○ Yes ⦿ No

From this page, you can also jump into your Account settings, change your mobile phone number, or add another number to your account.

Additionally, you can subscribe to receiving text notifications when particular friends change their status or upload mobile content. To subscribe to mobile uploads, opt-in to receive Mobile Texts (as described in the previous bullets) and then click Mobile from the Applications menu. At the bottom of the page, you see a text box to enter friends' names whose mobile uploads you'd like to be notified about. To subscribe to friends' statuses, navigate to your Home page and then click See All next to Status Updates on the right. Halfway down on the Status Updates page on the right you see a box under Mobile Status Updates.

> ▣» **Mobile Status Updates:**
>
> Whose status updates should go to my phone?
>
> | |
>
> Carolyn Abram remove
> Holly Ann Calloway remove
>
> Update status from your phone.
> Text "@" followed by your message to
> FBOOK (32665).

Enter friends' names here whose status you want to stay on top of. ***Note:*** If you subscribe to the status of someone who doesn't spell very well, you might receive several texts as they try to get their status just right.

Mobile uploads

In this section, we show you how to spend only one magical moment to capture, save, and publish the real magical moments in life.

Mobile Photos

Three types of people can be found at social events. The scrapbookers who always remember to bring their fancy-schmancy camera to every gathering. (You know who they are because they tell you to "Smile!" a lot or sometimes say "Act natural.") The person who never intends to take photos, but who, when the birthday girl blows out her candles, the host spills wine on himself, or someone arrives wearing a hilarious, slogan tee-shirt, is ready with the low-quality mobile phone camera. (Hey, it captures the moment, right?) And the person who doesn't take photos even though their phone has a camera because, "What good is a picture on a phone?" (Where do you go from there?)

For the scrapbookers of the world, we recommend Facebook Photos. After the social gathering, plug your camera into a regular computer, weed out the embarrassing photos, and upload the rest to a photo album. However, if you're the second or third type of person, we recommend you check out Mobile Photos:

1. **Make sure you have a phone with a camera and you know how to use it to take a picture.**

   If you're unsure, check your phone's instruction manual, or ask just about any teenager.

2. **Wait for something hilarious to happen and take a picture of it.**

3. **Send an *MMS*, which is an SMS with a picture attached, to** mobile@ facebook.com.

   Check your phone's manual to find out how to send an MMS. The subject of the message is the caption for your photo.

4. **(Optional) To make any edits or changes to your mobile uploads, go to your photo albums and click the Mobile Uploads album, which is where your phone's photos are located.**

5. **Make any changes to your mobile photos here, just as you do with any photos you upload to Facebook; see Chapter 7 for details.**

The front page of the Mobile application is a stream of your friends' mobile uploads. Just click Mobile from the Application menu to see your friends' recent mobile uploads.

Mobile Notes

If you have the Notes application added to your profile, write a note on the go. Simply follow the steps for sending photos via your mobile phone and upload your note to Facebook immediately by either sending an SMS to notes@facebook.com with the body of the MSS containing the text of the note or to mobile@facebook.com.

The best Mobile Notes are often written when someone finds himself trapped in some interesting situation with nothing but a mobile phone. We've seen several Mobile Notes written when someone is locked out of their house, for example. Another popular Mobile Note comes from someone in a long line, such as one for a new Harry Potter book, the latest Xbox release, or the next hot iToy from Apple. Mobile Notes also come from airports, runways, and sports games — even dentist, doctor, and hospital waiting rooms.

Mobile Videos

If you have Facebook Videos added to your profile and a video-capable phone, follow Steps 1 through 3 in the Mobile Photos section to upload videos. Because you send photos and videos to mobile@facebook.com, Facebook figures out where it belongs. View, edit, or delete your videos with the Videos application. (See Chapter 8.)

On the Phonebook tab of the Mobile application — that you access by selecting Mobile from the Applications menu — you see a list of your friends and their mobile phone numbers. This page demonstrates the value of adding your phone number to your Facebook Profile (provided you select privacy settings you're comfortable with). Consider how valuable this page becomes when you lose or switch your mobile phone.

Is That Facebook Mobile Web in Your Pocket . . . ?

Have you ever noticed how some things are smaller than other things? Bunnies are smaller than elephants; toy cars are smaller than real cars. How about the fact that your mobile phone is much smaller than your computer? If you haven't noticed *that,* then you clearly haven't tried to access the Web on your phone.

Viewing a Web page from your phone can be extremely difficult because the information that is normally spread across the width of a monitor must be packed into one tiny column on your phone. www.facebook.com is no exception to this, which is why the very first tip in this section is this: Never go to www.facebook.com on your mobile phone. You'll regret it. ***Note:*** iPhone users are the only exception to this rule.

But fear not, you still have a way to carry almost all the joys of Facebook right in your purse or pocket. On your mobile phone, open your browser application and navigate to m.facebook.com — a completely new window in Facebook designed specifically to work on a teeny-tiny screen.

The first time you arrive at m.facebook.com, you're asked to log in. After that, you never (or rarely) have to re-enter your login information unless you explicitly select Logout from your session, so make sure you trust anyone you lend your phone to.

If you plan to use the Facebook Mobile Web site frequently, we recommend that you have an unlimited Data plan that allows you to spend as much time on the mobile Web as you like for a fixed rate. The Facebook Mobile Web site is nearly as comprehensive and rich as the computer version. You could spend hours there and, if you're paying per minute, your life savings. Currently, Facebook Mobile Web is supported in the United States for people using Boost, Cingular, Nextel, Sprint, and Virgin USA. Bell Mobility, Aliant, Fido, Solo, Rodgers, Telus, saskTel, and MTS support Facebook Mobile Web in Canada. Facebook Mobile Web works with many other carriers besides these, but Facebook makes no guarantee about the quality of your experience if you use a different carrier.

Mobile Home

After you log in, you see the mobile version of the Facebook Home page. While the design of the mobile site is somewhat based on the design of the regular Web site, it has some significant differences. Some of the differences exist simply because of less space; the mobile site must cut to the chase while allowing you to get more information on a particular topic. For example, the mobile Home page shows only three News Feed stories rather than 25. You can get more stories if you want them, but you'll damage your thumb if you have to scroll through 25 News Feed stories to get to any of the links at the bottom.

The other differences arise because people using Facebook on a mobile phone often have different needs than those at a computer. For example, one of the first pieces of information you find on your friends' profiles is their phone number (if they have it listed), because if you're looking up someone on a mobile phone, you might be trying to contact them by phone.

To follow along with this section, explore the Facebook Mobile Web free of charge by entering **http://www.facebook.com/mobile/?web** into your browser. You can also navigate there by following these steps:

1. **Click Help at the bottom right of the Frame.**

2. **On the Help Topics page, click Mobile under Applications by Facebook.**

3. **Click Facebook Mobile Web under Mobile Web.**

Either way, the Mobile Web page appears, as shown in Figure 14-3. By default, the preview for the mobile Home page appears in the mobile phone graphic on the right. Click any of the other links (Profile, Friends, Inbox, and Photos) to see a preview of those pages. In this section, we detail what you see on the mobile Home page; we cover the other pages in the following sections.

Figure 14-3:
Explore
Facebook
Mobile Web
from the
comfort
of your
computer.

Currently, Facebook Mobile Web is supported in the United States for people using Boost, Cingular, Nextel, Sprint, and Virgin USA. Bell Mobility, Aliant, Fido, Solo, Rodgers, Telus, saskTel, and MTS support Facebook Mobile Web in Canada. Facebook Mobile Web works with many other carriers besides this, but Facebook makes no guarantee about the quality of your experience if you use a different carrier.

Scan this list for a tour of the mobile Home page:

- **New Messages:** When you reach the mobile site, you find whether you have any unread messages. The name of the sender links to the sender's profile, so be careful to select the word *Read* if you want to jump straight to the message.

- **Status Updates:** When you use Facebook from your mobile phone, you're probably not sitting at your home office, workplace, or school. You might be at a football game, out on the town, or waiting in line for a roller coaster. Facebook makes it super easy to spread the news the moment you're doing something that you want people to know or when you want people to meet you:

  - *Your Status:* Shows you what you're status is set to. If your status isn't set, you'll be encouraged to set it.

  - *Update Your Status:* Where you enter your status using the letter keys on your phone. When you're happy with what you've entered, select Update. If you don't want a status, select Clear.

- *Friends' Statuses:* The three most recent statuses set by your friends. To see more than this, select See All. To see a particular friend's status, we recommend going straight to their profile, which we show you how to do in a minute.

✔ **Search:** The search box on the mobile site is designed to help you find people. When you enter text, the search results show your friends, the people in your network, and everyone else — in that order. There's no full-blown search or browse functionality from your mobile phone, just the search box, which is usually good enough.

✔ **Upcoming Events:** If you've received (and have not declined) invitations to events that are in the next three days, you see the primary information here. If you have no events in the next three days, this section won't appear on the mobile site. To see your events, you have to get to them in another way, which we talk about later.

  - *Name of the Event:* Takes you to more information about the event.

  - *Location:* An extremely handy feature when you can't remember the address of where you're going.

  - *RSVP Status:* This makes it easy for you to change your mind at the last minute.

  - *Time:* The start time helps you avoid arriving too early or too late, which is good, because that's embarrassing. The end time helps you plan your after-party or arrange for a ride home.

  - *See All:* Shows your upcoming and past events.

✔ **New Wall Posts:** If anyone has written on your Wall recently, you can read up to three posts here. Select See All to see the rest of the comments on your Wall or to write on your Wall should you have something nice to say about yourself. The full text of the Wall post appears here, so you don't need to navigate to your profile. The name of the friend who wrote the Wall post is linked to their profile.

✔ **Mobile News Feed:** Shows you the three most recent stories that you would see on your computer. To save space, the stories have a little less information than the stories you're used to. Enter into the story to get more information about it. Select See All at the bottom of the Mobile News Feed section to see all the stories your heart desires and links to filter the stories by type. Certain types of stories don't appear on News Feed just yet because the information they link to can't be rendered (well) on a mobile phone.

✔ **On the Go:** Gives you quick access to the most popular ways people pass their time on a mobile phone.

  - *Photos of Friends:* Takes you to a random photo tagged with at least one of your friends. You can keep selecting Next Photo as long as it holds your attention. You can select My Photos to view your photos.

- *Friends' Notes:* Shows you the five most recent notes written by your friends. If any images are associated with those notes, select the Image link to see the photo. Links at the bottom take you to more notes. You can also select Write a Note, My Notes, My Friends Notes, or Notes about You.

- *Write a Note:* Takes you to a simple form for writing a mobile note. All you have to do is fill out the title and body. Don't worry about getting flashy; any note written from your mobile phone is flagged with a small mobile icon, so people will understand if its super short or you have some typos.

- *Groups:* Shows you the five groups you belong to that were most recently updated. However, you can navigate through all your groups. Select any group name to get more details about the particular group.

- *Inbox:* Where you see all the messages people have sent you. You can read entire threads and take action on a particular thread, including Reply, Mark as Read/Unread, and Delete. Navigate to Sent messages by scrolling to the bottom of the page.

✔ **Navigations Links:** The primary navigation links are at the bottom of every mobile page. The first four links are the same as the links on the blue bar at the top of the regular site. You won't see a Networks link because there isn't a version of the Networks page for the mobile phone. However, what the mobile site lacks in Networks, it makes up for with Contacts; we describe that in a moment.

✔ **Search:** Search is listed again at the bottom because people often use the mobile site to hop around among friends, so it's nice to be able to do that without scrolling all the way to the top to find the box.

✔ **Bottom Links:** Much like the bottom links on the regular site; a catchall of other stuff.

- *Settings:* Allows you to opt-in to applications that you'd like to use on your mobile phone. This list contains every application you've added to your profile. Not all of these applications have a mobile component, but if you check the box next to an application, you'll get access to that application on your phone if that application adds mobile support.

- *Logout:* The only way to end your mobile session. We recommend that you log out regularly if anyone else has access to your phone.

- *Help:* A misnomer on the mobile site — it's actually more like an About page that explains the value of the Facebook Mobile Web. We will recommend that Facebook update this page to make it actually *help*ful.

Navigation hot keys

You might be wondering why the primary navigation links on the mobile site are all the way at the bottom of each page. Maybe you're not wondering, but we explain anyway. If the links lived at the top, you'd have to scroll past them every time you landed on a page. Say, you select Friends' Notes, it'd be silly to show the navigation links first when it's clear you're trying to read a note. Another option could be to put the navigation links at the bottom of pages like Friends' Notes and at the top of the Home page, but this kind of inconsistency doesn't help with navigation either.

To solve the problem, each navigation link at the bottom has a *hot key,* which is denoted by the number before the link. Pressing the following numbers while you're on the mobile Home page jumps you to that link:

- ✔ **0 Home**
- ✔ **1 Profile**
- ✔ **2 Friends**
- ✔ **3 Inbox**
- ✔ **4 Contacts**

If you forget what the hot keys are, scroll down; most mobile browsers also have a hot key that takes you straight to the bottom (and top) of the mobile Web page. Check your phone's manual to find your phone's particular hot key.

Mobile Profile preview

Profiles on the Facebook Mobile Web are designed differently than profiles on the regular site. As we mention in the previous section, a lot of information from specific applications might be absent from your profile. Moreover, the structure is ordered such that the information you're after is closest to the top. When you arrive at any mobile profile, you see the most usable and actionable subset of the available information. A See Full Profile link at the bottom gives you access to the rest.

Access to information on mobile profiles is the same as on the regular site — when you look at your profile on the mobile site, you see your information, but that doesn't mean everyone has access to it. They have access only to what you specify via the privacy settings on the regular site.

- ✔ **Status:** At the top of a person's profile after their name, you see their status and the last time it was updated. When you see that your friend is *at Starbucks, come join,* the time stamp is helpful for knowing whether she updated it one minute ago or four days ago.

- ✔ **Profile Picture:** Next, you see the current profile picture. Selecting it shows you other photos used as profile pictures in the past.

✔ **Contact Information:** Located close to the top of the profile, because when you look someone up on a mobile phone, you're often after a number or address. If the person has their phone number listed here, you can select it to start the call.

✔ **Networks & Basic Information:** Have you ever been talking with friends when someone mentions a familiar name for which you can't quite recall the face? Or maybe someone suggests someone you should try to meet? This is a great time for Facebook Mobile Web. For these scenarios, it's handy that the networks and basic information are right on the abbreviated version of the profile. It helps you quickly identify key facts about the person you're looking at. These sections are identical to what appears on the normal site.

✔ **See Full Profile:** Where you access more information about a person, including their personal information and work information.

✔ **Wall:** The next time you're out and see something that reminds you of someone, rather than trying to remember it until you see them, go to their mobile profile and write it on their Wall. You see the three most recent Wall posts. To see more, select the Wall link from the set of action links that appear underneath the Wall. This is both interesting information and an easy way to ensure your Wall post appears as you meant. You can't delete Wall posts from a mobile phone, so have a nearby friend check your spelling before you post.

✔ **Photos, Albums, and Notes:** Beneath the main contents of the profile, you can jump into a user's applications. Photos shows pictures of the person whose profile you're looking at. Albums takes you to photos they've taken, and Notes takes you to notes they've written.

✔ **Message and Poke:** These are also at the bottom of the profile for quick *thinking of you* (or whatever your Poke means) communications. Your friend is guaranteed to get your message if they have Facebook Mobile Notifications set up, which we talk about earlier in this chapter.

Mobile Friends list

The Friends link takes you to a list of your friends with the most recently updated statuses. The reason for this default is that when you're out (and on your mobile phone), it's nice to see where everyone else is out and about. To view friends by how recently they've updated their profile (like the regular site), select Recently Updated at the bottom of the page. Selecting All Friends shows you an alphabetical list of your friends' names, which you can use to navigate to their profiles. From either of these views, you can message or Poke your friends without navigating to their profile.

Mobile Inbox

The mobile Inbox functions the same as the Inbox on the regular site, but you access it in a compacted view. In the mobile Inbox, your messages are sorted by the time the last message on a thread was sent. Each thread includes the subject, the sender's name, the time the last message was sent, a snippet of the message, and quick links to Reply, Mark as Read/Unread, or Delete. The Mark as Unread link is particularly handy because often times you read a message on your mobile phone, but don't have time or energy to type out a response. Marking it as Unread reminds you to respond when you return to your computer.

One major design difference between the Inbox on your phone and the Inbox on your computer: When you enter into the mobile thread, the newest message is at the top with the Reply box beneath it. You can scroll down to read the previous messages in the thread. In the regular Inbox, the order is flipped because it generally makes sense to read a conversation from the top of the page to the bottom. When you open a thread on the regular Inbox, the oldest message is at the top of the page, but the page automatically scrolls down to the newest message. This scrolling behavior isn't possible on a mobile phone, so the order of the messages is reversed.

On the Facebook site, the Inbox contains a Notifications tab. See Chapter 10 for more details on Notifications. We bring it up here to point out that Notifications aren't available on the Facebook Mobile Web because the content they point to isn't always available. Also, your Sent messages appear as a separate tab in the regular Inbox. In the mobile Inbox, you access your Sent messages by scrolling to the bottom of the Inbox and selecting the Sent link.

Mobile contacts

The Mobile contacts give you an easy way to access your friends' contact information, which is a popular task one is often trying to complete on their mobile phone. The contacts page shows a list of all your friends in alphabetical order by last name. For each name, you'll see that person's e-mail address and phone number (if they have listed those on their profiles). All three — name, number, and e-mail address — are hyperlinked so that if you click the name, you navigate to that person's profile, if you click the number you initiate a call, and if you select the e-mail address, an e-mail compose window opens with a prepopulated To: line. A quick alphabetical nav at the top allows you to jump to any section of your contact list; clicking C, for example, will take you to all friends whose last names begin with C.

Part IV
It's Not Personal: It's Business

The 5th Wave   By Rich Tennant

"That's the problem—on Facebook, everyone knows you're a dog."

In this part . . .

Businesses, like people, derive tremendous value from representing themselves online and connecting with people, specifically customers. In this part, you discover three unique ways in which your business can use Facebook to inform, connect, and engage your customers and grow your business as a result:

- ✔ **Facebook Pages** enable your business to have a free presence on the site to interact with your customers in a similar (but different) way that people connect with one another.

- ✔ **Social Ads** allow you to spread your business's message in a relevant, compelling, and effective way.

- ✔ **Facebook Platform** opens completely new types of business opportunities for companies looking to integrate and leverage the existing social connections on Facebook.

Chapter 15

Leveraging Facebook for Business

In This Chapter

▶ Discovering the major role Facebook plays for businesses

▶ Integrating with the Facebook Platform to grow and strengthen your business

▶ Connecting with your clientele

▶ Fueling success with Facebook Advertising

*W*hat do you do for a living? Are people important to your work? Does your livelihood *depend* on people appreciating your work so much that they tell all of their friends? Maybe you want them to tell a particular set of friends — say, their female, younger, or married friends; or their athletic, politically-minded, or Californian friends.

Here's another question for you: Could your business or craft benefit from an online presence? If you're selling something that can be delivered electronically or by mail, if your business exists at a location you want people to find, or if you have a message you need people to hear, the answer is yes.

If your business can, in any way, benefit from people, engagement, and the spread of information, it can benefit from Facebook. In the first section of this chapter, we explain why Facebook is uniquely positioned to help any business succeed. The rest of this chapter highlights three distinct yet related ways that different types of businesses leverage Facebook. The other chapters in this part detail each of these Facebook business strategies.

Even if you're not looking to use Facebook for business or promotion, read on. Understanding the roles these entities play on Facebook is valuable from a consumer perspective in the same way that it's useful to be able to tell a newspaper article from an advertisement.

In the very beginning of this book, we defined *social graph* — all people, their connections with one another, and the information that spreads between them. Because the social graph on Facebook enables each individual to efficiently connect and communicate with the people they know, the interactions between people become easier, richer, and more prevalent. By helping all people in this manner, information flows more and more efficiently while the barriers are reduced and the friction diminished. Because businesses are all about getting the word out about their products, art, or services, they have a lot to gain by plugging into a system with a vast and fast flow of information.

Facebook Pages, the Facebook Advertising Network, and the Facebook Platform are three distinct ways that Facebook enables businesses to leverage the power of the social graph. Read on to find out how.

Facebook Pages

Take a minute to think about someone in your life you like. Someone you like *a lot*.

Do you have a little smile on your face or a tingle in your chest? Now think about your favorite band, singer, or musician. Similar smile and feeling? Now think about a favorite song, movie, or book. Think about *your* coffee shop, brunch spot, or restaurant — you know, the one with the cozy atmosphere, friendly servers and desserts to die for. Think about your most comfortable shoes, your dream car, or the delicious cereal you eat any time of day, breakfast-food-be-damned. Who's your favorite author, the nonprofit you believe in, and the political figure you count on?

People have physical and emotional relationships with products, celebrities, and businesses as well as with other people. A social graph that doesn't capture those relationships would be incomplete. However, your relationship with a business, brand, or celebrity isn't the same as the relationship you have with your neighbor, co-worker, or cousin. The difference lies primarily in how you think about each other. Although you might worship Madonna, pray for Prada, or iDolize your iPod, what do the people behind these entities feel toward you? Individually, probably nothing. Darn. However, as a member of their fan base or clientele, maintaining a healthy relationship with you is crucial. Yay!

Facebook Pages are designed to meet this bidirectional goal of enabling individuals to connect directly with the bands, brands, and businesses they care about, while enabling the people behind those efforts to engage and recruit loyal supporters.

If you're interested in representing your business within Facebook, the following steps get you started:

1. **Be the appointed representative of some business, band, brand, product, or celebrity.**

   It's okay if Justin Timberlake doesn't update his page, but whoever does must be the authorized spokesperson for JT.

2. **Set up your free Page.**

   Click Advertisers at the bottom of Facebook, click the Get Started button beneath Facebook Ads, and follow the setup flow. The name you select should be *the exact name* of your band, product, or business in the same way that your name on Facebook is your real name.

   A Page isn't the same as a user account. You must create a user account to manage pages on Facebook. If you don't have one, you're led through the creation of one in this flow. (Check out Chapter 16 for more about Facebook Pages.)

3. **Customize your Page.**

   Based on the category you select for your business, your page is pre-loaded with a set of default applications. For example, a page in the Band category has a music player and discography application. A page in the Restaurant category has a menu application and hours of operation. Similar to customizing your user profile, you add and remove applications to your page.

4. **Publicize your Page.**

   Initially, after you create a page, you have to help a few people find it. Tell your friends and loyal patrons, e-mail the customers who've given you their e-mail addresses, or stick a Find Us on Facebook sign on your Web page or store window. When anyone lands on your page, they have the option to Become a Fan of *<your business>*, which means that your business is linked from their profile. Additionally, you can message fans en masse, and when you update your profile, they might read about it in their News Feeds. *Note:* Except through paid advertising, businesses can't use Facebook to ask Facebook users directly to become fans of their pages. (They can on other sites, such as MySpace.) This restriction protects the user from unwanted solicitations.

5. **Engage.**

   After recruiting some fans, the best way to grow is to provide a lot of content on your page, such as new photos, videos, and blog posts; or host events, offer coupons, and run contents. When fans of your page engage with it, their friends see News Feed stories that read, "So-and-so just reviewed *<Your business's>* new product." Because these stories serve as social endorsements, there's a good chance that your clients' friends or fans will check out your business's page, too. Engage *those* people, and even more News Feed stories will be generated, giving your business more free promotion.

If your curiosity is piqued, Chapter 16 details the *who, what, how,* and sometimes *why* of Facebook Pages.

Social Ads

Today, advertising has a well-deserved bad rap. While we go about our days driving down highways, watching TV shows, and cruising down the supermarket aisle, we're constantly bombarded with ads. For every ad that features a product we might care about, a hundred others feature something totally irrelevant to us. It's no wonder many people feel like shutting their eyes, plugging their ears, and singing, "LA, LA, LA, I can't hear you!" in the face of advertising. Unfortunately, the louder folks la-la-la, the louder the advertisers turn up their jingle, brighten their colors, and increase their invasiveness.

If we lived in an almost-perfect world, we would see advertising that is only informative, enticing, and above all else, relevant. A perfect-perfect world would probably have no advertising; instead, it would offer easy access or exposure to information about products and businesses we're truly interested in, accompanied by reviews and endorsements from experts, the public, and specific friends we trust.

In the spirit of that dream, Facebook Social Ads could be the hottest innovation on the advertising scene since the television — hotter than billboards, hotter than celebrity endorsements, and WAY hotter than renaming sports stadiums.

Granular targeting

The number one rule of good salesmanship is *Know Your Audience*. To formulate the most convincing message, you have to know whom you're addressing. This allows you to speak to their needs, desires, biases, and concerns — or whether to speak to them at all. Traditionally, advertisers have only been able to make broad generalizations about the people who see their messages. A late-night radio jingle might reach night owls, billboards might reach commuters, and inserts in Cosmo likely reach women — how's that for a broad generalization?

On Facebook, you scratch the guesswork. If your product is most popular among 20-year-old men who went to college and like sports, then create an ad that appears to people in only that demographic. If your product is ideal for politically liberal, married women, then Facebook ensures your ad appears to politically liberal, married women. Maybe your product is attractive to two groups but for different reasons. No problem. Create two different ads and target them differently.

You target your ad to a particular audience for two reasons. You pay less for more relevant attention, and you don't sabotage your brand by putting it in front of uninterested people. When people start to see ads actually relevant to them, they might start to pay more attention, making every company's advertising efforts that much more effective. Chapter 17 delves deeply into the Facebook Advertising options.

Social relevance

Think of the last purchase decision you deliberated over. It can be anything — sporting equipment, a sandwich, a movie ticket — anything. Which message would've been more likely to tip the scales?

> Buy our product!

Or

> Buy our product! Three of your friends did.

If you think the social context is important to consumers, you're absolutely right. In the preceding section, we introduce *Pages* on which people engage with the bands, brands, and businesses they like. Every action these people take — writing a good review, making a purchase, commenting on a discussion board, becoming a fan — are all passive endorsements. (An *active endorsement* is when a friend proactively tells you to try something, with the intent to endorse it; a *passive endorsement* occurs when a friend takes some action that incidentally lets you know they approve of the product.) If your business has an engaging page on Facebook, you have the option to roll these passive endorsements into the ads you run on the site. That is, whenever your ad is about to be shown to someone, Facebook sees whether that person's friends have interacted with your page in a positive way. If so, that information is included with the ad. So, rather than seeing

> Use our service!

the person might see

> Use our service! Jared and Naomi both gave it a 5 star review.

If you're a bit lost, don't worry. This concept doesn't exist anywhere else in the world of advertising. In Chapter 17, we spend a lot time going into how this system works and how much value it delivers compared to traditional advertising.

The Facebook Platform

Facebook Ads and Facebook Pages are two ways to *use* Facebook to help people discover and engage with your business in a casual way. The Facebook Platform deeply integrates your business with Facebook by allowing you to build an application that can leverage the most valuable components of Facebook, such as easy-to-design Web pages, user login, user-to-user communication, viral distribution, information by and about your users, including demographic info, photos, videos, and friends, while creating new functionality for your customers and users. The Facebook Platform might greatly benefit your business if:

✔ You provide a service that enhances people's interactions with their friends.

✔ You have a Web developer handy.

The following list can help you decide whether the Facebook Platform could be right for your business:

✔ **Do you have a Web site where people already sign in and interact?**
By integrating with Facebook, the actions they take on your site could be distributed to their friends through News Feed and Mini-Feed.

✔ **Does, or could, your business benefit from having people sign in to use your service?**
By building an application on Facebook, you grant secure and personalized access to your services without having to ask people to create yet another username and password.

✔ **When people interact with your service, could their experience be enhanced if they could access some of their information and data from Facebook?**
Examples of this are their demographic information, their photos, their list of friends, their relationships with other businesses, and more.

✔ **Could your business be enhanced by people interacting in various ways, such as commenting, rating, purchasing, sharing, dedicating, and more?**
Facebook Platform helps you easily figure how to incorporate this functionality into your site or application.

✔ **Are you looking to start a business?**
   If you want to start a venture where any of the features above would be
   valuable, then building a business on Facebook first is an easy way to get
   a Web site off the ground. Expand outside of Facebook later if you need,
   but we have a feeling the Facebook Platform won't leave you asking for
   very much.

Chapter 18 details how and why Facebook helps meet these goals. There, you
read about examples of applications that use Facebook in unique ways — all
of which have seen increased success and engagement as a result.

Chapter 16

Creating a Page for Your Business

*P*icture your town or city. Besides the occasional park or school, it's primarily made of buildings in which people live (like houses) and buildings in which people buy things (like stores). The world we live in is mostly composed of people and stuff that people need. People have real connections to all this stuff: the shops, the brands, the bands, the stars, and the restaurants and bars — everything that's important. These businesses have a significant stake in attracting and connecting with their fans, many of which are on Facebook. Facebook is all about people and their real-world connections; the social map wouldn't be complete without these types of relationships.

Facebook offers a way for businesses to have a presence that's similar to (yet different from) the one users have. Any legitimate business, band, or public figure can set up a Facebook Page, which is much like a user's Profile. Managers of a business can customize a Facebook Page to represent the business, informing and attracting customers. One primary difference between a business Page and a user's Profile is the means of interaction, which reflects and accommodates the different type of connection that people have with businesses in real life. Another difference is the set of detailed statistics — *metrics* — that reveal how people interact with a particular Facebook Page. Businesses use these numbers to understand their return on advertising investment.

We spend a lot of time in this book explaining exactly what people get from having a personal presence on Facebook. In the first part of this chapter, we show you the potential value of having your business present on Facebook. After that, we explain the features and functionality of Facebook Pages, often by comparing and contrasting them with other types of presence on Facebook. If you have spent a lot of time on Facebook or read the first few parts of this book already, you have an advantage while following along. In the last part of this chapter, we walk you through the steps to get your Facebook Page set up and active to further fuel the success of your business.

Why Create a Facebook Page?

Before we can answer why you should create a Facebook Page, first think about other things you can do to achieve success for your business:

- ✔ **Offer a quality product or service.** Quality, differentiated products attract repeat customers and referrals.

- ✔ **Locate your business on a busy street or in a dense shopping area.** Highly trafficked locations translate to attention and accessibility.

- ✔ **Clean and decorate your shop, carefully design your Web site, or dress up for a performance.** Quality presentation gains trust from customers.

In the end, all of these are examples of things businesses do to achieve growth: namely, growth of a loyal fan base. Giving your business a presence on Facebook ultimately has the same purpose: namely, driving growth.

Then again, lots of things *could* drive growth. Handing out flyers on the street, placing coupons in a newspaper, or running a commercial during the Super Bowl might get you customers. The trick is to figure out which, of all possible promotional efforts, has the biggest bang for your buck. We think we know the answer.

Speaking of bucks, it's time to get the uncomfortable money stuff out of the way: Facebook Pages are free. All you need is access to a computer, someone who knows how to use it, and a little time. Setting up your business Page could take five minutes or several hours, depending on how advanced you want to get. If that sounds daunting, remember that it would take several hours to make, print, and distribute flyers — and even longer to create a Web site or film a commercial.

Following are several goals you might have for your business. Throughout this chapter, we show how Facebook Pages help you achieve each goal.

- ✔ **Provide customers and potential customers with an accurate source of information about the business,** such as an e-mail address, product details, or hours of operation.

- ✔ **Communicate new promotions, products, and updates** with as many customers as possible while alienating as few as possible.

✔ **Engage your customers or audience** regularly and in compelling ways. When they think of your industry, they think of you.

✔ **Encourage customers to provide both positive and negative feedback** so you can continually improve.

✔ **Enable your customers to communicate with one another** about your business, product, or band in productive ways.

✔ **Impress your customers so much** that they come back again and again — and tell their friends to do the same.

Facebook Pages offers a suite of features that work together to help you achieve these goals. If you're in a position of promotional authority for a business and have even one of the preceding goals, you can find value in creating a Facebook Page. See an example of the Product (Red) Facebook Page in Figure 16-1.

Figure 16-1:
An example of a Facebook Page.

Pages versus Profiles versus Groups

In real life, how people interact and communicate with their best friends, favorite bands, or local neighborhood associations are unique, which is why people, businesses, and groups all have unique types of presence on Facebook. The way people interact with these entities on Facebook reflects those real-world differences. Because Pages, Profiles, and Groups offer different features and functionality, we want to make sure that you understand each type of presence. Then, based on your specific business goals, you can pick the presence (or presences) best for your goals. Before we highlight the specific functionality differences on Facebook, first think about the real-world differences between people, businesses, and groups:

- **Communication:** Communication with a friend is usually a conversation, where you say something, and then she responds, and so on. With a business, however, communication is often unidirectional: For example, your favorite band tells you about a new CD, or your favorite store has a sale. Comparatively, communication within groups tends to flow among all members with equal authority, relevance, and interest to all members.

- **Access:** You are welcome and encouraged to walk into a café or bookstore at any time during posted business hours. Quite the opposite is true of entering a friend's home unannounced. Additionally, a group usually meets at formalized meeting times agreed upon by all members (or a governing body), and at a venue accessible by all.

- **Information:** People are particular about which people know what information about them. Groups have varying degrees of privacy, depending on the group, but they generally fall into three buckets in which information is shared: only among members, only among members and the people they authorize, or the general public. With the exception of strategic future plans and some financial details, businesses usually want as many people to know as much about them or their product as possible.

These kinds of real-world differences determine the differences in design and functionality between a person, group, and business presence on Facebook.

Table 16-1 details the specific differences between these types of presence on Facebook.

Table 16-1	Comparison of User Profiles, Groups, and Pages	
Profiles	**Groups**	**Pages**
Have one administrator: you.	May have many admins, as arbitrarily appointed by the creator or other admins.	May have many admins, which are the appointed authority of the business.

Profiles	Groups	Pages
Represent a real person.	With the exception of copyrighted material or hate speak, represent anything. Seriously.	Represent a real business or promotional entity.
Have "friends." Friend requests must be accepted.	Have members. Member requests may be reviewed or automatic, depending on the group's setting.	Have fans. Fan requests are automatic.
Can send messages to other people, and up to 20 friends. If people are friends, they can always message each other.	Permit admins to message up to 500 members. Members can reply to the group admin. Members must leave the groups to opt-out of messages.	Allow admins to send updates to all subscribed fans. Fans cannot reply to these updates. Fans can opt-out of Updates.
Can expose or hide various information to the specific networks of which they're a part, and specific friends, but have no concept of being globally visible.	Can restrict privacy to members, members and friends, or opt to be globally visible.	Can restrict privacy based on age, but are otherwise always globally visible.
Must choose to accept or ignore each friend request.	May choose to review membership requests, or accept automatically.	Automatically accept all fan requests.
Can block people for inappropriate behavior.	Can block people for inappropriate behavior	Can block people for inappropriate behavior.
Can customize with applications and content.	Can customize with applications and content.	Can customize with applications and content.
Have no access to aggregate information about profile views and interactions.	Have no aggregate information about the page views and interactions with the group.	Have detailed insights about how people view and interact with a particular Facebook Page, aggregated and broken down by demographic.

Who should create a Facebook Page?

Simply put, anyone who is in a position of promotional authority can build a Facebook Page. Small business owners, event promoters, and advertising agencies can create a Page on Facebook to get attention and engagement from people. Facebook Pages are designed and optimized for the legitimate business seeking legitimate attention.

Popular categories for business profiles include

- **Local businesses,** such as restaurants, bars, clubs, shops, and recreational spots.
- **Big name or national brands,** such as those that distribute products or provide a service. Starbucks, Verizon, and Coca-Cola are examples.
- **Celebrities and public figures,** such as actors, authors, musicians, bloggers, consultants, thought leaders and politicians, and even folks running for student council. Stand-up comedians tend to create pretty enjoyable Facebook Pages.
- **Nonprofit or government organizations,** such as schools and religious organizations.
- **Specific products,** such as certain car models, business mascots (such as Ronald McDonald), or high-end designer clothing lines.
- **News, media, and entertainment companies** can create Pages for their brand or their various offerings, such as movies, TV shows, and magazines.

The preceding list demonstrates that Pages are equally suited for businesses as well as for their products. The NBA, for example, has an NBA Facebook page as well as a Facebook Page for each of its teams. CBS has a Facebook Page, as does each of its shows. The reason why many businesses promote themselves in this fractured way is because people might identify with particular parts of their business but not the business in its entirety. Creating different Pages for the different entities with which people might connect is important for maximizing engagement. Conversely, you want to avoid over-fragmenting your audience. For example, Six Flags amusement parks don't have to create a Page for every ride, Radiohead doesn't have to create a page for each album, and Starbucks doesn't have to create a page for every beverage.

Who shouldn't build a Facebook Page?

A Page, just like a user's Profile on Facebook, represents a real identity and is managed by the real-life appointed authority of that entity. For example, if you're not Chuck Norris (or his PR person), you can't create a Facebook Page called Chuck Norris. And if you didn't write or publish *Fight Club* (or weren't hired by someone who did), you can't create a page for it. It doesn't matter how much you love *lite-mocha Frappaccinos, extra whip-cream;* unless you're the marketing rep for Starbucks, you can't create a Facebook Page for them. Well, you can, but your Page — and/or your account — might end up being disabled.

Good examples of names for hypothetical Facebook Pages are

- ✔ Amazon
- ✔ Anthony's Pizza
- ✔ Stephen Colbert
- ✔ Buffy the Vampire Slayer

Bad examples of Facebook Page names are

- ✔ **Amazon's Facebook Page:** Like a user's Profile, Facebook Pages are an online representation of your business. When users navigate to your Page and click Become a Fan, they're a fan of your business, not the page. When you send fans an update, you're sending it on behalf of the business, not the Page. The Page isn't a destination: It's a means. When people interact with your Page, they're actually interacting directly with your business, and it's important that the name reflects this.

- ✔ **Anthony's Pizza at 553 University Ave.:** Just like the thousands of Joe Smiths on Facebook, there might be hundreds of Anthony's Pizzas — but that's okay. People will use the content on your Page, such as your photos or local address listed in your information fields, to identify the Anthony's Pizza they're after.

- ✔ **Stephen Colbert, Politician & Comedian Extraordinaire:** Stephen Colbert is welcome to specify his profession in his information fields. Additionally, in the body of his Page, he can declare himself *extraordinaire* over and over. However, his brand is his name, and that should be the name of his Page: *Stephen Colbert.*

- ✔ **Buffy the Vampire Slayer Is Awesome:** Buffy *is* awesome, and this would make a great name for a Facebook Group. However, there's no real-life entity with this name (that we know of); therefore, there shouldn't be a Facebook Page with this name.

Creating and Managing a Facebook Page

A Facebook Page isn't equivalent to an account. Rather, it's an entity on Facebook that can be managed by many people with their own distinct accounts. This section will take you through all the steps of Page creation, administration, and maintenance.

Creating a Page for your business

If you haven't already created an account on Facebook, we highly recommend that you do that first (although you don't have to). If you don't want to, you can start the process at Step 2 in the following steps; before completing Step 6, however, you're asked to create an account. The account you create here is a lesser version of a full Facebook user account, but it's still your account. You're asked to enter your e-mail address and birth date, and you should enter accurate information. That way, if you ever decide that you want a personal profile, upgrading the account you create here is much easier than starting from scratch.

Pages can have multiple admins. If you plan to have other people managing the Page you're creating, they can do so from their accounts. There's no reason to share the e-mail address or password with anyone. In fact, doing so violates the Terms of Use. We hope we've gained your trust enough at this point of the book that you trust us here: ***Use your real e-mail address and birth date.*** This information won't be revealed to anyone else, and it makes your future interactions on Facebook much easier.

1. **Navigate to** www.Facebook.com **and log in with your username and password.**

2. **Scroll to the bottom and then click Advertisers.**

   The page you land on (www.Facebook.com/ads) gives you an overview of the Facebook integrated advertising system, which includes Facebook Pages, Social Ads, and Insights. We talk about Insights later, in the "Know-It-All" section.

3. **Click the Create Facebook Page button, located at the bottom right.**

   You're welcome to read the copy on that page or click the Learn More link, but there's nothing there that's not in this book. (After all, we wrote both.)

4. **Specify what kind of business you're trying to promote, as shown in Figure 16-2.**

   The reason for making an accurate selection here is twofold:

   • Depending on the category you choose, your Facebook Page is created with a very specific set of fields and functionality. For example, specifying that your business is a restaurant allows you to specify your hours of operation, and specifying that you're a musician gives you instant access to a discography.

   • You can help users find and identify you.

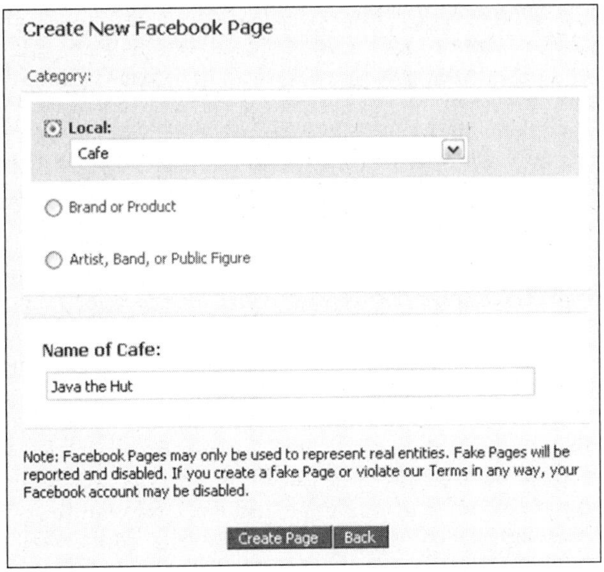

Create New Facebook Page

Category:

⊙ **Local:**
Cafe ▼

○ Brand or Product

○ Artist, Band, or Public Figure

Name of Cafe:

Java the Hut

Note: Facebook Pages may only be used to represent real entities. Fake Pages will be reported and disabled. If you create a fake Page or violate our Terms in any way, your Facebook account may be disabled.

Create Page   Back

Figure 16-2:
Categorize
and create
a page
for your
business.

5. Enter the name of your business and then click Create Page.

As we mention earlier, enter the exact name of your business, just like you'd sign up for Facebook with your real name.

As soon as you click Create Page, you're the proud admin of a Facebook Page. You're not done, though. Now you have to configure and customize. Both of these processes are complicated enough that we're punting those explanations to a separate numbered list.

If all the excitement has gotten the best of you, continue on to customize your Page right away; the next section guides you through that process. If you plan to take a break, you need to know how to get back here.

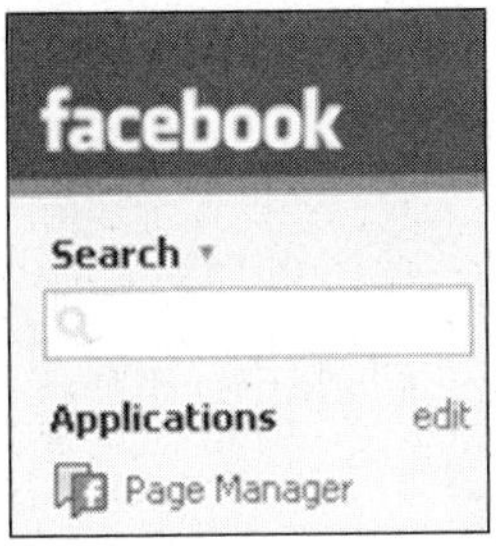

facebook

Search ▾

🔍

Applications   edit

📘 Page Manager

When you follow the preceding steps to create your first Facebook Page, you automatically have a new application added to your account called Page Manager, which is located (by default) at the top of your application list in the Applications menu (on the left side of the Frame). Whenever you're logged into Facebook, you can click this link to access, edit, and manage your Page. Page Manager is also where you go to see all the user-engagement statistics, which we talk about in the "Know-It-All" section, at the end of this chapter.

Making your Page yours

Since its beginning, Facebook has operated under a different principle than most of its competitors. Many other sites encourage people to customize their online presence with backgrounds, colors, layouts, and songs to express their individuality. Facebook encourages people to express their individuality through the content on their profile rather than through visual (or audio) display. The same is true for Facebook Pages. Most of the customization of your Page comes from the applications that you choose to add as well as the content that you include. Businesses that are used to branding and customizing their Web sites might find this limiting, but think of the trade-off. Potential customers who arrive at your Facebook Page know exactly how to get the information they need and how to interact with your Page because they're already familiar with the format. The unified look and feel of Facebook Pages is designed for ease of navigation and to provide a seamless experience for Facebook users. Rather than view these limitations as a disadvantage, try distinguishing your Page by offering rich and engaging content and functionality.

We mention earlier that while creating your Page, you're asked to categorize your business. This category determines which information fields and default applications appear on your Page. Keep reading as we summarize the information fields as well as all the default applications that your Page might start out with.

After completing the steps in the preceding section, you see your clean slate of a Facebook Page. An example is shown in Figure 16-3. At the top is your business, brand, or band's name, beneath which is a whole bunch of boxes waiting to be filled in with rich, informative, engaging information.

In some ways, your Page looks different to you than it does to your fans. Although any box you leave empty on your Page doesn't appear to fans, it appears to you, reminding you to put interesting content there. If you don't plan to fill the box with anything, remove it by clicking the X in its upper right. Some of the boxes aren't removable. We explain that shortly. After you begin to fill a box with content, your view is the same as your fans' except for the Edit links (which are for your eyes only).

Speaking of adding content . . . click Edit Page in the upper right of your Page. This takes you to the Control Panel, from which you can turn your Page from a blank slate into an engaging one, which you can use to connect with your fans and attract new ones.

Information

The very first thing that we recommend doing is to set up a photo for your Page. This brings your Page to life, helping your fans identify you when they find you in Search or read about you in their friend's News Feeds. Set your picture by clicking Edit in the upper right of the Profile Picture box; then follow the instructions to upload a photo. The column in which the Photo is placed is 396 pixels wide and can be up to three times the width of your picture. Keep these dimensions in mind when trying to make or choose a high-quality photo for your Page.

Most Pages have three sets of information boxes: Basic, Detailed, and Contact.

✔ **Basic information** appears in the upper right of your Page. Here, enter information that is core to your business. For Basic information, bands list members, local businesses list their address, and big name brands usually list their Web site, for example.

✔ **Detailed information** includes information fields unique to your type of business. This is where bands list their influencers, clubs state their dress policy, and movie studios list the awards they've won for certain films.

▼ Information	edit
✎ Add information to this page	

✔ **Contact information** is pretty self-explanatory. Depending on the type of business you have, you enter an e-mail address and/or phone number — and, in some cases, a mailing address.

Clicking Edit in the upper right of any of these boxes takes you to a tabbed page of fields where you fill in information. The more of these boxes that you fill out, the more your fans know about you. Any box that you don't fill out simply won't appear on the Profile page.

Applications

We spend a lot of time in this book talking about how applications integrate with your personal profile. Remember that when you first create your profile, you have some default applications (which you can remove if you don't find them useful) as well as more applications that you can use to meet your specific needs. The same is true for your Facebook Page. Most Facebook Pages come prepackaged with a default set of applications, as shown in Figure 16-4. Depending on the category you choose, you might get a few choice extras. You're free to keep any of the preinstalled applications or remove them (with the exception of the Reviews application, which is required for all Pages in certain categories), and you're encouraged to browse and add more applications that you think your customers will find engaging.

The more your customers are engaged with your Page, the more actions that generate in their friend's News Feeds, bringing you further attention and engagement.

Photos

Use the Photos application to create albums for your fans to use. If you own a restaurant, you might want to take photos of your most popular dishes, creating one album for breakfast, one for lunch, and one for dinner. Bands might make albums for their various concerts and events. Brands might use photos to show off people engaging with their products. For example, Nike might show women in Nike shoes, Starbucks might show a kid with whipped cream on his nose, and Blockbuster might show friends watching a movie. Add photos by clicking Edit in the upper right of the Photos box on the Control

Panel. If you choose, you can set the Photos application to allow your fans to add photos to your Page. These photos are shown in a separate section from the photos you add, which helps viewers distinguish the content you're adding to your Page from what your fans add.

Events

If you ever host any kind of event for your business, you'll get a ton of value from the Events application. Stores create events for their big sales, comedians create events for their shows, and clubs create events for their special-party nights. To create an event, click Edit in the upper right of the Events box on the Control Panel. Fill out the event information, upload a photo (see Chapter 13 for more details on event creation), and then — the final step — send an update to all your fans informing them about your event. A bit later, we talk more about what sending an update to your fans entails.

Discussion board

Every Page comes with a discussion board for their fans to congregate and discuss topics relating to your Page. A discussion board takes no setup on your side, which is why there's no box for it in the Control Panel. With the Discussion Board on your Page, users can instantly start topics and respond to others.

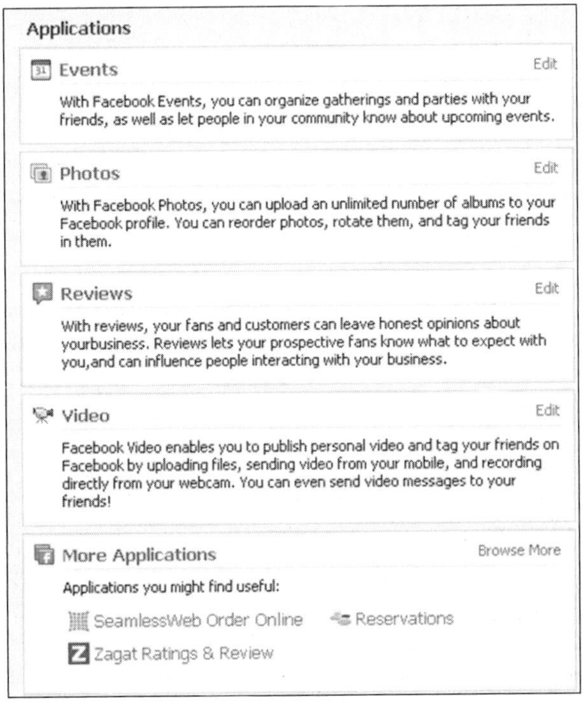

Figure 16-4: The Applications and settings portion of the Pages Control Panel.

Applications

Events   Edit
With Facebook Events, you can organize gatherings and parties with your friends, as well as let people in your community know about upcoming events.

Photos   Edit
With Facebook Photos, you can upload an unlimited number of albums to your Facebook profile. You can reorder photos, rotate them, and tag your friends in them.

Reviews   Edit
With reviews, your fans and customers can leave honest opinions about yourbusiness. Reviews lets your prospective fans know what to expect with you,and can influence people interacting with your business.

Video   Edit
Facebook Video enables you to publish personal video and tag your friends on Facebook by uploading files, sending video from your mobile, and recording directly from your webcam. You can even send video messages to your friends!

More Applications   Browse More
Applications you might find useful:
SeamlessWeb Order Online   Reservations
Zagat Ratings & Review

Video

The Video application for your Page works in a similar way that it does for your Profile (see Chapter 8). Just like with Photos, you can upload videos to your Page. For example, a coffee shop might show a video of a barista making a fancy drink, a singer might show clips from a recent concert, and a movie theater might show clips from an upcoming film. Add videos by clicking Edit in the upper right of the Video box in the Control Panel.

Wall

Although the Wall is a permanent fixture on every user's Profile, it's an optional application for a Facebook Page. Use of the Wall is encouraged because it provides a place for Fans of your Page to easily engage with your Page. You can always delete those Wall posts from your Page that you find disagreeable or in poor taste. If any user commits this offense regularly or tries to spam your Fans by putting links to other sites or pages on the Wall of your Facebook Page, we encourage you to block that person from contributing by clicking Block just beneath the offending Wall post.

Reviews

Besides being a way for you to represent your business or band, Facebook Pages are also a means by which real people get real information about the businesses around them. For this reason, users can count on the Reviews application on each and every Facebook Page in relevant categories. Unlike writing on the Wall (which must be done by someone who has already declared themselves a Fan of your page), anyone can write a review on any Facebook Page (although admins can't review their own business). Reviews are also different from the Wall in that each user can only ever write one review, although they can update that review if their impression of the business changes. When you click the Edit link at the upper right of the Reviews application, you can specify whether you want visitors to your Page to see all reviews when they land on your Page or only those written by their friends.

Music Player

The Music Player application is added by default to every band or musician Page, although it can be added to any other type of Facebook Page. It allows admins to upload songs for Fans and potential Fans to listen to. Note that songs in your Music Player never play by default on Facebook; someone must click Play to hear your tunes. These days, many people have copies of music they don't have the legal rights to, and it's actually illegal to upload a song to a social networking site if you don't hold the rights for distributing that song. To limit the amount of illegal song sharing on Facebook, Facebook can activate the Music Player for your Page only after receiving proof of identity. If

Facebook is sure you are who you say you are, then you can be held account-able if you upload content to which you do not own the rights. Here's how to become authorized for music upload:

1. **Take a picture of your government issued photo ID, load it onto your computer, and save the file as a JPEG.**

2. **Go to the Control Panel for your Page, and click Edit in the upper right of the Music Player application.**

3. **Click Verify Your Page and read the instructions.**

   The instructions tell you to upload the photo of your ID by clicking Browse and finding it on your hard drive.

4. **Wait a few days, during which the Facebook Customer Operations team verifies that you are who you say you are.**

   As soon as that happens, Music Player automatically appears on your Page.

5. **Add tracks by repeating Step 2.**

   This time, though, clicking the Edit link displays a button to Add a Track.

6. **After uploading a song, enter its name, artist, album name, and (if your music is for sale), a link to buy it.**

While looking at your Page, Fans can see all the songs that you added (see Figure 16-5). If you add a link to where they can purchase a song, they can go get it for themselves. If you're a band or musician, this is a great way to get your music heard and purchased. If you're any other kind of business, the Music Player is a great way to add some audio color and engagement to your Page. *Note:* Make sure that the music you upload is your own.

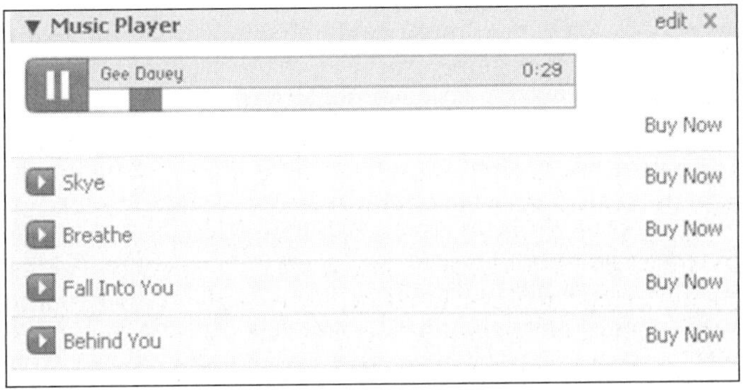

Figure 16-5:
Fans can listen to or buy music uploaded to Music Player.

▼ Music Player		edit X
❚❚ Gee Davey	0:29	
		Buy Now
▶ Skye		Buy Now
▶ Breathe		Buy Now
▶ Fall Into You		Buy Now
▶ Behind You		Buy Now

Discography

Like Music Player, the Discography application is primarily applicable to musicians, and comes pre-added to music pages only. To add information to your discography, follow these steps:

1. **Click Edit in the upper right of the Discography box.**

2. **Click Add Album, and follow the steps to filling out information about your discography, including album title, synopses, label, release date, duration, and album art.**

3. **Click continue to add information about each track on the album by clicking Add a Track in the bottom right of the Edit Track Listing tab.**

4. **To edit track information, click Edit on the right of each track listing. To change the order of songs, click the arrows on the left side of the track listing and drag the track up or down.**

5. **Click Save Changes before navigating away.**

6. **Choose which albums you want your fans to see by going back to the main Discography Edit page (click Edit at the upper right of the Discography box on the Control Panel or Page) and then clicking Show on Profile next to the albums you want to see.**

   If you're a musician with a large canon of work, you probably don't want your entire discography showing up on your Page.

   Your fans can access the rest of your discography by clicking See All on the Discography box when viewing your Page.

More Applications

At the bottom of the Applications section of your Page's Control Panel is the More Applications box (refer to Figure 16-4). Depending on the category you initially selected for your Page, this box might already be populated with applications that Facebook thinks could be appropriate for your type of business. Restaurants, for example, might be encouraged to add the OpenTable application, which allows your customers to make reservations straight from your Facebook Page. Restaurants can also show off their Zagat rating by adding the Zagat application.

The Discography application comes recommended for movies and TV shows because many have sound tracks. To discover more about these applications, click the title to go to the application's About page. From there, if you like what you see, you can choose Add the Application to Your Page. To see more apps than those recommended, click the Browse More link (shown in Figure 16-4) in the upper right to go to the Product Directory. You'll already be in the For Facebook Pages section of the directory, and every application you see listed there can be added to your Facebook Page to increase your fans' engagement with your Page.

Most applications in the Product directory are built by companies other than Facebook. Although many of them make fantastic applications that can add a ton of value to your Page, some of them might be, um, inadequate. Facebook has rules to protect you from *malicious* applications, but some might be low quality. After adding an application, we recommend that you check how it interacts with your Page and watch how your fans use it. Be sure that any application adds value before you decide to keep it.

Rather than browsing the Application Directory for good applications, some Page administrators check out their competitors' Pages to see what kinds of applications seem to be working well. If you do this and see one you like, click Add in the upper right of the Application box to add it to your Page.

Settings

The very last section of the Control Panel features a box for editing your Page's settings, of which, for now, there are only three (see Figure 16-6):

- ✔ **Gender Pronoun:** Depending on the category for your Page, you can change the pronoun that Facebook uses when referring to your business. For example, if you're a band with more than one member, using *they* makes the most sense. An actress would select *she*, and a shopping mall might choose *it*. This pronoun is used in sentences, such as those that appear in your Page's Mini-Feed. For example, "The Shins added a new album to their Discography," or "R.E.I. added photos to its Photo Album."

- ✔ **Age Restrictions:** Put an age restriction on your Page in case you're promoting something that's illegal or irrelevant to those under a particular age, such as bars or matchmaking services.

- ✔ **Published Status:** If you're the type who likes to make changes to your Page in private without your fans watching the transition, you can publish and unpublish your Page. When you're ready, use this settings box to unveil it.

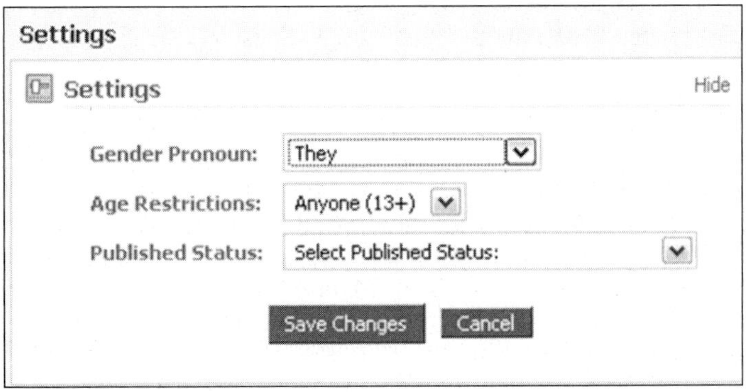

Figure 16-6:
Fine-tuning your Settings on a Facebook Page.

Settings			
▣ Settings			Hide
Gender Pronoun:	They ▾		
Age Restrictions:	Anyone (13+) ▾		
Published Status:	Select Published Status:		▾
	Save Changes Cancel		

Admins

Most businesses have more than one person sharing responsibility for promotion. Perhaps you're the co-owner of your restaurant, or you're part of a marketing team for several companies, or maybe you're the drummer of a band who's sick of the lead singer holding all the cards. Good news: Every Facebook Page can have up to 25 administrators, all of whom can admin the Page through their personal account. This means no password sharing and no creating fake accounts. Whoever initially creates the Page simply needs to invite all the appropriate people to help admin the Page. Here's how:

1. **Navigate to the Control Panel of your Page.**

2. **In the Admins section in the right column (under which only you are listed), click Edit.**

3. **Invite people to be the administrators of your Page.**

    You can invite any person who already has a Facebook account and with whom you're friends on Facebook to be an admin by entering their names into the Friend Selector in the upper right of the Invite Admins page. You can enter the-mail address of any person who isn't on Facebook or with whom you're not friends in the box on the bottom right. In either case, the person you invite must accept the invitation in order to become an admin.

Mini-Feed

Identical to the Mini-Feed on the user Profile (see Chapter 5 for details), the Mini-Feed on your Facebook Page shows all your visitors the more recent activity you've taken on your Page, such as adding photos or posting items. The Mini-Feed is mandatory for all Pages because users rely on it to quickly access the newest information on your Page.

Layout

Similar to a user's Profile, you use the layout of your Facebook Page to help emphasize what information is most important to you. Go to your Facebook Page by clicking Page Manager in your Applications menu and then clicking the Pages tab. There, you can then click the name of the Page that you want to configure. You can also search for your Page by name: It appears first. When you're looking at your Facebook Page, mouse over the light blue header of any box to see how you can rearrange it. If your cursor changes into two crossing arrows, you can click to drag that box around. On mouse-over, a little icon to the left of the light blue header indicates whether that box can be moved from side to side as well as up and down.

Promote your Page

To benefit from the viral nature of Facebook, you must seed your Page with Fans.

Tell customers electronically

If you have an existing Web site or a mailing list, you might want to add a link or send a message to alert your existing fans or customers that they can now find you on Facebook. For those in your fan base who already have a Facebook account, they'll probably find that connecting with you there is way more convenient that remembering to go to your site regularly. And having them connect with your Facebook Page doesn't preclude them continuing to visit your Web site; rather, a Facebook Page gives you an extra opportunity to communicate with them about changes and updates on your site.

Tell customers physically

If you have a physical store, try sticking a sign on the window that tells customers to find you on Facebook. That way, they don't have to remember yet another URL. As long as they remember your business name and Facebook, they can look you up and connect with your business on an on-going basis.

Tell your friends

If you run a business, you probably already spend a lot of time marketing it to your friends. We'll go out on a limb here and hypothesize that you don't enjoy sending mass e-mails or constantly promoting your business to your friends and family. You never know who really wants to hear about it or who is just being polite by not complaining. Directing your friends to your Facebook Page solves two problems. They can choose to become a *Fan of* your Page, and then they can choose whether to receive updates. This means the following:

- ✔ You update only those people who want to hear about it.
- ✔ You seed your Page with a slew of fans whose actions on your Page serve as passive referrals when their friends read about it in News Feed.

To share your Page with your friends:

1. **Navigate to your Facebook Page.**

2. **Scroll to the bottom and click Share.**

3. **Add up to 20 of your friends in the To line and welcome them to your Page.**

TIP

You can also stick the link in an e-mail. We don't recommend messaging your friends more than once in this way, though. If they want to hear from your business, they'll become a fan; if not, they're probably not great customers, anyway.

Advertise

In Chapter 17, we introduce you to the world of advertising on Facebook, with a special emphasis on how to advertise your Facebook Page. The beauty of advertising your Page on Facebook is that you're already targeting the audience most likely to understand what your Facebook Page is all about. Also, from the audience's point of view, it's a smoother experience to click an ad in Facebook, which navigates to another Facebook page. This is very different than how most Web advertising works, where clicking an ad opens a whole new window into a whole different Web site.

Engage your fans

If you've read this chapter to this point, you have your customized Facebook Page and are ready to drive traffic to your business. Now might be a good time to get up, take a little walk, a nap, or make a delicious turkey sandwich (extra cranberry, hold the mayo). You're done with the basic work required to allow people to find out about your business and connect with it.

To gain real attention and interaction, though, you can do a lot more. *Remember:* The richer your Page and the more you engage your fans, the more actions they take, which generates News Feed stories for all their friends to see, thus giving you more visibility and attention.

Add rich content

By *rich,* we mean informative and fresh. The more new and useful content you add to your Page, the more reason your fans have to come back and check it out. Here are some ideas to keep fans (that is, customers) lingering on your content:

- ✔ **Add Photos, Video, Notes, and Posted Items** to bring your Page to life, making it grow while your business does. If you sell stuff, you can continually add photos and videos of new products or of people using your existing ones. If you provide a service, you can add videos showing you or your employees at work — say, an expert barista pouring a latte, a sculptor whose fans would love to see you in action, or an auto technician offering tips on good car care. If your fans like what they see, they're very likely to use the Facebook communication tools to show your content to their friends, giving your business more attention.

✔ **Hold Events** to keep your patrons hooked. You use Facebook Events to invite fans to special parties, sales, or promotions. Some businesses hold events *just* for their fans on Facebook. When your fans RSVP your event, their friends might read about it on their News Feeds. They can easily invite their friends along as well, or else their friends might just read about it in their News Feeds.

✔ **Talk to your fans,** on behalf of your business. Your fans will be writing on your Wall and discussion board, and they'll be writing reviews. Wherever possible, feel free to contribute. If someone writes on your Wall about how they had a bad experience, don't delete it — respond! Apologize and tell them you'll give them a free meal if they come back (and show you their ID, which you'll know because their name is listed next to their Wall post). Other people who see the exchange will be impressed by your level of service.

If you're a shoe salesman and someone asks on your discussion board about finding the perfect shoe, fill them in. This public dialog has the benefit of informing other customers with the same questions. Any time you write on the Wall or a discussion board of a Page that you administer, your comments are listed on behalf of the business itself, rather than you. This helps viewers trust your voice of authority and doesn't expose your personal account to anyone.

Send Updates

When looking at the Control Panel for your Page, notice the Send an Update to Fans link to the right. Updates on Facebook are different than other types of mailing lists. By clicking this link, you can compose a message that goes out to all your fans. Before writing an update for your fans, however, you should understand how Updates works from the user perspective:

✔ **Fans can opt-in to Updates.** When users on Facebook find your Page, they choose to affiliate with it by clicking Become a Fan at the upper right of your Facebook page. Upon doing so, they're asked whether they would like to receive updates from your businesses. You can comfortably assume that anyone who clicks OK wants to hear what you have to say. If a business ever sends updates that a particular fan doesn't find valuable, he can opt-out of Updates by clicking Opt Out directly from the update itself.

✔ **Updates are kept separate from Friend-to-Friend messages.** When your fans log in after you send an update, a notice on their home Page alerts them that they have a new update. Clicking that notice takes them to the special tab in their Inbox where updates from businesses reside. The reason for sorting business updates differently from Friend-to-Friend messages is simple: They're different. We're all familiar with the disappointment that comes from discovering that a new e-mail is promotional. E-mails from our favorite bands or businesses could be very exciting, if not for the fact that we're usually expecting a personal message.

Updates

☐ 1 new update

✔ **Each business competes only with itself for its fans' attention.** The first time a fan receives an Update from a business, a new row for that business is created on that fan's Updates tab in their Inbox. Because every business gets exactly one row in its fans' Updates tab, even if you send ten messages in a row, you're not adding any clutter to their lives. More Updates simply means that your row bumps to the surface, putting your most recent subject and snippet at the top.

Updates are organized within the Updates tab similar to how messages are arranged in the Inbox (which we describe in Chapter 10):

✔ Each row contains the picture of the business's page, the title, and a snippet of the most recent Update.

✔ A blue dot next to the subject line of an update indicates that unread Updates are in that row.

✔ The rows are ordered by the time at which the most recent Update from that business was sent.

The narrow column on the right of the Updates tab acts like a table of contents, listing the businesses that have rows in the Updates tab. The number next to the businesses' names specifies how many new updates each business sent since the recipient last clicked through.

✔ As soon as a user clicks into a particular row, all updates from that business are immediately marked as read.

Okay, so fans experience updates from businesses very differently from how they experience promotional e-mails or paper mailings. What does this mean for you? It means to *update your fans.* They said they want to hear from you. The messages you send won't be misconstrued as spam because of the organization in the system, and users have full control to opt-out at any time.

In the next section, we show you how to track what effect your updates have on your fans' engagement. Use these metrics to help you monitor what types of updates and what frequency of updates optimizes your fans' attention.

Here are a few other things you need to know about updates:

✔ **You can include attachments in an update.** If you add a new photo, album, video, note, event, or other piece of content that you'd like your fans to know about, you can copy the URL for the page where that content lives and paste it into the message. In most cases, the content is automatically transformed into an attachment to your update, just like the Share feature we talk about in Chapter 10. Note that you can attach only one piece of content per update.

✔ **You can access your sent updates from your Page's Control Panel.** In the right column, just under the Send an Update to Your Fans link, you can click See All Updates (as shown in the image at the beginning of this section).

✔ **Fans who opt-in to receive your Updates have access to every Update you sent.** The first time someone receives an Update from your business, only that new update is marked as unread. If she clicks through on the row for your business, she sees all the updates that you sent before she became a fan. Cool, huh?

Know-It-All

In the beginning of this chapter, we mention various types of activities that business owners use to try to grow their customer base: running television and radio commercials; putting ads on buses, benches, and billboards; or hiring someone to dress like a chicken and dance outside your door. One of the hardest problems in advertising is figuring out what kind of effect your efforts have on your business. Facebook Insights are dedicated to unveiling this mystery. If you already set up your Page, follow along with this next section. If you haven't, this section might be the one that convinces you to.

Within 48 hours of publishing your Page, you start to see exactly how people are engaging with it. Click the Page Manager from the Applications menu to land on an *Overview page,* which gives you 24-hour feedback about the current success of your Page (or Pages, if you have more than one), and ads (if you're running any). By default, the big graph on the Overview page shows you how many views your Page received in the past two weeks. Click the arrow in the upper left next to Page Views to see all sorts of other interesting statistics, such as:

✔ **Unique Page Views:** This is how many different people have seen your Page over time. This number is likely to grow if your fans are *engaged,* meaning that more of their friends are seeing News Feed stories about your Page and coming to check it out. This number might also increase if people can find you in Search, or if you direct your fans or customers to check you out on Facebook.

✔ **New & Removed Fans:** Although you want this number to stay steady or rise, make sure that this number doesn't trend down. After users declare that they're fans of your business, they have very little incentive to revoke their *Fan of* status unless you do something to offend or bother them. Perhaps you sent out too many Updates that lacked good content, maybe you received some bad press, or perhaps the content you're putting on your site is offensive. Whatever is the issue, take it seriously. Fans have to go out of their way to disassociate with your business. If this number drops, action of some sort is probably in order.

✔ **Wall Posts and Reviews:** The higher this number, the more engaged your fans are, and you can count on each one of those Wall posts to generate publicity to those posters' friends.

✔ **Photo Views & Audio Plays:** Photos are far and away the most popular things for Facebook users to engage with. If you add a new album and your Photo Views numbers go up, it's a good indication that your fans are engaged. If not, you might want to send them an update letting them know that they should check out your new stuff. If your Page has music player, you might find it valuable to see which additions or reordering of tracks on your Page lead to increased listening.

Below the Graph on the Overview tab, you can find Insights comparing today's numbers with those from yesterday. On the Overview tab, you can see your Page's total number of fans, page views, and unique visitors from today (compared with yesterday). Clicking See More next to Recent Activity: *Your Page Name header* takes you to a page with detailed insights about activity on your Page. Here you can see the following:

✔ **Week-over-week metrics:** These appear for each week for as long as your Page has been published, and for each of the types of activity mentioned earlier.

✔ **Day-to-day comparisons of the same activity types.**

✔ **Your fans' activity, broken down by gender and age (provided that your Page has at least ten fans):** Perhaps you ran a few ads to drive traffic to your Page, each targeted at a different age demographic. While the ad is running, you might see growth in some age groups but not others, indicating which messaging is effective and which needs work.

That last point is a good transition to reiterating the importance of Insights. Although you should definitely take the time to pat yourself on the back if your Page is gaining attention (and ideally, your business growing as a result), always treat Insights as the tool you need for iteration and improvement. Each change you make to your Page, or your business, might bear good or bad effects. You need to know when something is resonating or alienating your fans so that you can make adjustments quickly to maximize your efforts, extracting the largest gain possible for your business.

Chapter 17

A New Kind of Advertising

*T*here are two kinds of people in America: those who watch the Super Bowl, and those who watch the Super Bowl commercials. It's odd that, for a few hours of every year, most of us actually seek out advertising, while the rest of the year we resent it. We fast-forward commercials, we change radio stations, we chuckle at the occasional billboards (but mostly we complain about how they ruin the skyline). What's the cause for prejudice? Is advertising inherently evil?

If you're someone who runs a business, or is responsible for driving customers to a business, you know the answer is *No*. Advertisers have no malicious intent (usually), and they're not out to annoy, distract, or interrupt us. They simply have a product or service that they believe could improve our lives, if we only knew about it. So they tell us. They tell us three minutes before the end of our favorite TV shows; they tell us with their tee-shirt logos, hood ornaments, and catchy jingles; they stand on the corner with a sign that reads *Lemonade 5 cents*. And if one person among us will respond well to an advertiser's particular message, that advertiser has no problem yelling across an entire crowded room to make sure that person hears it.

Advertising Improves

Yelling across a crowded room has been the model of advertising for years. Advertisers operate under the somewhat accurate principle that the wider the distribution, the better the chances of reaching someone who cares — the reason Super Bowl slots are the most expensive of the year. It's not because football fans are more likely to buy stuff; it's because more people simultaneously watch the Super Bowl than anything else on TV. More people equal more customers.

However, there is a cost. People have only so much attention to lend to advertising. Therefore, if two, three, four, or five million advertisers start yelling across the room, people hear none of it. When too many messages fly, people tune out, leaving advertisers with no recourse other than being the *loudest, brightest,* or *catchiest.* Anyone who has stood in the middle of Times Square in New York understands exactly what we're talking about. And that has certainly been the model of advertising on the Internet. The flashier an ad, the more in your face, the more distracting — the more likely you are to click it.

Advertising has a bad rap because of this. Every now and then, you see an ad for something you were craving, something that intrigues you, or features something that just entertains you. In those times, you probably don't mind the advertising at all; in fact, you might appreciate it. Nevertheless, 99 times out of a 100, an ad is a nuisance, which is how *ad* has practically become a dirty word.

Understanding these flaws with the modern advertising landscape led to the formulation of principles for the Facebook Ad system:

- ✔ Consumers will be happiest if they see fewer total advertisements and the ones they do see that are most relevant to them.

- ✔ Advertisers will be happiest if they *don't* throw away cash and *don't* dilute consumer attention. In other words, advertisers want to deliver their message primarily to those people who actually care.

- ✔ When consumers are exposed to relevant, high-quality advertisements, they're more likely to pay attention to advertising on the whole, making each ad that much more valuable.

- ✔ To get people's attention, advertising is usually weaved into some product or service that already has consumer attention, such as TV shows or Web sites. People will enjoy a TV show or Web site more if its ads are relevant, high quality, and not harmful to the user experience. As a result, they spend more time watching that channel or using that Web site, thereby seeing more total ads. Therefore, responsible TV stations or Web sites are rewarded for good advertising behavior. Customers are happier, advertisers are happier, and the product or service provider is happier.

Advertisers have to yell across the room because they don't know who, in a crowd, might be listening. Now, because each Facebook user enters so much personal information, Facebook can enable its advertisers to deliver their message only to the people most interested (while completely protecting its users' privacy).

No more yelling.

Imagine Times Square in this model. Rather than everyone looking at thousands of flashy signs, each person would see five or six messages about things that actually interest them, making more room for flowers, and sky, and, we'll say it, *non-commercialism*.

Defining Social Ads

On Facebook, users see two types of advertising. One is *syndicated advertising*. On a certain percentage of Facebook pages, Microsoft has a special location carved out in where they can run ads from their ad network. Microsoft pays Facebook for use of this location, and other businesses pay Microsoft for getting their ads exposure. For a while, this was Facebook's primary source of revenue. Most of this chapter is about the other kind of ads on Facebook. We mention syndicated ads so that you understand why you see two very different types of ads when you're browsing the site.

The other type of advertising is *social advertising*. A *Social Ad* is an ad that businesses create and upload to Facebook directly to circulate on Facebook. No middleman.

Social Ads have a number of interesting characteristics:

- ✔ Social Ads appear in one of two places: in a user's News Feed as a story (maximum of one ad per 24-hour window) or beneath the Applications menu on the left.

- ✔ Social Ads are composed of the same set of optional components: a title, a photo, an ad body, and the option for inclusion of Social Actions (which we explain in the next section). Therefore, Social Ads are uniform in their appearance, so advertisers must get your attention with content, not form.

- ✔ Social Ads are demographically targeted to users based on information they list in their profile, including age, sex, interests, geography, political views, relationship status, school, or workplace.

- ✔ Using Social Actions, Social Ads are targeted to people whose friends have shown an interest in the product or service.

Social Actions

Previously in this chapter, we refer to *Social Actions*. If you haven't heard this term in advertising before, don't be surprised. It's currently exclusive to Facebook — a concept so new that it's being released to the public while we write this book. Social Actions are best described via examples.

1. Wiley Publishing makes a Facebook Page (described in Chapter 16) to advertise *Facebook For Dummies*.

2. At some point, Carolyn publicly becomes a fan of the *Facebook For Dummies* page.

3. Wiley Publishing creates an ad on Facebook. Characteristics of the ad include:

   • A subject that reads, "Facebook For Dummies. Do you know someone who needs help understanding Facebook? More help than you can give?"

   • A picture of the book's cover.

   • A targeted audience of 30–40 year-olds.

   In addition, Wiley Publishing *opts-in* to appending Social Actions to the ad.

4. Because Carolyn has already pledged allegiance to Dummies, the Social Ad system tries to show the Wiley ad to Carolyn's friends who fit the 30–40-year-old demographic. The system automatically appends to the ad the Social Action, composed of Carolyn's Profile picture and the News Feed story, "Carolyn Abram has become a fan of *Facebook For Dummies*."

Social Ads plus Social Actions rules

Carolyn's friends are way more likely to be interested in *Facebook For Dummies* if they already know that Carolyn liked it. At the least, if they're intrigued, they might ask her for more information. When authorized by an advertiser, the Facebook system looks at all the people within the targeted demographic for an ad, and then tries to show the ad to people whose friends have already had a positive interaction with that company. A few important points about social advertising:

✔ **No one's actions will ever be shown to people who couldn't also have seen that action as a News Feed story.** In other words, no one would see the ad with the Social Action above unless they're friends with Carolyn.

✔ **You cannot append a Social Action to your ad unless you also have a Facebook Page or Application or a Web site that's Facebook Beacon enabled.** Users must have a place to interact to generate the Social Actions in the ad. (See Chapter 3 for more on Beacon.)

✔ **Even if you opt-in to Social Actions, this doesn't guarantee that a Social Action will always be appended to your ad.** To increase the likelihood that this happens, you must ensure that your Facebook Page or Application is seeing a lot of activity.

Who uses Social Ads?

Anyone who has access to a computer, a credit card, and something to promote is a great candidate for using Facebook Social Ads. People use Social Ads for all kinds of different things:

✔ Drawing attention to your Web site, or business.

✔ Telling people about a new deal or offering.

✔ Campaigning for an election.

✔ Promoting a college event.

✔ Driving traffic to a Facebook Event, Group, Page, or Application.

✔ Raising awareness of a cause.

✔ Wishing friends *Happy Birthday!*

✔ Promoting a concert or a new CD.

✔ Directing traffic to a listing on Marketplace.

✔ Recruiting for a job opening.

Social Ads target your ad to an audience as small as a single school or as wide as a whole country, and they're applicable to just about every promotional effort. The only audience Facebook can't currently target is people who don't use Facebook. But you can spread your message to them some other way — dress up like a chicken and hand out flyers in front of your store, perhaps.

Creating a Social Ad

Creating an ad on Facebook is extremely easy; creating a good ad might require some extra effort. In this section, we walk you through the basic how-to of creating an ad on Facebook, while providing lots of tips and tricks to ensure your ad is as effective as possible. We make sure to call out which steps are required, and which are recommended.

Step 1. Get started

Log in to Facebook, and navigate to www.Facebook.com/ads. You can access this page at any time by scrolling to the bottom of any Facebook page and clicking Advertisers. On the Facebook Ads page, shown in Figure 17-1, click Get Started.

Note: If you don't have a Facebook account, you can skip the login part, but you'll be asked to create a personal account (use your e-mail address, name, and birthday) before completing your ad purchase.

Step 2. Pick your destination

After you click Get Started, you're asked to pick the destination of your ad. That is, if someone clicks your ad, where will they end up? Your choices (shown in Figure 17-2) are as follows:

Figure 17-1: Creating a Facebook Ad.

✔ **I Have a Web Page I Want to Advertise.** If you already have a Web site for your business, select the first option and enter your business's URL (or the URL of the page you want people to land on when they click your ad). If you select this option and click continue, proceed to Step 3.

✔ **I Have Something on Facebook I Want to Advertise.** If you're trying to advertise something you have on Facebook, such as a Facebook Page (see Chapter 16) or an Application, select the second option and choose the relevant Page, Application, Group, or Event from the drop-down list. If you select this option and click continue, proceed to Step 3.

✔ **Help Me Make a Page.** This option is for people who want to advertise something but don't have a Web presence yet. If you select this option, you're taken down the path of creating a Facebook Page (as we describe in Chapter 16) before continuing with Step 3. After you create your Page, clicking the Promote Your Page button on the Page Manager takes you straight to where you need to be to follow Step 3.

After you make your choice, click Continue.

Figure 17-2:
Choosing
the landing
destination
for your ad.

Step 3. Target your ad

On Facebook, an engaged man or woman is likely to see ads for wedding photographers, while sports lovers may see an ad for coverage of the big game. An older married man might see an ad about anniversary presents, and if you're a 23-year-old female who likes poetry and traveling, don't be surprised if you see an ad for a women's writing workshop in Europe. (Recently, this happened to Carolyn, who was so thrilled by the ad, she went on to get more info about the workshop.)

As we mention in the beginning of this chapter, targeting your ad may be the key to good advertising. If you narrow your message to the specific people most likely to respond, you pay much less for the same amount of attention.

The goal of targeted advertising is to try to be as specific as possible, without alienating anyone who might be interested. To that end, Figure 17-3 shows the options for the Facebook Targeting system, and this list helps demystify them:

- ✔ **Target audience:** At the top of the page, in the light blue bar, a sentence dynamically tells you the exact audience you're going to reach while you set targeting parameters. Because the default target is everyone in the United States over 18, that sentence reads *I want to reach people age 18 and older in the United States.* When you select various options, the sentence changes to reflect your new criteria. Before you navigate away from this page, read that sentence aloud to assure yourself you chose the right options. We hope no one sees you talking to your computer.

- ✔ **Size of demographic:** In the upper right, a number shows the size of the Facebook demographic that meets your targeting specifications. When you add more targeting parameters, such as gender, age, schools, or keywords, the number decreases. If you add more flexibility *within* a particular targeting type, such as adding five keywords, instead of just one, the number increases. For example, specifying that you want to target your ad at people who have *Laughing* listed in their profile narrows your audience. If you specify that you also want to target people with *Smiling* in their profile, your audience expands again.

- ✔ **Location:** If your product or service is relevant to consumers only in a particular location, then be sure your ad is shown only to those people. A traveling circus, for example, might make a whole series of ads targeted at different locations to let people know when to break out their clown noses and floppy shoes. Currently, Facebook doesn't allow an ad to be targeted at more than one country at a time, so if you have an international company, you need to make separate ads.

- ✔ **Sex:** Selecting either male or female ensures your ad goes to only men or only women. Checking both of these boxes works as if you hadn't selected anything. Leave both unchecked, and both females and males are counted.

- ✔ **Age:** Specify the minimum and maximum age for your ad. The default is 18 years old because any ads targeted at people under the age of 18 are reviewed before being shown.

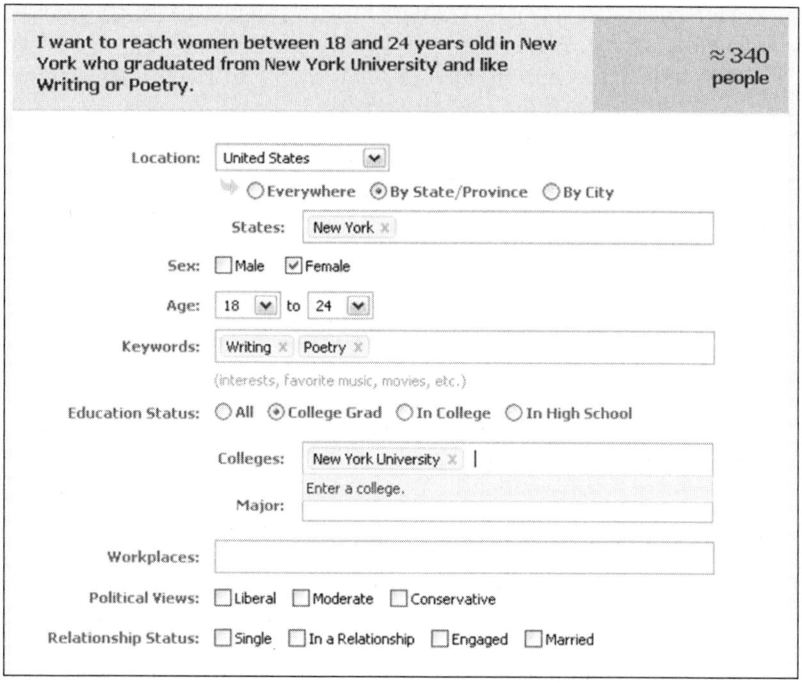

Figure 17-3:
Your ad's
targeting
options.

✔ **Keywords:** When Facebook users create their personal profiles, they enter various terms that describe their activities and interests. When enough people enter the same term, that term is used for keyword targeting. You know a term is valid for targeting if you start to enter it and a drop-down list appears to autocomplete the word. If the word you're thinking of doesn't appear, come up with a synonym. If the word you're looking for *does* appear, you probably still want to come up with a few synonyms and target those as well. For example, if you sell books, you may want to target to *Reading, Read, Books, Reading Books,* and *Literature.* Definitely play around with this step and see how the audience size estimator fluctuates with various combinations.

✔ **Education Status:** This field allows you to reach the people in a particular life stage, such as high school, college, or college graduate. You can also target people at (or from) a particular school. If you're targeting kids in college, you can reach out to a particular graduation year if that's relevant. You can target particular majors. For example, a computer company could create an ad and target it to all the computer scientists and engineering seniors from the top schools. If you're planning an alumni event for Amherst College, you can target everyone who is listed as alumnae of Amherst. If you want to wish your collegiate child a public *Happy Birthday!,* you can buy an ad and target it only at her school.

To specify a specific school or major, select the education level and then start typing the name of the school in the field. The name of the school most likely autocompletes for you; if not, then it's not in the system and can't be targeted.

✔ **Workplaces:** You can target everyone who works at a particular company by filling out the Workplaces field. This is most relevant for those who want to target an ad at their own company (or another company) for recruiting purposes. If the company you're looking for isn't listed, click Help in the footer, and suggest it to the User Operations team.

✔ **Political Views:** To spread a political-type message, you may want to target your ad toward those who've specified their political leanings in their profile. Note that when you leave all the check boxes blank your ad reaches people regardless of what they have listed as their political view, but that when you select all the boxes you also end up targeting people regardless of their political views. Checking all or none of the boxes leads to identical targeting.

✔ **Relationship Status:** People with different relationship statuses are likely to respond differently to different products and different messaging. There are many good examples of advertisers who effectively change the tune of their messaging depending on the relationship status. Just like Political Views, selecting all or none of the check boxes leads to identical targeting.

After making your selections for your targeted ad, click Continue. ***Note:*** Whenever you see the Back button, you can click it to go to the previous screen and make changes, if necessary.

We spend a lot of time emphasizing how valuable targeting can be if you have a message that's relevant to only certain kinds of people. However, what if you have a product everyone can enjoy? You still target your ad — with tailored messaging for different people. Say, for example, you are the promotion's manager for The Jewelry Store. You can create one ad targeted at women with a message about treating one's self, and another ad targeted at men that emphasizes gift giving. You can be more specific by targeting married men with an ad about buying gifts for their wives, or targeting young men with an ad about gifts for their mothers, for example.

Step 4. Create your ad

After you target your ad and have a clear understanding of your audience, it's time to create the ad so that it speaks to that particular audience.

Figure 17-4 shows where you add some basic information about your ad, as described here:

✔ **Title/Body:** When you enter the ad title in the Title field and body in the Body field, use the preview on the right to see what your ad will look like.

✔ **(Optional) Photo:** You can upload a photo — the way your photo shows up in the Preview is how people see it in your ad.

✔ **Add Social Actions to My Ad:** If you're the Admin of a Facebook Page or have developed an application, then you see a check box at the bottom of the Create Your Ad step, asking if you want to include Social Actions on your ad. (We describe Social Actions in the earlier "Social Ads" section. Way cool.) After checking the box, you must click Choose Sources. Check the Facebook Page (or pages, if you're the admin for more than one) or Application that houses the ad you want Social Actions appended to. It's important that the Page or Pages you select are obviously relevant to the ad you're running. If you're the administrator of pages for two different restaurants, The Peach Pit and The Bronze, you don't want actions taken on The Bronze restaurant's page to be associated with ads for The Peach Pit.

Figure 17-4:
Creating
your ad's
content.

Create Your Ad

Title:	Are you a Dummy?
Body:	... needs help understanding Facebook? / Facebook for Dummies will unDummy you fast.
Photo:	Upload a Photo Browse...

Images will be resized to fit inside a 110px by 80px box. Use 3:4 or 16:9 aspect ratio for best results.

Are you a Dummy?

Facebook DUMMIES

Do you know someone who needs help understanding Facebook?

Facebook for Dummies will unDummy you fast.

Click the ad preview to test your link.

☑ Add social actions to my ad. (What's this?)
Actions from Facebook for Dummies will automatically be added.
Choose Sources

Back   Continue ▶

Your ad appears either in the vertical column beneath the Applications menu or in the horizontal space in News Feed, so the layout of your ad is adjusted to fit either spot. Therefore, the preview you see while you create your ad might not be the same layout that your audience sees.

After making your choices here, click Continue to go to Step 5.

Step 5. Set your budget

Paying for ads isn't quite as straightforward as, "Hot dogs, 99 cents, get your hot dogs!" The amount you pay for your ad depends on all kinds of factors, including how you target it, whether you care that people click your ad or just see it, and your budget. We can best explain how pricing works on Facebook by breaking down the options you have while setting your advertising budget (check out Figure 17-5 to follow along with this list):

- ✓ **Pay for Clicks versus Pay for Views:** When you set your budget, you see two tabs: Pay for Clicks and Pay for Views. Select Pay for Clicks if the goal of your ad is that the audience ends up on your actual Web site or Page. Amazon is an example of a company that would likely choose Pay for Clicks because customers buy products on Amazon.com.

  Other examples of Pay for Clicks advertisers would be application developers who want people to use their application, bands who want people to try their music, or non-profits who want people to contribute to their cause. Coca-Cola might be the kind of company that would use Pay for Views to get their brand and slogan in front of people. Someone selling their car might use Pay for Views after putting a photo and all contact info in the ad.

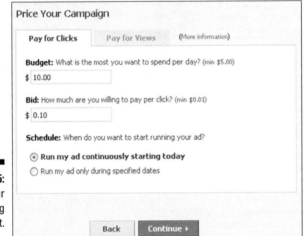

Price Your Campaign

| **Pay for Clicks** | Pay for Views | (More information) |

Budget: What is the most you want to spend per day? (min $5.00)

$ 10.00

Bid: How much are you willing to pay per click? (min $0.01)

$ 0.10

Schedule: When do you want to start running your ad?

- ● **Run my ad continuously starting today**
- ○ Run my ad only during specified dates

Back   Continue ▸

Figure 17-5: Set your advertising budget.

- ✓ **Budget:** You're charged based on how many people click or view your ad (up to your maximum daily budget, which you set by entering it into the Budget field). If you set a maximum daily budget of $10, and offer to pay up to 10 cents per click, you hope that approximately 100 people click on your ad. The Facebook Ad system does some fancy behind-the-scenes math to figure out how many people must see your ad to get you your 100 clicks. If the system shows your ad to too few people, then you won't end up paying the full $10, Facebook makes less money, and you might not get the response you were hoping for. If the system shows your ad to too many people, then you might end up getting some free attention you don't have to pay for. Good for you; less good for Facebook. So the system is constantly being improved to deliver your ad to exactly as many people as it takes to get the response you're willing to pay for.

✔ **Bid:** Besides filling out your daily budget, you also specify how much you want to bid for a click or a set of 1,000 views. Let's say that five advertisers want to target men who have the text *tattoos* in their profile. All five advertisers bid differently for clicks. Each time men with *tattoos* in their profile log in, the ad system shows them the ad from the highest bidder, until that advertiser's budget is exhausted. Then the system shows the ad of the next highest bidder. For each click or view, advertisers are charged the price of the next highest bid beneath their own (except that the second-to-lowest bidder pays 1 cent higher than the lowest bid). If an advertiser bids 10 cents per click, and another bids 5 cents, and all the others bid 3 cents, the first advertiser ends up paying 5 cents, the second advertiser 4 cents, and all the others 3 cents as well.

Facebook has a lot of users, but it doesn't show each user very many ads. The value in bidding high is that it's the safest way to get the response you're after. The value in bidding conservatively is that you might pay less for the same number of clicks or views. The bid system helps advertisers pay exactly what a click or impression is worth to them. Moreover, the companies who take the time to make highly targeted and quality ads often end up bidding higher than those companies that produce low quality ads; therefore, users are more likely to see high quality and relevant ads.

✔ **Schedule:** You can choose to either start running your ad right away or specify the start and end dates for your ad. When you select Run My Ad Continuously Starting Today, you stop your ad when your goals are met; otherwise, you're charged per day continuously.

Make your budget choices and click Continue to move to Step 6.

The first ad you create on Facebook is automatically put in a campaign. When you create more ads, you're able to add them to various campaigns or create new campaigns. You can set your budget at the campaign level rather than just the individual while setting the budget for your ad.

Step 6. Review your ad

After you choose your audience, create your ad, and set your own budget, it's time to admire all your handiwork on the Review Ad page. Rather than just applauding yourself for a job well done, review all the information carefully to make sure you're getting exactly what you're about to pay for. Speaking of which, when you're done reviewing all the information, fill out the standard credit card information on the bottom half of the page and place your order.

But first! We highly recommend you read the advertising guidelines and advertising policy linked on the right side of this page before you begin your Facebook advertising adventures. When you're confident all the information is accurate, click Finish.

Managing Your Social Ads

After you start running an ad on Facebook, you're more than welcome to cross your fingers and hope for the response you're after. However, with the Ads Manager, if you want to know exactly what kind of responses your ads are getting, and if you want to improve the performance of your ads, you can always pause ads while you make changes to optimize your efforts.

✔ To manage your ads, sign into Facebook and click Ad Manager (also called Ads and Pages if you're the admin of a Page in addition to running ads) in the Applications menu.

Applications	edit
📇 Ads and Pages	

✔ On the Overview page, you see a graph of the performance of your two most active Ad campaigns. The overview graph shows clicks, impressions, and the click-through-rate over time. The bottom of the Overview page shows the performance of your ad today compared to yesterday.

✔ Ad Campaigns (at the top) shows you much more detailed information about each of your ads (grouped by campaigns), as shown in Figure 17-6. Information here includes the following:

- Your bid (which you can change inline at any time)

- Type of ad (Cost per Click versus Cost per View)

- The number of total *impressions* (the number of times someone sees your ad)

- The number of clicks so far

- The click-through-rate

- The average cost you're paying per click (if your ad is a Cost per Click ad)

- The average cost per million views

- Your total spent so far

You can specify whether you want to see all these metrics for the last 24 hours, 7 days, or to date.

	Overview	**Ad Campaigns**		Pages				**Create an Ad ▶**	

Ads Internal Promos rename

Campaign is ▶ **running.** │ ▼

Daily Budget: $1000.00 edit
Schedule: 11/14/2007 to the end of time.

Stats: ◉ Last 24 hrs ○ Last 7 days ○ All | Ads | Daily Stats | Insights |

Name	Bid ($)	Type	Imp.	Clicks	CTR (%)	Avg. CPC ($)	Avg. CPM ($)	Spent ($)
▶ Advertise Here UK	2.00	CPC	832096	540	0.06	0.24	0.15	128.41
▶ Advertise Here US	2.00	CPC	408081	290	0.07	0.30	0.21	86.30
▶ Advertise Here CA	2.00	CPC	298246	50	0.02	0.63	0.11	31.57
▶ Advertise Here AU	2.00	CPC	5637	0	0.00	0.00	0.00	0.00
✕ Show Deleted Ads			147081	4	0.00	0.89	0.02	3.54
Totals			1691141	884	0.05	0.28	0.15	249.82

Figure 17-6: The Ad Campaigns page enables you to track your ad's statistics.

- ✔ Clicking Insights in the upper right of any campaign shows you the same information from the Overview page for the particular campaign that you selected.

- ✔ Clicking the name of an individual ad shows you all the detailed information at the campaign level, but this time about the performance of that particular ad in a campaign. This page also shows the preview of the ad, and reminds you of your targeting information. From this detailed view of an ad's performance, you can choose to pause or stop your ad at any time.

Between graphs and detailed statistics, the ad management interface gives you all the information you need to help customize your ads to get the absolute best return on your investment. This isn't as selfless as it sounds. If you're having the most success possible, it's likely you're making extremely high-quality ads with accurate targeting; therefore, a better experience for Facebook users and a better experience for Facebook. To this end, Facebook plans to continue building out these tools to create one of the most robust, valuable advertising networks on the Web.

Spam Is Not Delicious

Good user experience is key to the success of Facebook and, therefore, key to the advertisers who advertise on Facebook. In order to preserve good user experience, Facebook puts most ads through a review process before they're allowed on the site. Your ad must be generally relevant to the people you target. The text and image of your ad must not be misleading in any way. The content of your ad, and the site that it links to, must be appropriate for any audience. Ads may be rejected for other quality metrics, such as misspellings, too much capitalization or punctuation, and so on. Generally, if your ad is clear and tasteful, you won't have any problems.

Chapter 18

Facebook Platform

*F*acebook made headlines in May of 2007 when it announced it was opening up its platform such that any developers anywhere in the world could develop applications on top of its social graph. If that sounds like a lot of buzzwords, that's because it is. What this really means is that applications — features like Photos, Events, and Marketplace — that in the past have been built only by Facebook engineers can now be built by engineers who don't work for Facebook and still integrate into the Facebook experience.

In this chapter, we first give you the basic breakdown of what a platform is and how it works for both users and developers. After that, we go into more depth about what developers need to know when they're building applications. We also cover a lot of these topics from a user's perspective in Chapter 8.

Understanding What Facebook Platform Is

The most basic example of a platform is a soapbox. In ye olden times, people would take a crate that soap was shipped in, set it down in the middle of ye olde towne square, step on top of it, and shout out their ideas to ye olde crowde. There are three players here: the soapbox, the person, and the crowde. While you keep reading, here are a couple things to keep in mind:

▶ **The soapbox didn't create the ideas.** The ideas belonged to the person shouting, the soapbox literally giving them a platform from which to enumerate them. A person could stand in the middle of the crowd, at the same level, yelling at everyone else, but they wouldn't be heard as well.

▶ **The soapbox means nothing without the crowd.** No matter how high the soapbox boosts you up and allows you to project your voice, if there's no one there to listen, your ideas can't spread.

If you've ever used a PC, you've probably used some version of Microsoft Windows (something like Windows 95, Windows XP, or Windows Vista). Windows is what's known as an *operating system*. It's the graphical interface used to access files and programs on your computer. You don't technically need an operating system. You could manually give your computer text commands to navigate the various files and systems, but that's much harder than using the interface that Microsoft provides. The operating system offers some core functionality that can then be used by various applications.

You've also probably used some version of Microsoft Word. This program was developed by Microsoft. However, you might have other programs on your computer that weren't built by Microsoft — maybe some sort of game, or something like Quicken, which you can use to track your spending. Because both Microsoft and Quicken can build applications, or programs, that work within Microsoft Windows, Windows is a platform for applications — whether built by Microsoft or by a third party.

Facebook Platform, like a soapbox or an operating system, also offers core functionality that can be accessed to create applications. Facebook refers to its core functionality as the social graph. The *social graph* is the series of connections — profiles linked to other profiles via friendships — that makes up Facebook. Information spreads across the social graph via News Feed, which tells you the most recent information about all your friends based on your closeness and the relevance of the information.

For a long time, Facebook was the only company that could build on its own platform. And it did; it built Photos, Notes, Events, and Groups. All these applications use the connections that exist between individuals on the site to spread more information. These connections are what set Facebook applications apart from other sites, even ones specialized for various applications.

The classic example of this is Photos. Facebook has the number-one photo sharing application on the Web. Facebook Photos doesn't have all the features of specific photo-sharing sites, like high-resolution storage or anything like that, but it's still more popular. This is because of the connections — your ability to tag your friends in photos. When you do this, your friends are notified and they look at the pictures. This information is also spread through News Feed, where your friends can see your photos and comment on what they see. This, in turn, makes your friends more likely to use the Photos application the next time they want to share photos.

When Facebook opened up its platform in May 2007, it enabled third-party developers anywhere to build applications that fit into Facebook as easily as Facebook Photos fits in. Like the soapbox, Facebook Platform lets application developers get their ideas and creations out to a crowd of people quickly and easily.

The soapbox — the platform — doesn't create the ideas or applications, and the platform means nothing without the crowd. We cover the "crowd" aspect more in the next few sections.

Harnessing the Power of Facebook Platform

The "Power" of Facebook Platform lies in Facebook's ever growing and deeply connected user base. At the time of this book's writing, this user base is over 50 million strong. By the time you read this, it will be well over 60 million. In the Photos example in the preceding section, we mention that the information contained in photos as well as the Photos application itself spread across the social graph. The mechanism that spreads this is News Feed. While you take actions and your friends are notified of those actions, they also take actions, and their friends find out about it. This happens quickly and to a lot of people.

Case Study: iLike

Before Facebook Platform launched, one of the most requested features by Facebook users was that Facebook make a way for them to add music to their profiles. iLike, a music-sharing Web site, created an application that enabled users to add favorite musicians and music clips to their profile, just like they'd always been requesting. What happened next is best described in a blog post from iLike's Web site posted on May 26 (Platform launched on May 25):

> In our first 20 hours of opening doors, we had 50,000 users sign up, and it is only accelerating. (10,000 users joined in the first 12 hrs. 10,000 more users in the next 3 hours. 30,000 more users in the next 5 hours!)

> We started the system not knowing what to expect, with only 2 servers, but ready with backup. Facebook's rabid user base chewed up our 2 servers almost instantly. We doubled our capacity to catch up. And then we doubled it again. And again. And again. Oh, crap — we ran out of servers! Although iLike.com has a very healthy level of Web traffic, and even though about half of all the servers in our datacenter were sitting unused, idle, as backup capacity, we are now completely maxed out.

> We just emailed everybody we know across over a dozen Bay Area start-ups, corporations, and venture firms in a desperate plea to find spare servers so we can triple our capacity for the continued onslaught.

Tomorrow we are picking up over 100 servers from different companies to have them installed just to handle the weekend's traffic. (For those who responded to our late night pleas, thank you!)

Today was a critical day in iLike's history. The Facebook Platform enabled us to build a service that in a single day matched and beat the impressive traffic we built on iLike.com in over 6 months. iLike is now growing at more than twice the pace it was yesterday, and accelerating. Fasten your seatbelts everybody, here we come!

Mass distribution

The first aspect of the viral growth of any Facebook Platform application is that it gets mass distribution across the social graph. As people add your application, their friends get News Feed stories about it. The average person on Facebook has about 120 friends, so if Leah adds your application, some portion of her friends find out about it. If Carolyn sees this story in her News Feed, and chooses to add the application as well, two things happen:

✔ Some portion of Carolyn's friends find out about it.

✔ Friends that Carolyn and Leah have in common are more likely to find out about it because News Feed believes that it's more relevant when your friends have taken the same action.

Say you're building some sort of Web application that lets people create slide-shows of photos. You could launch your own Web site, with your state-of-the art tools and features, and ask friends to spread the word to their friends. You could launch a massive advertising campaign to drive people to your site. Either way, you need to grow a user base from scratch.

With Facebook, you don't have to start from scratch. In fact, an active user base is right there waiting for you. The act of friends telling friends is taken care of, too. Without even trying, people can tell their friends, "Hey, I like this slideshow application," and their friends can decide if they want in, too. By building your application on top of Facebook Platform, you get access to Facebook's enormous user base and distribution across it through News Feed.

News Feed Optimization, or NFO, is a term that's occasionally thrown about by developers to explain that getting stories about an application into News Feed is the most important way to grow that application's user base. Keep in mind these important types of News Feed stories that optimize your growth via News Feed:

✔ **Add application stories:** These stories are shown to friends of people who've added your application. The way to keep these stories going is to keep getting people to add your application.

✔ **Stories for people who've already added your application:** After folks add your application and opt-in to have your application generate News Feed stories, you can publish as many stories as you'd like for News Feed to consider for any particular user's News Feed. These stories are the best way to keep people engaged with your application.

For example, if Carolyn sees a story that Leah drew on Blake's Graffiti Wall, she might think, "Oh yeah, I love Graffiti Wall, let me draw on someone's Wall." News Feed is a way to keep people reminded of the options they have on Facebook. This directly benefits your application because the Popular section, or the front page of the Application Directory, is based on a metric of both number of users and engagement levels of users. Therefore, if all your users are using your application every day, your application moves up in the Recently Popular list.

✔ **Stories for people who haven't added your application:** These stories help your application grow virally; an interesting story about friends using your application (not just adding it) can attract many new users.

Deep integration

The comparison we keep making is that your application can hook into Facebook and be just as successful as Facebook Photos and Facebook Events. This sort of comparison wouldn't be fair if Facebook didn't give access to most of the same integration points that users are accustomed to for the applications built by Facebook. Your application can hook into a user's experience in several places on Facebook. Please note that these are all ways to integrate *after* a user has added your application to his account. Additionally, you access these points only with express permission.

✔ **The Application box:** Adding a box to a user's profile is one of the most basic ways to integrate an application into Facebook and gain visibility for a user's friends. The Application box can contain anything you wish. Moreover, any user should be able to interact with — and add — your application straight from an Application box on someone else's page. An example of an Application box is shown in Figure 18-1.

✔ **The Wall:** The Wall is a public forum for leaving people notes or messages on their profiles. You can add content from your application to the Wall as an attachment. A good example of this is the Video application, which lets you record a video Wall post straight onto your friends' Walls. You can see how your application integrates into the Wall in Figure 18-2.

✔ **Profile Action links:** Profile Action links are usually found directly beneath a user's profile picture. Depending on a user's settings, you can insert extra links here so that people can instantly start interacting with someone through your application after they arrive on a profile. You can see an example of this (Play Scrabulous with me) in Figure 18-3.

Figure 18-1:
Adding an
Application
box to the
user's page
adds visibility
to an app.

Click to watch the video.

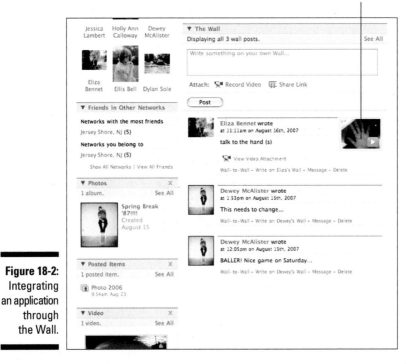

Figure 18-2:
Integrating
an application
through
the Wall.

✔ **Message attachments:** Similar to how a Wall post can include media from your application, you can include an attachment in messages between individual users. Again, Video is a great example of this integration, as shown in Figure 18-4.

Figure 18-3:
Interact with a friend through an application by clicking a Profile Action link.

Figure 18-4:
Use Facebook messaging to send videos.

✔ **The Notifications page:** Facebook sends people notifications when someone writes on your Wall, or tags a photo of you. You can also send people notifications when others interact with them via your application. All these notifications appear together in a list on the Notifications page. However, people can block notifications and mark them as spam. If you send too many notifications, you might find that people start ignoring them, or worse, you could be marked as a spammer. The two ways in which people control these notifications are shown in Figure 18-5.

✔ **News Feed:** News Feed can give people stories about other people using your applications. For example, a story about Leah drawing on Carolyn's Graffiti Wall, may prompt someone else to draw on either Leah's or Carolyn's Graffiti Wall, too. Figure 18-6 shows a sample News Feed story.

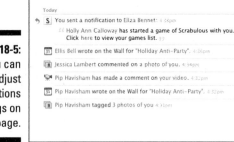

Figure 18-5: You can adjust notifications settings on this page.

Figure 18-6: Check the News Feed to see which apps your friends have used lately.

✔ **Mini-Feed:** Mini-Feed only publishes stories about one profile owner, but the ability to publish Mini-Feed stories means that all the people visiting that profile see the interaction with a variety of applications. Figure 18-7 shows a sample Mini-Feed with stories about several different applications.

✔ **Applications menu links:** The links in the left-hand Applications menu are some of the fastest ways for people to navigate to the applications they use the most. You can insert a link here for your application. You can see the expanded Applications menu in Figure 18-8.

✔ **Requests:** Facebook Requests are interactive notifications that require the second party to take an action. For example, inviting someone to an event requires that person to RSVP. Requests appear on the right column of the Home page and are listed individually, unlike the notifications flag, which keeps count of all notifications listed. Some Requests examples are shown in Figure 18-9.

✔ **The Canvas:** The Canvas is covered in Chapter 3 as well; it's the area within the Facebook Frame that you fill however you wish. Most Facebook applications have what are called *splash pages,* which highlights content that a user's friends have recently added via that application. You can put any content you think is relevant on Canvas pages, and your application can have as many Canvas pages as you wish.

Figure 18-7: The Mini-Feed also shows information about apps being used.

Figure 18-8:
Use the left-
hand menu
links to
navigate
between
applications.

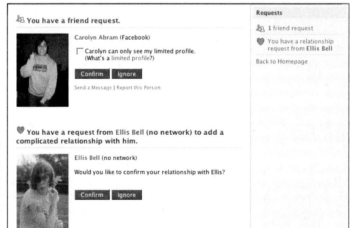

Figure 18-9:
Requests
appear in
the right
column.

✔ **Privacy settings:** Facebook users are very accustomed to having granular control over their information and content they add to the site. For
example, when a user begins to create a photo album, the first screen
includes a privacy setting for that album. Integrating privacy options
into your application makes people more comfortable using it.

✔ **Application-to-application integration:** Many applications built by Facebook integrate into one another. For example, you can add photos to a group or event. Facebook is working on creating hooks for all of its applications, so that admins can choose to add other applications to groups and events. To integrate with non-Facebook applications, the application you want to integrate into needs to have its own hooks or integration points.

Business opportunity

Facebook makes its money from advertising. Facebook doesn't charge developers for their use of Facebook Platform but encourages people to use their applications to make money. The two main ways to use Platform to make money are selling advertisements on your Canvas pages and selling goods or performing transactions directly from your Canvas pages. Either way you get to keep all the revenue.

You can only serve ads on your own application's Canvas pages, not inside people's profiles via the Profile box.

The Application of Applications

You can build a few high level types of applications on top of Facebook Platform. The distinction among these is in terms of who's using the application — businesses, users, or both — and where the application is being used — on Facebook, another Web site, or a user's desktop. We talk briefly about these types and offer some examples in this section.

Applications for users on Facebook

When people sign up for Facebook, they have certain applications that are pre-added to their account — Photos, Notes, Groups, Events, Posted Items, and Marketplace. All the other applications need to be *added* by each user individually before they can fully interact with the application.

If you choose to develop an application for within Facebook, re-read all the integration points outlined in the previous "Deep integration" section. A great example of an integrated Facebook application is (fluff)Friends. (fluff)Friends showcases the adorable artwork of Julie Zhou (a Facebook engineer) and allows people to add a small pet — a (fluff)Friend — to their profiles. Users can pet each other's (fluff)Friends, generating notifications for the pet owners as well as producing a change in the mood of that friend. This is the basic functionality of an app that appeals to the profile owner (Hey, check out my pet, I named him Thor.) and has a social element to it (people can pet and feed their friends' (fluff)Friends).

(fluff)Friends took it one step further in engagement, however, by allowing people to earn *munny* (tender) by petting each other's friends. The munny is used to buy food and habitats. Additionally, people can bet munny on races between (fluff)Friends. People can also fill out a profile for their friends — creating a (fluff)Book within Facebook.

(fluff)Friends takes advantage of almost every integration point in a manner that isn't spammy but simply engaging. The sale of (fluff) tee-shirts helps cover the developer's server costs, and the users of (fluff)Friends are provided with a great application. Everyone wins.

Applications for businesses on Facebook

In November of 2007, Facebook introduced the concept of a *Facebook Page,* which is a place for businesses, celebrities, and artists to establish a presence on Facebook. Along with this change came a new place where developers could focus their efforts. Maybe users don't need a Menu application, but restaurants do. Similarly, not-so-famous folks might not need to list *public appearances*, but celebrities do. Developing applications for businesses provides a brand new opportunity for you as a developer. Take heed of the following integration points:

- ✔ **Pages Application Box:** Similar to a user's Application box on the Profile, Page admins can add boxes to their Pages showcasing the functionality of your application, and enabling people to interact with that application there.

- ✔ **Pages Mini-Feed:** Just like users, Pages have Mini-Feeds, which serve as a constantly updating list of actions the Page has taken — whether updating its information, adding a photo album, or somehow creating content with your application.

- ✔ **News Feed:** Stories that appear on a Page's Mini-Feed can become candidates to appear in the News Feed of that Page's *fans* (people who have established a connection to that Page). Again, this can bring more users to your application.

Applications elsewhere on the Web

You might already have a Web site where it doesn't make sense to port all of your information into Facebook, but maybe you can enhance your users' experience if they bring information from Facebook to your site. An example of this might be an interface that maps where your friends are based on their region networks. A user can log into that Web site with their Facebook credentials and see the mash-up of friends and maps. These types of applications can also allow your customers to publish the actions they take on your site back onto Facebook for their friends to see. Chapter 19 gives a detailed example of how Pandora.com has integrated with this type of application.

Desktop applications

You might also want to help a user integrate Facebook with something happening on her desktop, say, displaying on her profile what she's listening to on iTunes. Alternatively, it might bring information from Facebook to the desktop in the form of a screensaver of friends' Facebook photos.

Facebook Branded Applications and Third-Party Applications

Facebook Platform is moving toward creating a level playing field for third-party applications and Facebook applications. However, now that everyone has access to the playing field, there's a lot of competition. Facebook has a few advantages over third-party applications, but the biggest one is its brand. People trust Photos and Events. They've used these applications without even thinking twice. Additionally, these particular applications are pre-added to a user's Facebook account upon registration.

However, third-party developers can have a huge impact and be very successful in several places. First, when an application is simply better than Facebook's version of the same application, it outperforms Facebook's version. Second, Facebook serves an audience of 60 million plus users, and strives to build applications that appeal to everyone. An application developer can develop for specific groups with specific desires and discover huge pockets of untapped opportunity. For example, Facebook recently shut down its Courses application, which allowed students to list their classes and find other students to study with. Facebook couldn't maintain Courses for only a minority of the user base. Several Courses applications have sprung up from third parties to fill that void. Your niche might be sports fans or poker enthusiasts, and your attention to their needs means that you can get incredible traction with that base.

Helping users to find your application

Users find applications through their friends' profiles, integration points (discussed previously), and the Application Directory. Figure 18-10 shows the front page of the Application Directory.

The Application Directory has four browse tabs on top: Recently Popular, Most Activity, Most Active Users, and Newest. The metrics that Facebook uses to rank these measure user *engagement* — not just number of users. Engagement is the number of users that touch your application every day. *Touch points* include

- ✔ **Canvas page views:** Your Canvas pages are the screens within Facebook that you control. Views of these pages count as an engagement metric.

- ✔ **Link clicks on the profile:** Anytime someone clicks on a link in your application's box in a user's profile is a touch.

- ✔ **Mock-Ajax form submission:** A form that a user can submit from a Profile box. Anytime a user puts in some sort of content via your application is a touch.

- ✔ **Click to play Flash:** Flash is not allowed to auto-play on Facebook; however, if a user actively starts a Flash interface, this is considered a touch on your application.

Facebook measures engagement instead of total number of users to provide developers an incentive to build applications that are more than just a box on a profile that's never revisited. Engagement gives prospective users a better sense of how useful or entertaining an application is, and they can better decide if they want that application, too.

Facebook also holds itself to engagement standards for the site as a whole, measuring Active Users on a monthly basis rather than just Number of Accounts. Accounts that aren't used aren't included in Facebook's activity measurements.

Users can also browse the Application Directory by using the keywords on the right-hand side. Whether a user arrives on a keyword-based browse page, applications are still ranked by engagement. You can choose up to three categories for your application.

From anywhere that users find your application, they can click through to its About page. A sample About page is shown in Figure 18-11.

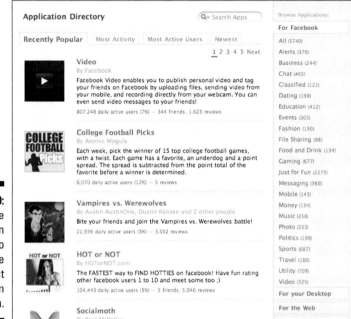

Figure 18-10:
Browse the
Application
Directory to
find the
perfect
application
for you.

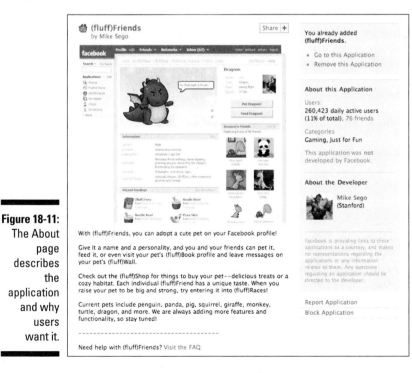

Figure 18-11:
The About
page
describes
the
application
and why
users
want it.

While your application's About page isn't as important as your application's actual functionality, it's worth putting in some time to explain what it is your application does and why it's worthwhile for a user to add it. Users want to know what your application means for them before they add it, so this is a great way to explain it in your own words.

The About page also contains a space for reviews and discussion boards. These two spaces are an invaluable way for you to get feedback and respond to criticism. We talk about this part more in the upcoming "Best Practices for Developers" section.

Getting users to trust your application

For a user, adding an application is kind of a big deal. First, they're allowing a third party access to a good portion of their information (though not contact information). Facebook encourages people to add only applications that they trust.

Here's some of the advice we give to users in Chapter 9: How do you decide whom to trust? The same way you decide how a profile is trustworthy or real — you look at the available data. When you look at an application's About page in the Application Directory, look for things like who built the application. Was it a company you've heard of and trust, such as Amazon.com? If not, check out the reviews and the discussion boards. Are people reporting problems with the application, such as spam or inappropriate content? If not, you can probably feel comfortable adding the application and allowing it to access your information.

As a developer, understand what users are looking for and answer their questions up front and openly. In the end, it's better for a user to decide not to use your application because of the information you provide than for the same person to add your application under false pretenses, and then report it as a malicious application after they figure out what your application does.

Also, keep in mind that users have the ability to authorize only parts of your application's integration. Figure 18-12 shows the confirmation screen that users see when adding an application. They can opt-out of News Feed and Mini-Feed stories, the Profile box, and the Applications menu links. The more they trust your application, the less likely they are to opt-out of these features, making it more likely they help spread your application.

Developing on Facebook Platform

Developing on Facebook Platform is both challenging and rewarding. Facebook Platform is constantly iterating to make things better for both users and developers; therefore, your application has to keep up with the changes. The popularity of your application can soar overnight, so you need to be prepared to keep up with server loads and traffic to your application's Canvas page.

To get started as a developer, head to `developers.facebook.com`, which is full of detailed resources including the Developer Wiki and a forum for getting help, tips, and collaborating with other developers. After you reach the site, click the big, yellow Get Started button on the left side of the page. You can then add the Developer application to your account. The landing page for the Developer application provides many helpful links — this is also how you access your application after it's built. Figure 18-13 shows the landing page after you add the Developer application.

Figure 18-12:
Users have choices when adding an application to their profile.

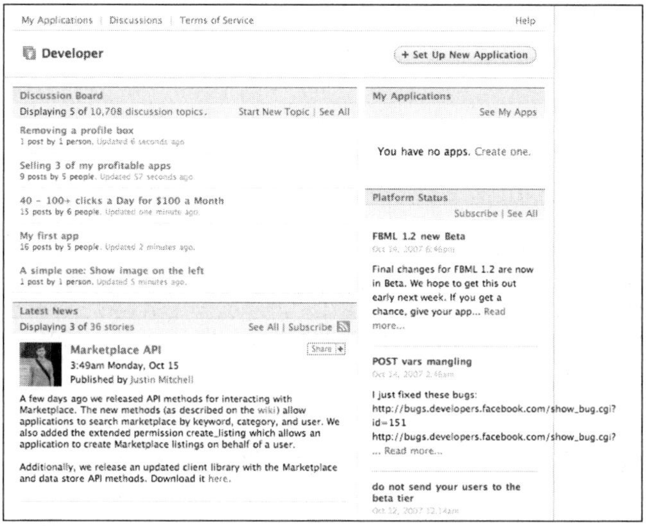

Figure 18-13:
The Developer page is the starting point for adding an application to Facebook.

Developing an application on Facebook Platform has many nuances. This list highlights some of the bigger concepts that you need to know before you start:

✔ **API:** Facebook's Application Programming Interface (API) uses a REST-based interface, which means method calls are sent over the Internet using HTTP GET or POST request sent to Facebook's REST server.

✔ **FQL:** Facebook Query Language allows you to use an SQL-style interface to access data available through Facebook Platform. Facebook developed its own query language to give developers a more consistent interface, even though you're accessing data you can get through other API functions. FQL respects all the privacy limits of Facebook users.

✔ **FBML:** Facebook Markup Language is a subset of HTML with some functions removed (and others added) to make it specific to Facebook.

If you're looking for help after you add the Developer application, the best resource is the developer community. The Developer Wiki and the discussion boards are maintained by a group of passionate and intelligent developers, so don't be afraid to ask questions and get help. The Developer Wiki can be found at `http://wiki.developers.facebook.com`. You can also use the discussion boards to look for developers to partner with or employ. The discussion boards are part of the Developer application. Part of the Discussion Board is shown in Figure 18-13.

Best Practices for Developers

The most general advice we have for developers is this: Fit into the existing Facebook Experience for a user, and your application will have more traction. The following tips speak to that point:

✔ **Don't spam.** Users hate spam. If they associate spam with your application, they will probably hate your application. When Platform launched, there were methods of notifying users about applications that were abused by developers, and users started to complain of spam. As a result, invite limits were introduced, as was the ability to block notifications from certain applications. Obviously, it can be hard to strike the right balance between notifying people of something interesting (which Facebook wants you to do) and over-notifying people. However, it's very important that every developer try to find this balance. It's best for the entire developer community if Facebook users associate third-party applications with utility and fun, and not with spam and annoyance.

✔ **Don't be obnoxious.** Facebook has always been known for its clean interface. Some people wanted a bit more color, and it's good that Platform enabled that. Nevertheless, Platform applications that are too flashy or obnoxious decrease engagement on all of Facebook, which harms the entire developer community. Also, don't develop obnoxious actions, such as presenting people with a page to notify all their friends of something, with no way off the page (except to do so). When Carolyn receives a page like this, she immediately removes the application and reports it for spam.

✔ **Be useful.** People use Facebook as a way to keep in touch with friends and get the information they need about people. If your application is useful, it is more likely to spread virally. For example, Facebook recently removed the Courses box from the profile, instead letting various Courses applications pick up the slack. These applications provide high value to specific communities.

Facebook develops applications that everyone can use, leaving Platform applications with a lot of room to grow in niche markets, providing utility for people with specific needs. For example, Facebook frequently had to shut down fake profiles that people created for their dogs and cats. Developing a Profile feature to accommodate pets wouldn't have served everyone on the site. With Facebook Platform, the Dogbook and Catbook applications were created, finally allowing the group of people with pets to express their love and affection for their dogs and cats.

✔ **Be social.** Folks use Facebook to keep in touch and interact with friends and family in a new way. Your application spreads quickly if it has an inherent social aspect to it. For example, an application that lets a user upload content, but doesn't let him tag friends or share that content easily will quickly be forgotten in the ever-expanding list of applications. People want to connect with their friends. Give them new ways to do so.

✔ **Be clear about what you do.** This almost could be crammed into the *Don't be obnoxious* category, but it's very important that people understand what they're doing when they add your application or interact with it. An application that advertises itself as tracking who comes to your profile not only freaked out many users, but also deliberately misled them to make them click on a link on others' profiles that notified the profile owner who had been there. While this wasn't a violation of our Terms of Use, it wasn't fair to the people interacting with that application.

✔ **Be competitive.** Numerous people are developing on Platform, so to distinguish your application from others that may be similar, make sure it has the absolute best feature set you can build. Good applications take time to build, so giving yourself a little extra time to do it right might make all the difference in the world.

The fbFund

The fbFund was announced in September of 2007 as an initiative to help entrepreneurs build applications and businesses on Facebook Platform. You can apply to the fbFund for non-recourse grants from $25,000–$250,000. The only restrictions are that you build your business on Facebook Platform and that you haven't received any previous venture funding.

Facebook decided to start the fbFund to nurture the developer community and encourage people to build quality applications. Building quality applications takes time — and time is money — so we hope the fbFund gives you the boost you need to get started.

To get started with the fbFund, add the Developers application and head to `http://www.facebook.com/developers/fbfund.php`.

✔ **Listen to your users.** Facebook users are passionate and vocal. Use that to your advantage. Read the reviews and discussions on your application's About page, and respond to negative posts when you can. As your customers (and people who can help you get at what you need to build), users are an asset to you and a way for you to stay competitive. Take their suggestions seriously.

✔ **Be reliable.** No matter how good your application is, if a user is always hit with a *Down for Maintenance* message, she stops using your application. Spend time and resources planning on how to scale quickly for a large user base.

✔ **Be fast.** Users prefer things that go quickly. For example, Carolyn enjoyed a quiz feature of an application that tested her trivia knowledge of *Arrested Development*. Unfortunately, the quiz took a very long time to reload after each answer. So, despite her competitive instincts, she stopped playing.

Part V
The Part of Tens

The 5th Wave   By Rich Tennant

"Jim and I do a lot of business together on Facebook. By the way, Jim, did you get the sales spreadsheet and little blue pony I sent you?"

In this part . . .

In the earlier parts of this book, we focus heavily on options and hypothetical situations. So, to ensure that you have some concrete examples of what's really happening on Facebook, we present to you the Part of Tens.

In this part, we don't make claims about what's the *best* of anything on Facebook because every experience is unique. However, you can see how much your taste matches ours by checking out our favorites groups and applications. Additionally, you can see how Facebook has made an impact on people's lives — and how it might just have an impact on yours.

Chapter 19

Ten Great Third-Party Applications

· ·

*T*raditionally, Facebook has focused on offering the most general types of functionality that just about anyone would find useful. But, in life, different people have different needs and desires. Students like to know what courses their friends are taking. Athletes sometimes trade exercise tips; some record their workouts. Foodies often swap recipes. Music lovers share new music discoveries, movie buffs rate and review films. In an attempt to be all things to all people, Facebook has empowered the masses to add all the specialized functionality that can transform Facebook from a general social network into a specific, tailored tool for managing one's lifestyle — no matter what that lifestyle consists of. This specialized functionality includes all of the examples above, tools for students, business people, hobbyists, families, and more. Here's a sampling of some of the best.

Scrabulous

Scrabulous is an online board game modeled after the Parker Brother's original game of Scrabble. What makes it a particularly good Facebook application is that it manages to appropriately leverage many of the most compelling Facebook components.

First, you can use the Facebook Friends selector to start a game with up to three of your friends. Therefore, unlike the board game, you're not limited by space and time. For example, Leah, who lives in California, can play a game with her parents in Colorado and her brother in New York. Leah takes her moves late at night, her brother takes his turn after the kids go to school the next morning, and her parents take their respective turns before dinner. Carolyn can play a game with her grandmother in Minnesota and her sister in New York. Again, they each take turns as their schedules permit.

Scrabulous uses the Facebook notification system to alert players when it's their turn and the Facebook messaging system to talk smack about the game, and it plugs into News Feed to let mutual friends know who is playing who. Finally, those who are particularly good at Scrabble appreciate the running tally of their wins that live on their profile.

Quotes

Think about the last time a friend said something hilarious, and your first thought after "hahaha" was, "I should write that down." Some people underline poignant quotations when they read them in books. Others hang inspirational quotes in visible places in their homes. Quotes is a Facebook application that lets you attribute quotations to the friends or famous people who said them. When you enter a quotation into the application, you're asked to type the name of the friend or famous person who said it. Quotes has two major components that make it a good application.

- All the quotations you enter are aggregated in a box on your profile, so your friends can see what kinds of sentiments you find funny or poignant.

- For anyone who is tagged through the Quotes application, a link appears underneath their profile picture that says, "Things I've said."

As your friends tag you in quotes, others will see all the clever things you've said (with your permission) by clicking this link on your profile. When you attribute quotations to your friends, others will see these on their profiles. Quotes is a Facebook application that helps you document and memorialize the meaningful things you, your friends, and your role models say.

Graffiti

Graffiti is a simple and beautiful application that allows users to install a blank canvas in a box on their profile where their friends can draw pictures for them. It's very simple and mimics all the features of the Profile Wall. A friend can leave a little visual gift for another friend, and mutual friends can discover the art in their News Feeds.

We like Graffiti because it's a mix of the *thinking of you* Poke and the more labor- and time-intensive tasks of writing a card and mailing it. Receiving a Graffiti drawing is rewarding because someone dedicates time to you in a public way, which shows the world that person cares about you and that you are worth their time. Goosebumps.

Pandora

Pandora (`www.pandora.com`) is a Web site that allows its users to enter a song or musician they like, around which a radio-like station is created. The station streams the songs the Pandora machine deems similar to the entered song or artist. For example, entering *Dave Mathews Band* yields a string of songs heavy on the acoustic guitar. Entering *Shakira* provides hours and hours of Spanish pop songs.

As the songs stream, users can add them to a favorites list, purchase the songs, and learn more about the bands or albums. They can also express an opinion about a particular song, which helps Pandora fine-tune their music-machine to make the stations closer to what users want to hear.

If you're a Pandora user or want to become one, download the Facebook Pandora application. After that, when you use Pandora on Facebook or on Pandora's Web site, your friends discover through their News Feed what new stations you create and what songs you like. Through your News Feed, you see your friends' Pandora activity, which introduces you to great new music. On the Pandora application Home page, you see all the stations that your friends listen to, songs and artists they marked as their favorites, and stations that you recently listened to. Additionally, you can search for more music on the Home page.

Causes

The creators of Causes state their mission as *creating equal opportunity activism.* The Causes application allows anyone who believes in a cause (and can register that cause as a nonprofit) to run a fundraising or awareness campaign on Facebook. Users of the Causes application list the causes they care about on their profile to raise awareness among their friends.

A friend may list *Stop Global Warning* on her profile, the news of which is distributed to her friends via News Feed. If, as a result, one of her friends decides to add *Stop Global Warning* to his profile, this news is distributed to his friends. This system can generate great awareness of various causes throughout the social network. Sometimes, though, awareness is not enough. The Causes application enables people to easily donate to the causes they care about. Again, these donations can, if one chooses, be distributed via News Feed, which may encourage friends to do the same.

List as many causes on your profile as you choose. Each listing gives viewers the option to learn about the cause, donate to the cause, and see how many people have donated to the cause — and how much. Each listing also shows how many people have joined or donated to the cause through your profile.

(fluff)Friends

Imagine owning a pet you don't have to pick up after, find a sitter for, or keep away from the mailman. A Caribou named LoveMePleaseIGotNoArms and a bunny, Thor, are Leah and Carolyn's respective (fluff)Friends on Facebook. For those not ready for a real pet or another real pet, owning a (fluff)Friend affords you many of the joys of owning a pet, without the hassle. You can spend your free time dressing him up, developing his personality, and accepting compliments on how adorable he is. Feed your fluff(Friend) if you have enough munny to buy it food, but you only get munny if you interact with your friends' (fluff)Friends — by virtually petting them or racing your pet against theirs. You also need munny to buy your (fluff)Friend a habitat to live in, or give a gift to your friends' (fluff)Friends.

Create a rich profile for your fluff(Friend), give it clever things to say, and have it interact in more creative ways with your friends' (fluff)Friends. (fluff)Friends is a great way to interact and stay in touch with your friends in a fun, silly, and addictive way. One word of warning: avoid petting the (fluff)Friend from someone you don't know; it's considered pretty forward.

Picnik

While the other applications primarily focus on helping you interact with your friends in new ways, Picnik focuses on enhancing your own Facebook experience, and content. The Facebook Photos application is a great way for getting your photos off your camera and in front of your friends. Adding Picnik to your profile gives you a fancy set of tools for improving your photos for more enjoyable consumption. Take any photo you add to Facebook (or that someone else has tagged you in) and edit it in cool ways. The basic tools allow you to adjust coloring, fix red eye, resize, and crop the photo. The advanced tools let you get crazy-creative by applying filters, drawing on the photos, or cutting your photos into shapes. Additionally, you can add speech bubbles, text, or cool frames. When you're all done, you can share the photos, create slideshows, or post them back to your profile. Useful *and* cool.

Extended Info

When Facebook first launched, it offered a set of basic information fields that seemed to be the most general facts people would want to share and know about one another. Those fields have not changed much, except to match the changing nature of Facebook's demographics (for example, it no longer offers a section to list your dorm room). People are different, though, and have different requirements for the kind of information that they find important to share.

As a result, users have often asked Facebook for various additions and modifications to these fields. The Extended Info application solves the problem. Users can create any information fields they desire, and then fill out the information. People who want to share more information (but can't decide what) can click the Insert Random Title button to generate a random information field to fill out.

Extended Info also allows people to organize the information fields to highlight what's most important to them. Examples of popular Extended Info fields include Languages Spoken, Currently Reading, Pet Peeves, and Things That Make Me Happy.

OpenTable

OpenTable, a service that existed long before Facebook, enables restaurants to allow people to easily make reservations online. When Facebook welcomed businesses onto the site in Facebook Pages, OpenTable built an application that any restaurant owner can add directly onto their Facebook Page. This means that you, as a hungry diner or plan maker, can make your reservations on the Facebook Page for any restaurant that uses the OpenTable application.

Which FB Employee Are You?

This application was developed by a Facebook engineer as a recruiting tool for the company. Anyone can answer a series of questions, and, based on the set of answers, the quiz-taker meets (sees the picture and bio of) the Facebook employee to whom they are most similar. If your answer to *Your alarm clock goes off at . . .* is *11 p.m.*, you might be most similar to Chris Putnam, who prefers to code by moonlight. If you respond to *Daily diet includes* with *Peanut Butter Twix,* you're probably most similar to Ezra Callahan. If you finish *Your average day at work includes . . .* with *At least one e-mail to more than twenty people just to get in a good punchline,* you're a lot like Yishan Wong, the engineer who built the application.

The Which FB Employee Are You application is a great example of how an application can be worth building even if it meets the needs of only a very small set of people.

Chapter 20

Ten Ways Facebook Uniquely Impacts Lives

Sometimes people are dismissive of Facebook saying, "I keep up with my friends by calling them and visiting them, I don't need a Web site to do that for me." This is true. However, we try to make the point throughout this book that Facebook doesn't replace real friendships — it supplements them. You can still communicate and share information with your friends without Facebook; however, it's easier and faster to do with Facebook. Some things are always a part of life; Facebook just makes them better, faster, and stronger.

Camp Friends Forever

Carolyn recently spent a summer leading a troupe of 7th graders into the wild. After two weeks of backpacking, kayaking, climbing, and bonding, the kids were given a big list of e-mail addresses and phone numbers, said their goodbyes, and were packed off to their respective homes. Carolyn (about to return to Facebook headquarters to begin her job) lamented the fact that the kids were too young to be on Facebook because they almost assuredly would lose that sheet of paper. Carolyn quickly "friended" her co-counselors (who were all old enough to be on Facebook) and keeps up with them through photo albums, notes, and the occasional Poke war.

Not just for Carolyn, but for thousands of high school students, the best-friends-for-the-summer — who had a tendency to fade away as school and life took over — are now a thing of the past. Camp friends immediately become Facebook friends, and on Facebook, no one gets lost. If you're interested in finding out what's new with your camp friends, they're only a click away. Additionally, it's easy to plan camp reunions without needing to find everyone's new info.

Not with only summer camps but all sorts of one-time programs — study abroad or volunteer experiences — people can hold on to a piece of that experience and bring it back with them to everyday life.

Heading Off to School

Everyone has a story about leaving for college. Whether they're dropping off a child, an older sister, or themselves, people remember some form of anxiety, nervousness, or blinding fear of the unknown. Who were these people in the hallway or sharing the bathroom? Who was this so-called roommate?

Now, college students go off to school having been introduced to their future dorm mates, roommates, and RAs via Facebook. Students can list their residences and easily pick out the people they'll most likely meet on the first day, thus dulling the fear that they won't know anyone.

In the time between acceptance letters and orientation, college freshmen spend their time Wall posting, friending, and getting to know their future classmates. Therefore, they join groups and support one another through a big transition. Suddenly school is less scary.

Not-So-Blind Dates

Ever been a matchmaker? Ever had a particularly difficult client? Ever been embarrassed because you didn't realize just how picky your client was until after the date? Enter Facebook. Now, "He's smart, funny, has a great job, lots of cool hobbies, a nice family, and nice friends" can be condensed into a Facebook message with a shared profile. From there, both parties can decide based on the profiles — looks, interests, or the combination of all the information — whether they want to go on a date.

Some of our friends have gone so far as to say, "No profile, no date." Given the circumstances, this is reasonable. Not only do you get a little window into a person's world, you also prepare for talking about the various interests and activities that you see there. This way, "So I saw you like snorkeling. Where does one do that when you live in Idaho?" can be a much better conversation starter than, "So, what do you do?"

Think of it as *far-sighted* dating rather than blind dating.

We've Moved!

When Leah moved to California from Seattle, the first thing she did was look up all the people she knew who were in both the Brown University and San Francisco networks. She figured it was as good a place as any to get a handle on what her new social life was going to be.

Many people are making themselves comfortable this way in new cities around the world. Carolyn got the following message from her friend, Shelby, who was living in Abuja, Nigeria, at the time.

> So I was friends with this Marine in Liberia. We lost touch when I left Liberia. He joined Facebook two weeks ago, and requested me as a friend. We started talking again. He put me in touch with a friend who works for the U.S. Consulate in Lagos, Nigeria. I Facebooked her. She found my blog address on my Facebook profile, and forwarded it to her friend who works for the U.S. Embassy in Abuja.
>
> Tonight, I went out with this girl from the Embassy and a bunch of other Embassy people. And I have plans (finally!!) for a couple of days next week with these people.
>
> And all of this is because of Facebook.

Shelby's story is just one example of how Facebook makes moving less of an ordeal — a neighborhood is waiting for you when you arrive.

Reconnecting

Long-lost friends. The one that got away. I wonder whatever happened to her. Have you heard about him? These are just some of the ways people talk about the people they somehow lost track of along the way. Whatever the reason for the loss, this sort of regret can be undone on Facebook. Finding people is easy and getting in touch is, too.

Many recent graduates exclaim that going to a reunion is unnecessary — you already know what everyone is doing five years later; you found out from Facebook. But even for the not-so-young alums, the Find Classmates and Find Coworkers feature provides a direct line to search anyone who's on Facebook that you remember from way back (or not so way back) when.

Facebook gets e-mails every so often about people who find birth parents or biological siblings on Facebook. However, the majority of the time, people are looking for and finding their old classmates and reminiscing about the good old days. Better yet, they are reigniting a spark in a friendship that can last far into the future.

Keeping Up with the 'rents

Face it, keeping your parents in touch with everything that's going on is difficult. However often you speak, it sometimes feels as though you're forgetting something. And visits often feel rushed, as though you don't have enough time to truly catch up.

Facebook Photos and Video applications are two of the best ways to easily and quickly share your life with your parents. Because you can upload photos so quickly, they can feel as though they were present at the <*insert activity here*>. Whether a dance, party, or concert, it's as though you came home and immediately called to tell them about it.

Additionally, Facebook creates the casual interactions that are so often missing from a long-distance parentship. The *How was your day?* is reinstated by daily status updates. The *Good morning* replaced with Poke. You still might not feel as though you're actually home for a visit. That's when you add Scrabulous, an application that lets you play Scrabble with anyone (at any time) from anywhere in the world. It's perhaps the best way to keep in touch with your parents. Check out Chapter 19 for more about Scrabulous.

Keeping Up with the Kids

If you've read much of this book, you know (from your authors' gentle reassurances) that everyone is welcome on Facebook and that Facebook is for everyone. If you happen to be the parent of a teenager, you might hear a distinctly different story, something more along the lines of, "Stay out of my life! <door slam>"

Well, Facebook is for everyone, and it can be a great way to keep up with your children when they go away to college and beyond. Our parents love the ability to look at our photos, Poke us when we haven't called, and say things like, "Your status said that you're stressed. Is everything okay?" If you're looking to be friends with your child on Facebook, here are some tips:

- ✔ **Respect their boundaries.** At some ages, kids just don't want their parents to have access to their social life. Don't be hurt if your child doesn't accept your friend request or puts you on her Limited Profile. Like all relationships on Facebook, share what you're comfortable with, and your kids can share what they're comfortable with.

- ✔ **Don't friend all of their friends unless given permission.** As funny as it can be to say, "See? Johnny thinks it's cool that I'm on Facebook," this can also be really irritating and breaks Rule 1: Respect boundaries.

✔ **Have your own social life.** Yes, Facebook can be a great way to feel connected with your child at any distance, but use Facebook to connect with your own friends and share content with everyone — friend and family alike.

✔ **Don't worry too much.** Yes, you might see some parts of your child that you didn't know about. Just as you're a wonderful, multi-faceted human (as represented by your profile), so too is your child. Get excited that you're getting to know the person you helped shape.

Assuming that your child accepts your friend request, start keeping up. It's easy to check their Mini-Feed if you haven't heard from them in a few days, weeks, or months. A simple *Carolyn is writing Dummies all the time* can explain a lot of lost phone time. (Sorry Mom and Dad!)

Will Facebook for Food

If you've ever found yourself job hunting, you probably are acquainted with the real-world version of *networking*. You ask friends for their friends' numbers and job titles; you take people out to coffee; you go on interviews; you decide whether the company is right for you; you repeat the whole process.

Although finding the right job hasn't gotten any easier with Facebook, a lot of the intermediate steps have. Asking friends for friends' info is as easy as writing a note. Better yet, scan through your friends networks to see whether any of them are working at companies that interest you. After you receive some names, Facebook message them (or e-mail, whichever is most appropriate) to set up the requisite "informational coffee date."

After interviewing, a great way to get information about a company is to talk to people who work there. Use Find Coworkers to search people who've listed that company in their profiles.

The only caveat here is that you're now using Facebook to represent a professional portion of your life. If you contact people via Facebook and they feel a little uncomfortable with the number of exclamation points you use in your profile (some people have a thing for punctuation), it could make a bad first impression — just as if you'd shown up to the interview in torn jeans and the shirt you slept in. As a well-educated user of Facebook (because you *have* read all previous 19 chapters without just skipping directly to this one, right?), you're well aware of the myriad privacy settings that enable you to tailor what different parties see and don't see. However, if anything on your profile might be particularly misunderstood, simply hide it until you sign your offer letter.

We're Goin' to the Chapel

A small bit of Facebook trivia: There has, in many circles, arisen the idea of *Facebook Official* — the act of moving from *single* to *in a relationship* and listing the person that you're in a relationship with on your profile. For any fledgling couple, this is a big deal for their personal lives; however, becoming Facebook Official also serves notice to friends and anyone who happens upon one's profile: I'm taken.

Because of this relationship function, Facebook has become the fastest way to spread a wedding announcement to extended friend groups. Of course, people still call their parents and their closest friends, but *everyone* can find out and share in the happiness via News Feed. Congratulatory Wall posts ensue, as do copious amounts of photos with *the ring* tagged front and center.

Hey, Facebook Me!

Before Facebook, in both romantic and platonic contexts, it was hard to get from "Nice to meet you" to "Will you be my friend?" Now, the simple phrase, "Facebook Me!" expresses this sentiment and so much more. "Facebook Me!" can mean, *get in touch, look me up,* or *I want you to know more about me* but in a pressure-free way. It doesn't mean *take me to dinner,* or *let's be best friends forever and ever.* It's simply a way to acknowledge a budding friendship.

"Facebook Me!" can also be how good friends say, "Keep up with my life, I want you to know about it," which acknowledges that people are busy and that it's hard to find time to see each other or talk on the phone. However, even when people are incredibly busy, a quick check on Facebook can make you feel connected again and secure that your friend is doing well.

Chapter 21

Leah and Carolyn's Favorite Groups

. . . .

*P*erhaps it's a testament to human ingenuity that, when faced with a particular need, people look through their arsenal of tools to find something to meet the need — even if that something was designed for an entirely different task. This is how phone books become booster chairs, Perrier becomes stain remover, and forks become hair brushes (other people do that, right?).

In this vein, Facebook users found creative ways to use Facebook Groups other than those initially intended. While some groups on Facebook serve the intended purpose of providing a way for people to virtually convene around common interests and activities, many groups — the majority of them in fact — have come to meet two additional needs:

✔ **To evangelize or garner support for a cause.** Many groups raise money and awareness for worthy causes, such as cancer research or environmental issues.

✔ **To publicly pledge allegiance to some fact or idea.** People join these types of groups to endorse a sentiment they agree with. Joining such groups adds little value other than the badge it places on one's profile and the News Feed story that shows off the allegiance, but it's fun and keeps people involved.

The following top ten groups are our favorites from all the groups on Facebook.

When I Was Your Age, Pluto Was a Planet

For the first time, on August 24, 2006, the International Astronomical Union (IAU) agreed on a definition of *planet*. Before this definition, schoolchildren around the world (Earth, to be exact) had been memorizing the names, in geographical order, of nine planets. When the IAU settled on a strict, more formal definition based on physical properties, eight of the nine planets made the cut. One did not: Pluto. The creation of the Facebook Group, When I Was Your Age, Pluto Was a Planet, may have been motivated by the nostalgia we feel for days of yore. Goodbye Tooth Fairy, so long hole-punch voting machines, peace out Pluto.

There's also a secondary interpretation of this group. At the time of its creation, the Facebook user base consisted primarily of students. When I Was Your Age, Pluto Was a Planet, however, was comprised of a minority of Facebook users: those who were already out of school. The age difference may be small, but as the group's name implies, sometimes a few years makes a perceptible difference. Currently, When I Was Your Age, Pluto Was a Planet has more than 1.1 million members. Pluto is no longer the smallest planet in the solar system, but in the world of Facebook, it's a big star.

For Every 1,000 That Join This Group I Will Donate $1 for Darfur.

A number of groups on Facebook have similar names and intentions that follow a similar naming convention: For Every *X-number* That Join This Group I will Donate *$Y* to *Z-cause*. For Every 1,000 That Join This Group I Will Donate $1 for Darfur is the largest at nearly 500,000 members. This group is up to $500 in donations from the pocket of one NYU student. The Breast Cancer Awareness group is also up to $500. The Canadian Cancer Society, North Korean Refugees, Lupus Awareness, and Victims of Katrina will also receive donations from Facebook Groups. Although $500 doesn't sound like much, many of these groups are primarily set up to generate awareness. Each group provides links to much more information and explains how to make further donations should members find the cause compelling.

I Flip My Pillow Over to Get to the Cold Side

Much like When I Was Your Age, Pluto Was a Planet, this is a group created for solidarity. We sometimes refer to these kinds of groups as *bumper sticker groups* because joining them gives the same pleasure as slapping a clever bumper sticker on the back of your car.

Meta-League (and Members of the Meta-League)

To understand Meta-League, you have to be familiar with *meta-art* — art with content that describes the form. For example, *Adaptation* is a movie about making a movie. *Stranger Than Fiction* is a book about a character in a book. *One Down* is a song in which Ben Folds sings about writing the song *One Down*. Meta-League encourages any form of meta behavior. One member uploaded a photo of a poll he ran on Facebook asking, "Do you answer polls?" 59% responded, *No*. Someone else uploaded a photo of a car license plate that read, *LCNS PLT*. Another person started a discussion topic named *How do I start a discussion topic?* The Meta-League is the kind of group that provides a new center for creative interaction among people.

I Will Go Slightly Out of My Way to Step on That Crunchy-looking Leaf

Besides being one of the funnier bumper sticker groups, this group is particularly funny because of its spin-off groups: a group for stepping on a leaf that looks *particularly* crunchy; one for stepping on a leaf that *is* crunchy; one for going *significantly* out of one's way for the crunchy leaf; a corollary group whose members profess *If I step on a leaf that looks particularly crunchy and it isn't, I get sad;* and, finally, a group that says *I will avoid the crunchy leaves in order to be more stealthy and ninja-like.* (This may explain why autumn is the ninja off-season, but we'll check it out in *Being a Ninja For Dummies* just to be sure.)

Facebook Ultimate Frisbee

Ultimate Frisbee is a sport that sprang up in the late 1960s and is quickly gaining widespread popularity. Imagine soccer with a Frisbee, with people throwing instead of kicking, and you start to get the picture. These days, Ultimate Frisbee seems to be particularly popular among techy types. One hypothesis for this is that techie types don't often show an interest in team sports until adult life. But it's hard to break into team sports, such as baseball or soccer, when everyone playing has had years of practice. Ultimate Frisbee is quite open to beginners because it's so new it hasn't penetrated into most school athletic programs. Almost everyone is a beginner or started recently enough that they can relate to the new guy.

Ultimate Frisbee happens to be very popular among Facebook employees — particularly engineers. It's so popular, in fact, that the small company has no problem fielding more than two teams for a weekly pickup game, nor beating rival teams from much bigger companies. (We won't name names.) The Facebook Ultimate Frisbee administrators use the group to message interested people about weekly game times, locations, opponents, and more. When new people are interested in playing, they join the group; those who decide Frisbee is not for them, leave the group. Facebook Ultimate Frisbee is exactly the kind of group that Facebook Groups was initially designed to support. Your authors are avid Facebook Ultimate Frisbee fans, both the group and the game.

1 Wish 1 Were Your Derivative So 1 Could Lie Tangent to Your Curves

Yet another bumper sticker group that, like the leaf groups, yields a lot of spin-offs, such as I Wish You Were sin^2x and I Were cos^2x So Together We Would Be 1.

Like Meta-League, this group encourages a lot of ongoing engagement. Members continually add other mathematical humor to the group, which is often laced with innuendo.

Addicted to Quoting Lines from Arrested Development

The beauty of Addicted to Quoting Lines from Arrested Development is that it's one of the few groups that has reliably on-topic discussions. Members write to the group only to quote lines from the popular TV show *Arrested Development*. We went through the group's discussion board looking for a good quote to put here, but, honestly, they'll all be a lot funnier if you just watch the show.

Students Against News Feed

When Facebook launched its News Feed feature, people were a little freaked out. It took a few key additional Privacy options and a *lot* of user education to explain that News Feed wasn't sharing any information than what was already being shared; it was simply aggregating the actions one's friends took on Facebook and presenting them in an easy-to-read way. Before the education process began, however, a few users attempted to rally and unite the Facebook community in order to convince the company of their misstep.

Initially, Students Against News Feed was wildly popular; it grew faster and larger than any group on Facebook had before. The reason for this was *not* that rallying against News Feed was the most popular cause that had ever been promoted on Facebook. The group garnered so much popularity because it was one of the first groups to be created after News Feed was launched. That meant that as people joined, all of their friends were reading about it. Where? In their News Feed, of course. Students Against News Feed was the first validation that News Feed was capable of spreading information from person to person more efficiently than ever before across the social graph.

Today, News Feed is probably the most popular feature on Facebook. It's a tremendous contributor to the current user base's loyalty and the Web site's success. Students Against News Feed continues to lose members daily.

1 Was Doing Homework and Then 1 Ended Up on Facebook

This is a final bumper sticker group made up of 20,000 members, but we know it deserves many, many more. However, now that Facebook is no longer a site just for students, it's probably about time someone starts a group named I Was Doing My 9–5 and Then I Ended Up on Facebook. Your authors would be among the first to join.

Index

• F •

BUSINESS, CAREERS & PERSONAL FINANCE

0-7645-9847-3   0-7645-2431-3

Also available:
- Business Plans Kit For Dummies
  0-7645-9794-9
- Economics For Dummies
  0-7645-5726-2
- Grant Writing For Dummies
  0-7645-8416-2
- Home Buying For Dummies
  0-7645-5331-3
- Managing For Dummies
  0-7645-1771-6
- Marketing For Dummies
  0-7645-5600-2

- Personal Finance For Dummies
  0-7645-2590-5*
- Resumes For Dummies
  0-7645-5471-9
- Selling For Dummies
  0-7645-5363-1
- Six Sigma For Dummies
  0-7645-6798-5
- Small Business Kit For Dummies
  0-7645-5984-2
- Starting an eBay Business For Dummies
  0-7645-6924-4
- Your Dream Career For Dummies
  0-7645-9795-7

HOME & BUSINESS COMPUTER BASICS

0-470-05432-8   0-471-75421-8

Also available:
- Cleaning Windows Vista For Dummies
  0-471-78293-9
- Excel 2007 For Dummies
  0-470-03737-7
- Mac OS X Tiger For Dummies
  0-7645-7675-5
- MacBook For Dummies
  0-470-04859-X
- Macs For Dummies
  0-470-04849-2
- Office 2007 For Dummies
  0-470-00923-3

- Outlook 2007 For Dummies
  0-470-03830-6
- PCs For Dummies
  0-7645-8958-X
- Salesforce.com For Dummies
  0-470-04893-X
- Upgrading & Fixing Laptops For Dummies
  0-7645-8959-8
- Word 2007 For Dummies
  0-470-03658-3
- Quicken 2007 For Dummies
  0-470-04600-7

FOOD, HOME, GARDEN, HOBBIES, MUSIC & PETS

0-7645-8404-9   0-7645-9904-6

Also available:
- Candy Making For Dummies
  0-7645-9734-5
- Card Games For Dummies
  0-7645-9910-0
- Crocheting For Dummies
  0-7645-4151-X
- Dog Training For Dummies
  0-7645-8418-9
- Healthy Carb Cookbook For Dummies
  0-7645-8476-6
- Home Maintenance For Dummies
  0-7645-5215-5

- Horses For Dummies
  0-7645-9797-3
- Jewelry Making & Beading For Dummies
  0-7645-2571-9
- Orchids For Dummies
  0-7645-6759-4
- Puppies For Dummies
  0-7645-5255-4
- Rock Guitar For Dummies
  0-7645-5356-9
- Sewing For Dummies
  0-7645-6847-7
- Singing For Dummies
  0-7645-2475-5

INTERNET & DIGITAL MEDIA

0-470-04529-9   0-470-04894-8

Also available:
- Blogging For Dummies
  0-471-77084-1
- Digital Photography For Dummies
  0-7645-9802-3
- Digital Photography All-in-One Desk Reference For Dummies
  0-470-03743-1
- Digital SLR Cameras and Photography For Dummies
  0-7645-9803-1
- eBay Business All-in-One Desk Reference For Dummies
  0-7645-8438-3
- HDTV For Dummies
  0-470-09673-X

- Home Entertainment PCs For Dummies
  0-470-05523-5
- MySpace For Dummies
  0-470-09529-6
- Search Engine Optimization For Dummies
  0-471-97998-8
- Skype For Dummies
  0-470-04891-3
- The Internet For Dummies
  0-7645-8996-2
- Wiring Your Digital Home For Dummies
  0-471-91830-X

* Separate Canadian edition also available
† Separate U.K. edition also available

Available wherever books are sold. For more information or to order direct: U.S. customers visit www.dummies.com or call 1-877-762-2974.
U.K. customers visit www.wileyeurope.com or call 0800 243407. Canadian customers visit www.wiley.ca or call 1-800-567-4797.

SPORTS, FITNESS, PARENTING, RELIGION & SPIRITUALITY

 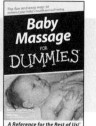

0-471-76871-5   0-7645-7841-3

Also available:

- Catholicism For Dummies
  0-7645-5391-7
- Exercise Balls For Dummies
  0-7645-5623-1
- Fitness For Dummies
  0-7645-7851-0
- Football For Dummies
  0-7645-3936-1
- Judaism For Dummies
  0-7645-5299-6
- Potty Training For Dummies
  0-7645-5417-4
- Buddhism For Dummies
  0-7645-5359-3

- Pregnancy For Dummies
  0-7645-4483-7 †
- Ten Minute Tone-Ups For Dummies
  0-7645-7207-5
- NASCAR For Dummies
  0-7645-7681-X
- Religion For Dummies
  0-7645-5264-3
- Soccer For Dummies
  0-7645-5229-5
- Women in the Bible For Dummies
  0-7645-8475-8

TRAVEL

0-7645-7749-2   0-7645-6945-7

Also available:

- Alaska For Dummies
  0-7645-7746-8
- Cruise Vacations For Dummies
  0-7645-6941-4
- England For Dummies
  0-7645-4276-1
- Europe For Dummies
  0-7645-7529-5
- Germany For Dummies
  0-7645-7823-5
- Hawaii For Dummies
  0-7645-7402-7

- Italy For Dummies
  0-7645-7386-1
- Las Vegas For Dummies
  0-7645-7382-9
- London For Dummies
  0-7645-4277-X
- Paris For Dummies
  0-7645-7630-5
- RV Vacations For Dummies
  0-7645-4442-X
- Walt Disney World & Orlando
  For Dummies
  0-7645-9660-8

GRAPHICS, DESIGN & WEB DEVELOPMENT

0-7645-8815-X   0-7645-9571-7

Also available:

- 3D Game Animation For Dummies
  0-7645-8789-7
- AutoCAD 2006 For Dummies
  0-7645-8925-3
- Building a Web Site For Dummies
  0-7645-7144-3
- Creating Web Pages For Dummies
  0-470-08030-2
- Creating Web Pages All-in-One Desk
  Reference For Dummies
  0-7645-4345-8
- Dreamweaver 8 For Dummies
  0-7645-9649-7

- InDesign CS2 For Dummies
  0-7645-9572-5
- Macromedia Flash 8 For Dummies
  0-7645-9691-8
- Photoshop CS2 and Digital
  Photography For Dummies
  0-7645-9580-6
- Photoshop Elements 4 For Dummies
  0-471-77483-9
- Syndicating Web Sites with RSS Feeds
  For Dummies
  0-7645-8848-6
- Yahoo! SiteBuilder For Dummies
  0-7645-9800-7

NETWORKING, SECURITY, PROGRAMMING & DATABASES

0-7645-7728-X   0-471-74940-0

Also available:

- Access 2007 For Dummies
  0-470-04612-0
- ASP.NET 2 For Dummies
  0-7645-7907-X
- C# 2005 For Dummies
  0-7645-9704-3
- Hacking For Dummies
  0-470-05235-X
- Hacking Wireless Networks
  For Dummies
  0-7645-9730-2
- Java For Dummies
  0-470-08716-1

- Microsoft SQL Server 2005 For Dummies
  0-7645-7755-7
- Networking All-in-One Desk Reference
  For Dummies
  0-7645-9939-9
- Preventing Identity Theft For Dummies
  0-7645-7336-5
- Telecom For Dummies
  0-471-77085-X
- Visual Studio 2005 All-in-One Desk
  Reference For Dummies
  0-7645-9775-2
- XML For Dummies
  0-7645-8845-1

HEALTH & SELF-HELP

0-7645-8450-2

0-7645-4149-8

Also available:

✔Bipolar Disorder For Dummies
0-7645-8451-0

✔Chemotherapy and Radiation
For Dummies
0-7645-7832-4

✔Controlling Cholesterol For Dummies
0-7645-5440-9

✔Diabetes For Dummies
0-7645-6820-5* †

✔Divorce For Dummies
0-7645-8417-0 †

✔Fibromyalgia For Dummies
0-7645-5441-7

✔Low-Calorie Dieting For Dummies
0-7645-9905-4

✔Meditation For Dummies
0-471-77774-9

✔Osteoporosis For Dummies
0-7645-7621-6

✔Overcoming Anxiety For Dummies
0-7645-5447-6

✔Reiki For Dummies
0-7645-9907-0

✔Stress Management For Dummies
0-7645-5144-2

EDUCATION, HISTORY, REFERENCE & TEST PREPARATION

0-7645-8381-6

0-7645-9554-7

Also available:

✔The ACT For Dummies
0-7645-9652-7

✔Algebra For Dummies
0-7645-5325-9

✔Algebra Workbook For Dummies
0-7645-8467-7

✔Astronomy For Dummies
0-7645-8465-0

✔Calculus For Dummies
0-7645-2498-4

✔Chemistry For Dummies
0-7645-5430-1

✔Forensics For Dummies
0-7645-5580-4

✔Freemasons For Dummies
0-7645-9796-5

✔French For Dummies
0-7645-5193-0

✔Geometry For Dummies
0-7645-5324-0

✔Organic Chemistry I For Dummies
0-7645-6902-3

✔The SAT I For Dummies
0-7645-7193-1

✔Spanish For Dummies
0-7645-5194-9

✔Statistics For Dummies
0-7645-5423-9

Get smart @ dummies.com®

- **Find a full list of Dummies titles**
- **Look into loads of FREE on-site articles**
- **Sign up for FREE eTips e-mailed to you weekly**
- **See what other products carry the Dummies name**
- **Shop directly from the Dummies bookstore**
- **Enter to win new prizes every month!**

* Separate Canadian edition also available
† Separate U.K. edition also available

Available wherever books are sold. For more information or to order direct: U.S. customers visit www.dummies.com or call 1-877-762-2974.
U.K. customers visit www.wileyeurope.com or call 0800 243407. Canadian customers visit www.wiley.ca or call 1-800-567-4797.